Footprints
in Faith

Lectionary Activities for Kids Ages 7-12 for Every Sunday of the Three-Year Cycle

KATIE THOMPSON

TWENTY
THIRD 23rd
PUBLICATIONS

First published by
KEVIN MAYHEW LTD
Buxhall
Stowmarket
Suffolk IP 14 3DJ

Reprinted under license in North America by
TWENTY-THIRD PUBLICATIONS
A Division of Bayard
One Montauk Avenue, Suite 200
P.O. Box 6015
New London, CT 06320
(860) 437-3012 or (800) 321-0411
www.23rdpublications.com

ISBN 978-0-89622-986-0

Library of Congress Catalog Card Number: 99-73813
Printed in the U.S.A.

Occasionally during our lives we have the good fortune to meet people who inspire us. *Footprints in Faith* and its companion book, *Step by Step*, are the result of just such an encounter I had with a dedicated and enthusiastic group working with the children in their parish. This book was written in response to their vision, and I am grateful to them and to everyone who has worked so hard to make this vision a reality.

Introduction

Do not be afraid;
come and follow me.
MARK 10:14

Footprints in Faith is a practical resource that faithfully follows the Sunday gospels, introducing children (ages 7-12) to God's word and encouraging them to learn about Jesus in an imaginative and enjoyable way that is both suited to their age and sensitive to their level of understanding.

Week by week a double-sided activity sheet (which can be folded to produce a leaflet) reveals each Sunday's gospel message and reinforces its teaching using picture and number puzzles, word games, quizzes, and codes. Together, children and adults are encouraged to share in a positive and stimulating experience of discovery and understanding.

The sheets may be photocopied and used in a variety of ways whenever and wherever the gospel-based activities are needed. Teachers, group leaders, and parents will find this book ideal for use with this age group, whether as individuals or in groups. Copy them to take home and share within families; introduce them as an additional resource for children's liturgy celebrations; use them to produce a children's newsletter or include them in the parish newsletter or magazine; use them in parish groups or at school. Above all, use them with flexibility and imagination according to your own particular needs.

Each sheet includes a reference for the text of the day, and, wherever practical, a "Look Ahead" page encourages the children (and adults) to use their Bible during the week to complete a simple activity that relates to the following Sunday. You may find it useful to give the children a photocopy of the following page, which will help them to find their way around their Bible.

To help you use this book, the Contents details the Sundays of the three-year cycle as well as the principal celebrations of the liturgical year, together with their scriptural references and themes.

I hope that *Footprints in Faith* will help children to discover the gospels for themselves in a way that is positive and enjoyable, encouraging their natural curiosity and creativity to lead them to know Jesus and to recognize his love in their young lives as they set out on their journey of faith.

KATIE THOMPSON

Finding your way around the gospels

To help you find your way around the gospels and use the references given in this book, let's begin by looking for Matthew 5:1-10.

First, look at the Contents page of your Bible and find Saint Matthew's Gospel, which is in the New Testament.

Go to the page where it starts and turn the pages slowly until you find a large number 5 in bold type. This tells you where chapter 5 of this gospel begins.

The smaller numbers you see tell you the verse numbers. So, for Matthew 5:1-10, go to chapter 5 in Saint Matthew's Gospel and start reading at the first verse of this chapter and continue until you reach the end of verse 10.

With practice you'll soon get quicker at looking up references!

Contents

Sixth Sunday of the Year	Matthew 5:17–37	Rules for life
Seventh Sunday of the Year	Matthew 5:38–48	Love your enemies
Eighth Sunday of the Year	Matthew 6:24–34	Do not worry
Ninth Sunday of the Year	Matthew 7:21–27	Build your lives on me!
Tenth Sunday of the Year	Matthew 9:9–13	Jesus makes a friend
Eleventh Sunday of the Year	Matthew 9:36—10:8	The twelve apostles
Twelfth Sunday of the Year	Matthew 10:26–33	Do not be afraid!
Thirteenth Sunday of the Year	Matthew 10:37–42	Make Jesus welcome
Fourteenth Sunday of the Year	Matthew 11:25–30	Jesus is gentle and kind
Fifteenth Sunday of the Year	Matthew 13:1–23	The parable of the sower
Sixteenth Sunday of the Year	Matthew 13:24–43	The wheat and the weeds
Seventeenth Sunday of the Year	Matthew 13:44–52	Priceless treasure!
Eighteenth Sunday of the Year	Matthew 14:13–21	The miracle of the loaves and fish
Nineteenth Sunday of the Year	Matthew 14:22–33	Have faith!
Twentieth Sunday of the Year	Matthew 15:21–28	The Canaanite woman
Twenty-first Sunday of the Year	Matthew 16:13–20	Who am I?
Twenty-second Sunday of the Year	Matthew 16:21–27	God's way!
Twenty-third Sunday of the Year	Matthew 18:15–20	I am with you
Twenty-fourth Sunday of the Year	Matthew 18:21–35	Be forgiving
Twenty-fifth Sunday of the Year	Matthew 20:1–16	Workers in the vineyard
Twenty-sixth Sunday of the Year	Matthew 21:28–32	Making choices
Twenty-seventh Sunday of the Year	Matthew 21:33–43	Listen to God's message
Twenty-eighth Sunday of the Year	Matthew 22:1–14	The wedding party
Twenty-ninth Sunday of the Year	Matthew 22:15–21	Give to God what belongs to God
Thirtieth Sunday of the Year	Matthew 22:34–40	The greatest commandment
Thirty-first Sunday of the Year	Matthew 23:1–12	Practice what you preach!
Thirty-second Sunday of the Year	Matthew 25:1–13	Be ready
Thirty-third Sunday of the Year	Matthew 25:14–30	Gifts from God
The Feast of Christ the King	Matthew 25:31–46	Christ is King!

YEAR B

ADVENT

First Sunday of Advent	Mark 13:33–37	Stay awake!
Second Sunday of Advent	Mark 1:1–8	Prepare for Jesus
Third Sunday of Advent	John 1:6–8, 19–28	A witness for Christ
Fourth Sunday of Advent	Luke 1:26–38	God's messenger!

CHRISTMAS

Christmas Day	Luke 2:1–14	A Savior is born!
The Feast of the Holy Family	Luke 2:22–40	Jesus is presented in the Temple
The Baptism of the Lord	Mark 1:7–11	John baptizes Jesus

LENT

First Sunday of Lent	Mark 1:12–15	Jesus in the wilderness
Second Sunday of Lent	Mark 9:2–10	"This is my beloved Son"
Third Sunday of Lent	John 2:13–25	Anger in the Temple!
Fourth Sunday of Lent	John 3:14–21	God loves the world
Fifth Sunday of Lent	John 12:20–30	A grain of wheat
Palm (Passion) Sunday	Mark 11:1–10	Hosanna! Hosanna!

EASTER

Easter Sunday	John 20:1–9	Jesus is alive!
Second Sunday of Easter	John 20:19–31	Thomas has doubts!
Third Sunday of Easter	Luke 24:35–48	Christ's witnesses
Fourth Sunday of Easter	John 10:11–18	The Good Shepherd
Fifth Sunday of Easter	John 15:1–8	Jesus is the true vine
Sixth Sunday of Easter	John 15:9–17	Love each other
Seventh Sunday of Easter	John 17:11–19	Jesus prays for us
The Feast of Pentecost	Acts 2:1–11; John 15:26–27; 16:12–15	The Holy Spirit comes!
The Feast of the Trinity	Matthew 28:16–20	Father, Son, and Holy Spirit

ORDINARY TIME

Second Sunday of the Year	John 1:35–42	Lamb of God
Third Sunday of the Year	Mark 1:14–20	Follow me!
Fourth Sunday of the Year	Mark 1:21–28	The power of Jesus!
Fifth Sunday of the Year	Mark 1:29–39	Jesus cures the sick
Sixth Sunday of the Year	Mark 1:40–45	Jesus cures a leper!
Seventh Sunday of the Year	Mark 2:1–12	Don't give up!
Eighth Sunday of the Year	Mark 2:18–22	Jesus pours love into our lives
Ninth Sunday of the Year	Mark 2:27—3:6	Choose God's way
Tenth Sunday of the Year	Mark 3:20–35	The family of God
Eleventh Sunday of the Year	Mark 4:26–34	God's kingdom
Twelfth Sunday of the Year	Mark 4:35–41	Lord of wind and sea
Thirteenth Sunday of the Year	Mark 5:21–43	Jesus gives us new life!
Fourteenth Sunday of the Year	Mark 6:1–6	Jesus is rejected
Fifteenth Sunday of the Year	Mark 6:7–13	Messengers for Jesus
Sixteenth Sunday of the Year	Mark 6:30–34	Jesus cares for the people
Seventeenth Sunday of the Year	John 6:1–15	Jesus feeds the people

Eighteenth Sunday of the Year	Exodus 16:2-4; John 6:24-35	Bread from heaven
Nineteenth Sunday of the Year	1 Kings 19:4-8; John 6:41-51	God cares for his people
Twentieth Sunday of the Year	John 6:51-58	The Bread of Life
Twenty-first Sunday of the Year	John 6:60-69	We believe in you
Twenty-second Sunday of the Year	Mark 7:1-8, 14-15, 21-23	A clean heart
Twenty-third Sunday of the Year	Mark 7:31-37	Jesus cures a deaf man
Twenty-fourth Sunday of the Year	Mark 8:27-35	Jesus is the Son of God
Twenty-fifth Sunday of the Year	Mark 9:30-37	The last shall be first
Twenty-sixth Sunday of the Year	Mark 9:38-50	All goodness comes from God
Twenty-seventh Sunday of the Year	Mark 10:2-16	The children's friend
Twenty-eighth Sunday of the Year	Mark 10:17-30	The camel and the needle!
Twenty-ninth Sunday of the Year	Mark 10:35-45	A place in heaven
Thirtieth Sunday of the Year	Mark 10:46-52	Master, let me see!
Thirty-first Sunday of the Year	Mark 12:28-34	The two greatest commandments
Thirty-second Sunday of the Year	Mark 12:38-44	The generous widow
Thirty-third Sunday of the Year	Mark 13:24-32	Jesus will return
The Feast of Christ the King	John 18:33-37	Jesus is King!

YEAR C

ADVENT

First Sunday of Advent	Luke 21:25-28, 34-36	Be ready to welcome Jesus!
Second Sunday of Advent	Luke 3:1-6	Be prepared
Third Sunday of Advent	Luke 3:10-18	Turn back to God
Fourth Sunday of Advent	Luke 1:39-44	A special visitor

CHRISTMAS

Christmas Day	Luke 2:15-20	Jesus is born!
The Feast of the Holy Family	Luke 2:41-52	Jesus goes missing!
The Baptism of the Lord	Luke 3:15-16, 21-22	Jesus is baptized

LENT

First Sunday of Lent	Luke 4:1-13	Jesus is put to the test
Second Sunday of Lent	Luke 9:28-36	Jesus shines like the sun
Third Sunday of Lent	Luke 13:1-9	God gives us another chance
Fourth Sunday of Lent	Luke 15:1-3, 11-32	The son who came back

Fifth Sunday of Lent	John 8:1–11	Jesus forgives a woman
Palm (Passion) Sunday	Luke 19:28–40	Jesus enters Jerusalem

EASTER

Easter Sunday	John 20:1–9	Jesus is risen!
Second Sunday of Easter	John 20:19–31	Peace be with you!
Third Sunday of Easter	John 21:1–19	Jesus on the shore
Fourth Sunday of Easter	John 10:27–30	The Good Shepherd
Fifth Sunday of Easter	John 13:31–35	A new commandment
Sixth Sunday of Easter	John 14:23–29	Do not be afraid
Seventh Sunday of Easter	John 17:20–26	May they all be one
The Feast of Pentecost	John 14:15–16, 23–26 Acts 2:1–11	The Holy Spirit comes!
The Feast of the Trinity	John 16:12–15	One God, three persons

ORDINARY TIME

Second Sunday of the Year	John 2:1–11	A wedding party
Third Sunday of the Year	Luke 1:1–4; 4:14–21	Jesus begins his work
Fourth Sunday of the Year	Luke 4:21–30	Good News for everyone!
Fifth Sunday of the Year	Luke 5:1–11	The marvelous catch
Sixth Sunday of the Year	Luke 6:17, 20–26	Happiness is...
Seventh Sunday of the Year	Luke 6:27–38; Samuel 26:2–23	Love your enemies
Eighth Sunday of the Year	Luke 6:39–45	The fruits of goodness
Ninth Sunday of the Year	Luke 7:1–10	The faithful centurion
Tenth Sunday of the Year	Luke 7:11–17	Jesus takes pity
Eleventh Sunday of the Year	Luke 7:36—8:3	Jesus forgives a sinner
Twelfth Sunday of the Year	Luke 9:18–24	The Son of God
Thirteenth Sunday of the Year	Luke 9:51–62	Make Jesus welcome
Fourteenth Sunday of the Year	Luke 10:1–12	Share the Good News
Fifteenth Sunday of the Year	Luke 10:25–37	The good Samaritan
Sixteenth Sunday of the Year	Luke 10:38–42	Making time for Jesus
Seventeenth Sunday of the Year	Luke 11:1–13	Teach us to pray
Eighteenth Sunday of the Year	Luke 12:13–21	The foolish man
Nineteenth Sunday of the Year	Luke 12:32–48	Be ready!
Twentieth Sunday of the Year	Luke 12:49–53; Jeremiah 38:3–6, 8–13	Jeremiah in the well
Twenty-first Sunday of the Year	Luke 13:22–30	Few will be chosen
Twenty-second Sunday of the Year	Luke 14:1, 7–14	Put others first
Twenty-third Sunday of the Year	Luke 14:25–33	Consider the cost
Twenty-fourth Sunday of the Year	Luke 15:1–32	Lost and found!
Twenty-fifth Sunday of the Year	Luke 16:1–13	Always be honest!
Twenty-sixth Sunday of the Year	Luke 16:19–31	The poor man at the gate
Twenty-seventh Sunday of the Year	Luke 17:5–19	Have faith

Twenty-eighth Sunday of the Year	Luke 17:11–19	Thank you, Jesus
Twenty-ninth Sunday of the Year	Luke 18:1–8	Don't give up
Thirtieth Sunday of the Year	Luke 18:9–14	The Pharisee and the tax collector
Thirty-first Sunday of the Year	Luke 19:1–10	The story of Zacchaeus
Thirty-second Sunday of the Year	Luke 20:27–38	Heaven is...
Thirty-third Sunday of the Year	Luke 21:5–19	Believe in me!
The Feast of Christ the King	Luke 23:35–43	King of the Jews

YEARS A, B, AND C

Mary, Mother of God (JANUARY 1)	Luke 2:16–21	Mary, Mother of God
Second Sunday after Christmas	John 1:1–18	God sends his Son Jesus
The Epiphany (JANUARY 6)	Matthew 2:1–12	Visitors for Jesus
The Presentation of the Lord (Candlemas) (FEBRUARY 2)	Luke 2:22–40	Jesus is presented to the Lord
Solemnity of Saints Peter and Paul (JUNE 29)	Matthew 16:13–19	Peter and Paul
The Feast of the Transfiguration of the Lord (AUGUST 6)	Matthew 17:1–10	God's glory on the mountain
The Solemnity of the Assumption (AUGUST 15)	Luke 1:39–56	Mary is taken into heaven
The Solemnity of All Saints (NOVEMBER 1)	Matthew 5:1–12	The saints in heaven

Year A

Be ready!

MATTHEW 24:37-44

Noah listened to God and was ready when the flood came. *What happened to the people who were not ready?*

Use the code cracker to find the answer

▲	A	T	W	E	Y
○	L	H	M	O	C
□	N	S	D	F	P
◆	✔	✚	☆	◗	

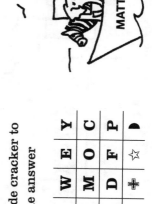

MATTHEW 24:39

THINK and LOOK ahead

Where did John the Baptist preach his message?

Find out in **MATTHEW 3:1**

_____ _____ _____
13   5   3

___ ___ ___ ___ ___ ___ ___ ___ ___
15 6   8   2   3   11 9   3   12 12

___ ___ ___ ___ ___ ___ ___
10 4   7   14 2   1   3   1

Use the code cracker to check your answer

A	D	E	F	H	I	J	L	N	O	R	S	T	U	W
1	2	3	4	5	6	7	8	9	10	11	12	13	14	15

Only God knows when Jesus will return!

Fit these jigsaw pieces together to read the advice Jesus gives us in Matthew 24:44

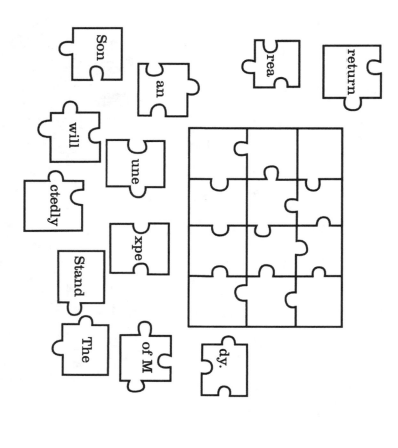

Son

an

will

rea

une

ctedly

return

xpe

Stand

The

of M

dy.

Today is the First Sunday of Advent. What does the word "Advent" mean?

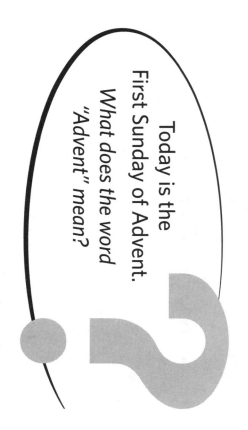

Write the letter that is missing from the second word in the box

In **CARROT** but not **PARROT**

In **OTHER** but not **THERE**

In **MAN** but not **PAN**

In **PIE** but not **PEN**

In **NICE** but not **MICE**

In **GOAL** but not **LOAF**

John the Baptist

MATTHEW 3:1-12

John appeared in the wilderness and preached to the people.

S	A	I	M	L	H	E
R	P	K	N	O	F	A	V
E	E	G	D	S	R	E	A
F	N	H	B	I	N	E	N
O	T	T	S	C	S	M	B
D	R	E	G	L	O	F	L

Follow the arrows to find his words

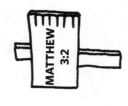

MATTHEW 3:2

THINK and LOOK ahead

John could not go to see Jesus himself.

Why not?

Unscramble the words below and check your answer in Matthew 11:2

EESUABC _____ EH _____

_____ ONSIPR

ASW _____ NI _____

John called the people to say sorry
for turning away from God
and to change their hearts.

John knew that the time had come
to "prepare a way for the Lord."
We must be prepared too!

Use the code to read the warning he gave them

z y x w v u t s r q p o n m l k j i h g f e d c b a
A B C D E F G H I J K L M N O P Q R S T U V W X Y Z

$\overline{z}$ $\overline{m}$ $\overline{b}$ $\overline{g}$ $\overline{i}$ $\overline{v}$ $\overline{v}$ $\overline{g}$ $\overline{s}$ $\overline{z}$ $\overline{g}$

$\overline{w}$ $\overline{i}$ $\overline{v}$ $\overline{h}$ $\overline{m}$ $\overline{l}$ $\overline{g}$ $\overline{y}$ $\overline{v}$ $\overline{z}$ $\overline{i}$

$\overline{t}$ $\overline{l}$ $\overline{l}$ $\overline{w}$ $\overline{u}$ $\overline{i}$ $\overline{f}$ $\overline{r}$ $\overline{g}$

$\overline{d}$ $\overline{r}$ $\overline{o}$ $\overline{o}$ $\overline{y}$ $\overline{v}$ $\overline{x}$ $\overline{f}$ $\overline{g}$

$\overline{w}$ $\overline{l}$ $\overline{d}$ $\overline{m}$

MATTHEW
3:10

How much do you know about time? Try this quiz!

How many seconds in a minute?

How many hours in a day?

How many days in a year?

How many minutes in an hour?

How many weeks in a year?

How many minutes in a day?

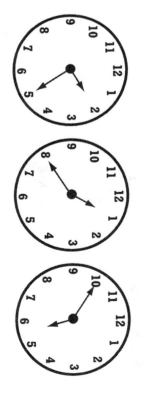

Jesus is the promised one

MATTHEW 11:2-11

John the Baptist sent some of his followers to ask Jesus a question.

Add or subtract letters to see what they asked

A B C D E F G H I J K L M N O P Q R S T U V W X Y Z

___ ___ ___   ___ ___ ___   ___ ___
F-5 M+5 G-2   W+2 Z-11 P+5   S+1 Q-9 S-14

___ ___ ___   ___ ___ ___   ___
K+4 U-7 C+2   X-1 J-2 P-1   B+7 V-3

?

___ ___   ___ ___ ___
R+2 Y-10   H-5 J+5 L+1 L-7

MATTHEW 11:3

THINK and LOOK ahead

Next week who appears to Joseph in a dream?

Write the first letter of each picture.
Check your answer in Matthew 1:20

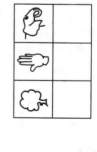

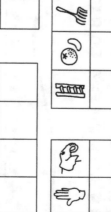

Use the picture code to find the missing words
from Matthew 11:4–5

= **hear** = **see** = **lame** = **deaf**

= **blind** = **walk** = **Good News**

= **lepers** = **John** = **proclaimed**

"Go and tell _____ what you

_____ and _____ !

The _____ can _____ , the _____ can

_____ , the _____ are cured, the _____

can _____ , and the _____

is being _____ !"

All these things happened just as the Old Testament prophets had foretold.

Decode these Old Testament Scriptures

KEY

A B D E F G I M N O P R S T U W Y
✿ † ❋ ▶ ✦ ◆ ✽ ○ ■ □ ☆ ♣ ▲ ▼ ➥ ♪ ❋

The angel's visit

MATTHEW 1:18–24

God sent an angel to visit Joseph in a dream.

Use the secret code pad to find the angel's message

SECRET CODE PAD

A (1) B (9) D (14) E (10) F (8) I (11) K (4) M (16)
N (2) O (17) R (22) S (19) T (5) U (12) W (26) Y (6)

$\overline{(14)}$ $\overline{(17)}$ $\overline{(2)}$ $\overline{(17)}$ $\overline{(5)}$ $\overline{(9)}$ $\overline{(10)}$

$\overline{(1)}$ $\overline{(8)}$ $\overline{(22)}$ $\overline{(1)}$ $\overline{(11)}$ $\overline{(14)}$ $\overline{(1)}$ $\overline{(19)}$ $\overline{(5)}$ $\overline{(17)}$ $\overline{(5)}$ $\overline{(1)}$ $\overline{(4)}$ $\overline{(10)}$

$\overline{(16)}$ $\overline{(1)}$ $\overline{(22)}$ $\overline{(6)}$ $\overline{(1)}$ $\overline{(19)}$ $\overline{(6)}$ $\overline{(17)}$ $\overline{(12)}$ $\overline{(22)}$

$\overline{(26)}$ $\overline{(11)}$ $\overline{(8)}$ $\overline{(10)}$

MATTHEW 1:20

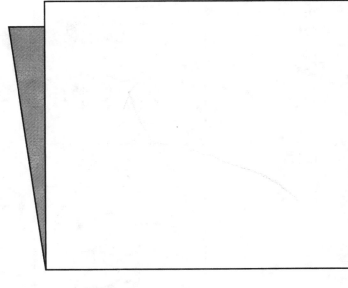

Christmas Day is almost here as Advent ends for another year!

Design a birthday card for Jesus

The angel told Joseph
to call the baby Jesus
(Matthew 1:21).

Unscramble the letters to find another name given to Jesus,
and then find what it means

A	M	E	M	L	N	E	U
4	3	1	2	8	5	7	6

1 2 3 4 5 6 7 8
_____

WHICH MEANS

9 10 11 12 13 14 15 16 17 18 19
_____

S	O	S	W	G	T	U	I	D	H	I
19	10	13	14	9	16	18	12	11	17	15

These pictures tell today's gospel story but they have
been mixed up. Can you put them in the right order?

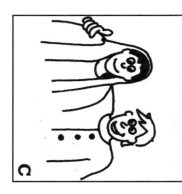

C

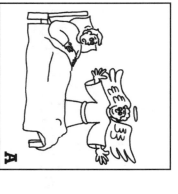

A

D

B

The order is _____ _____ _____ _____

The Light of the World!

JOHN 1:1-18

Who was sent by God to speak for the Light of the World?

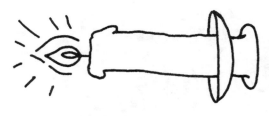

JOHN 1:6

Write the letter missing from the sequence

H I K L M	
L M N P Q	
E F G I J	
J K L M O	

R S U V W	
G I J K L	
C D F G H	

A C D E F	
X Y Z B C	
L M N O Q	
P Q R S U	
G H J K L	
R T U V W	
P Q R S U	

Merry Christmas, everyone!

Draw a picture of you and your family celebrating Christmas Day!

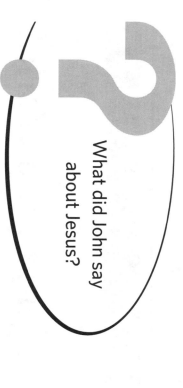

What did John say
about Jesus?

Match the numbers with the words

1 ____ 2 ____ 3 ____ 4 ____ 5 ____

6 ____ 7 ____ 8 ____ 9 ____ 10 ____

11 ____ 12 ____ 13 ____

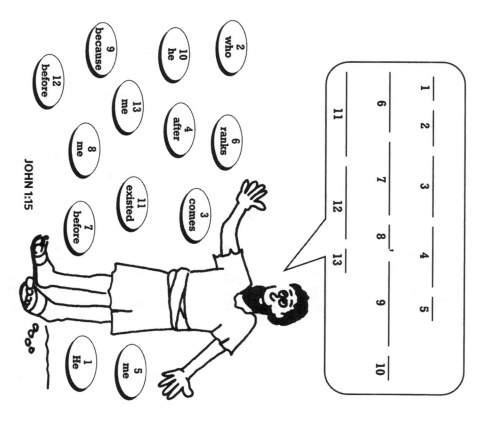

2 who

10 he

9 because

12 before

13 me

4 after

6 ranks

8 me

11 existed

3 comes

7 before

1 He

5 me

JOHN 1:15

Jesus is described as
"a light that shines in the dark"
(John 1:5).

Color this picture of the Advent wreath and Christmas candle

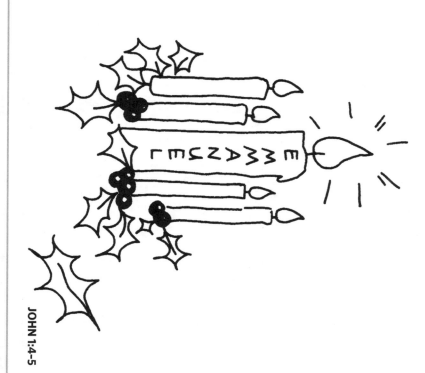

WELCOME

JOHN 1:4–5

Escape from danger!

MATTHEW 2:13-15, 19-23

An angel appeared to Joseph and warned him to take his family and escape from Bethlehem.

Where did they go?

Write the letter that is missing from the second word in the box

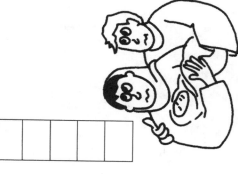

In <u>P</u>EN but not <u>PAN</u>
In <u>G</u>AME but not <u>MANE</u>
In <u>P</u>ONY but not <u>PONG</u>
In <u>P</u>IECE but not <u>NIECE</u>
In <u>T</u>OAD but not <u>ROAD</u>

Where did the Holy Family finally make their home?

Write the first letter of each picture to spell out the answer

IN

in

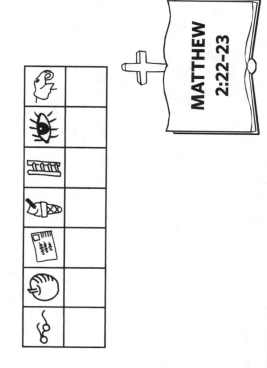

MATTHEW 2:22-23

What warning did the angel give to Joseph?

Use the numbers written under the lines to find the missing letters and spell out the angel's words

H K I M N E A R F L D C O T G S W

1 2 3 4 5 6 7 8 9

Examples: 8,9 = S   9 = W

"

___ ___ ___ ___ ___ ___ ___ ___ ___
1,2 2 3 8 1 3,4 4,5 7 6

___ ___ ___ ___ ___ ___ ___
9 4 3 7,8 8,9 7,8 7

___ ___ ___ ___ ___ ___ ___
5 2 3 6 7,8 1 3,4

___ ___ ___ ___ ___ ___ ___ ___
6,7 1 2 5,6 6 4 3 6

___ ___ ___ ___ ___ ___ ___ ___ ___ !"
1,2 2 5,6 5,6 1   1 2 2,3

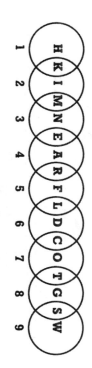

MATTHEW 2:13

When Herod died, Joseph and his family returned to Israel, but they were still afraid of the new ruler.

Write the word that fits the clue. The missing letters of the words will spell out the name of the new ruler of Judea

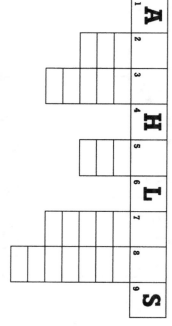

A (1) (2) (3)   **H** (4) (5)   **L** (6) (7) (8)   **S** (9)

CLUES

2. Water that falls from clouds
3. An orange-colored vegetable
5. Hens lay these
7. The opposite of never
8. Something used on a rainy day

He was Herod's son!

MATTHEW 2:22

Jesus is baptized

MATTHEW 3:13-17

Jesus came to the River Jordan to be baptized by John.

Use the code cracker to find John's words to Jesus

	A	Y	I	S
△				
○	R	L	E	U
□	B	T	P	N
◇	Z	D	O	P
	1	2	3	4

"

___ ___ ___ ___ ___
△4 ○4 ○1 ○3 ○2 △2 △3

___ ___
□2 ◇3 □1 ○3

___ ___ ___
□1 △1 □3 □2 △3 ◇1 ○3 ◇2

!"

___ ___
□1 △2 △2 ◇3 ○4

MATTHEW 3:14

□4 ○3 ○3 ◇2

THINK and LOOK ahead

How does John describe Jesus next week?

Add or subtract letters to check your answer!

A B C D E F G H I J K L M N O P Q R S T U V W X Y Z

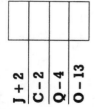

Look in
JOHN 1:29

Y – 5		
F + 2		
M – 8		

J + 2		
C – 2		
Q – 4		
O – 13		

I + 6		
E + 1		

P – 9		
R – 3		
X – 20		

How did the Holy Spirit appear when Jesus had been baptized?

Find the word DOVE in the word search below.
How many other types of birds can you find?

MATTHEW 3:16

```
S  R  O  B  I  N  L  C  M
A  N  O  E  G  I  P  U  W
W  E  N  A  E  S  P  R  T
O  E  A  V  A  G  E  L  S
R  V  O  R  G  N  A  E  P
R  D  W  O  L  L  A  W  S
A  N  L  K  E  T  H  N  W
P  H  S  U  R  H  T  I  G
S  F  P  N  O  E  S  L  R
```

Then a voice from heaven spoke!

MATTHEW 3:17

Write every second letter in turn on the lines below to read what the voice said

↓

KTAHMINSSIPSRM

AYBBLEDLROZVXE

TDBSDOENCMFYGF

IAHVGOKRPRSEBS

DTESFOLNNHPIRM

``

___ ___ ___ ___ ___

___ ___ ___ ___ ___ ;

ANSWERS There are eight hidden names:
robin, curlew, eagle, pigeon, sparrow, swallow, thrush, wren

Jesus is put to the test!

MATTHEW 4:1-11

Jesus spent forty days and nights
fasting in the wilderness.
The devil came and put him to the test!

TEST 1
Turn these stones
into bread

(MATTHEW 4:3)

Match the words with the
answer Jesus gave

NOT   ON   MAN
ALONE   LIVE   BREAD
DOES

THINK and LOOK ahead

Look in
MATTHEW 17:1

Next week

which three disciples
go with Jesus to the
top of a mountain?

1. _____   2. _____   3. _____

Check your answer by writing the first letter of each picture

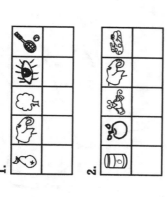

AND

The devil did not give up!
He tempted Jesus
for a second time.

TEST 2
If you are
God's Son throw
yourself down
(MATTHEW 4:6)

TEST 3
I will give you
the world if you
worship me
(MATTHEW 4:9)

Then Jesus was tested
for a third time!

ADAO NAOAT
APAUAT AAGAOIDA ATAO
AATHAE ATAEAASAT

Cross out the
letter that
rhymes with
"day" to read
Jesus' reply

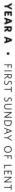

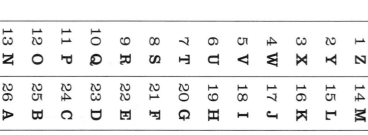

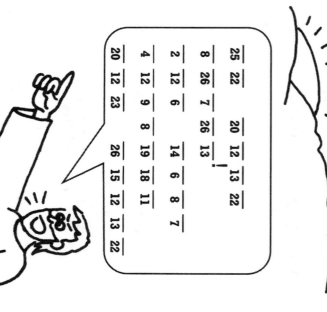

1 Z	14 M	
2 Y	15 L	
3 X	16 K	
4 W	17 J	
5 V	18 I	
6 U	19 H	
7 T	20 G	
8 S	21 F	
9 R	22 E	
10 Q	23 D	
11 P	24 C	
12 O	25 B	
13 N	26 A	

Glory on the mountain

MATTHEW 17:1-9

Jesus took Peter, James, and John to the top of a mountain to see something amazing!

Help them to find the way to Mount Tabor by completing the directions

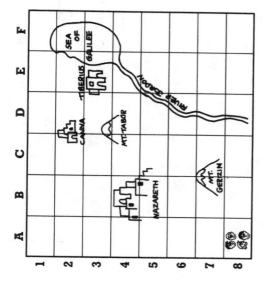

Directions:

8A, 7A, 7B

_____

MATTHEW 17:1

THINK and LOOK ahead

Look in
JOHN 4:6

Where does Jesus stop to rest next week?

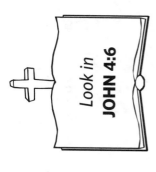

1. _ _ _ _ _ _ ,

2. _ _ _ _ _ _

CLUES

1. Isaac's son and Esau's brother

2. The opposite of sick

Jesus shone like the sun, and his clothes became brilliant white—he was transfigured!

Use the clues to spell a word that explains what "transfigured" means

1. The fourth letter of
2. The first letter of
3. The second letter of
4. The third letter of
5. The fourth letter of
6. The fourth letter of
7. The first letter of

MATTHEW 17:2

What did the three disciples glimpse on the mountain that day?

The answer has been written backward! Write the letters in reverse order on the lines below to read what they say

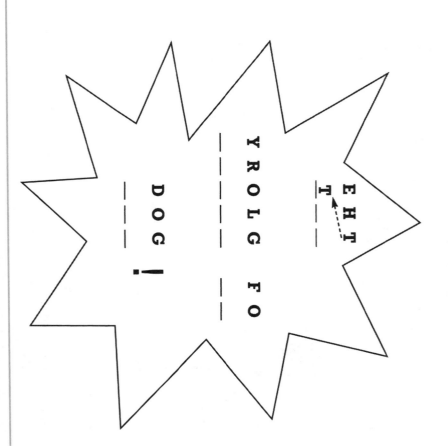

T ← E H T

Y R O L G   F O

D O G   !

The Water of Life

JOHN 4:5-42

Jesus stopped to rest at Jacob's well when a woman came to fill her water jug. Jesus asked her for a drink.

Use the code cracker to find out why the woman was surprised when Jesus spoke to her

	B	A	C	R	E
1	★		◇	★	◈
2	T	N	S	M	W
	◈	◷	★	◻	◎
3	E	H	I	U	A
	✳	◷	◉	1◷	◇

1✳ 3◎ 1★ 1◷ 3◇2★ 1◉   2★ 3◷ 1◎

2◉1◷ 2★   1◷

2★ 1◷ 2◇3◉1◉1◇3★ 2✳ 1◷ 2◷

JOHN 4:9

THINK and LOOK ahead

Look in **JOHN 9:7**

Next week Jesus sends a blind man to wash in a pool.

What was its name?

The pool of ___ __ __

Find the missing letter in each group

P	Q	R	T	U
F	G	H	J	K
K	M	N	O	P
N	P	Q	R	S
X	Y	Z	B	C
L	N	O	P	Q

What did Jesus say to
the Samaritan woman?

Follow the arrows
to find his words

B	E	H	E	I	R	L	N
M	S	T	A	W	L	I	E
K	O	R	E	L	N	K	A
P	N	I	G	V	E	A	G
M	I	K	E	I	Y	Z	J
N	Y	R	H	R	B	T	R
A	D	O	W	A	E	I	S
J	O	N	E	S	B	T	H

"A ___ ___ ___

___ ___ ___ ___ ___

___ ___ ___ ___ ___

___ ___ ___ ___ ___

___ ___ ___ ___ ___

___ ___ ___ ___ ___

___ ___ ___ ___ ___"

Jesus told the woman
many things that
no one else knew,
and she believed in him.

What did the other Samaritans say when they met Jesus?
Choose the right words and write them in the spaces

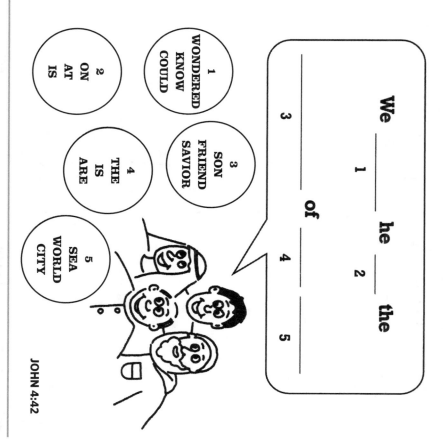

We ___ he ___ the ___
    1   2

3   of   4   5

1 WONDERED KNOW COULD

2 ON AT IS

3 SON FRIEND SAVIOR

4 THE IS ARE

5 SEA WORLD CITY

Help us to see!

JOHN 9:1-41

Jesus met a man who had been born blind.

Add or subtract letters to complete the words and find out what Jesus did

A B C D E F G H I J K L M N O P Q R S T U V W X Y Z

__E__ __A__ __E__ __A__ __S T__ __I T__
J-2 H+5 A+3 W-7 D-3 D+1 X-1 L-4

__M__ __A N D__ __P I T__ , __N__
Q+4 H-4 P+3 F+0 I+3 N-9 H-7 C+1

__U T__ __T O__ __H E__ __M A__
R-2 F+3 K+3 V-2 G+7 G+12

__Y__ S . __T__ __E N__ __E__ S __T__
F-1 A+4 D+4 O-7 I-4 M+1

__I__ __T__ __A S__ __I__ __H__
P-3 C+10 J+5 Z-3 X-16 O-1 Q+3 M-3

__O O__ S __L__ __M__ .
L-4 Q-5 F-1 I-4 E+4 E+10 J-9

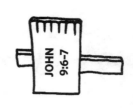

JOHN 9:6-7

THINK and LOOK ahead

JOHN 11:13-14

Next week a good friend of Jesus dies.
What was his name?

Use the picture clues to check your answers

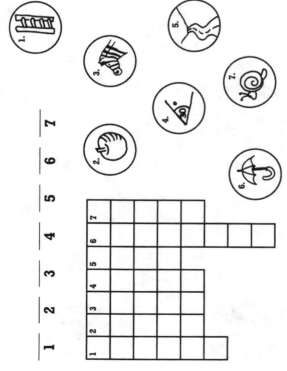

1 __ 2 __ 3 __ 4 __ 5 __ 6 __ 7

To his amazement, the man could now see! He told everyone what had happened but many would not believe him.

Later, Jesus found the man sitting alone.

Fit the letters into the boxes below to see what the Pharisees said about Jesus

THIS M☐ ANN BE
HE S ☐ ☐ T K
FR ☐ D !
THE SAB ☐☐☐☐☐☐☐

GO BATH AN EEP DOE C OT OM NO

Figure out the math problems and use the answers to decode what they said to each other

Number				
4 x5	7 +4	8 -6	8 x2	12 +5
Letter A	E	I	O	U

D̲ Y̲ ̲ B̲ L̲ V̲ ̲ N̲
16 16 17 2 11 11 2

TH̲ ̲ S̲ N̲ ̲ F̲ G̲ D̲?
11 16 16 16

SH̲ W̲ H̲ M̲ T̲ ̲ M̲ ̲ ND̲
16 2 11 11 11 20

W̲ LL̲ B̲ L̲ V̲
2 11 11 2 11

Y̲ ̲ R̲ ̲ L̲ ̲ K̲ NG̲
16 17 20 11 16 16 2

T̲ H̲ M̲!
20 2

L̲ RD̲, ̲ B̲ L̲ V̲
16 2 11 2 11 11

N̲ Y̲ ̲!
2 16 17

Lazarus is alive!

JOHN 11:1–45

Martha and Mary's brother, Lazarus, was very ill,
so the sisters sent a message to Jesus.

Can you decode their message?

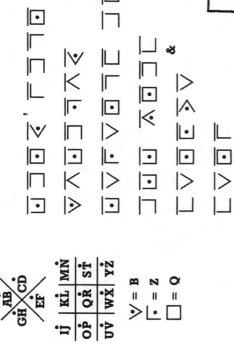

JOHN 11:3

THINK and LOOK ahead

What is one name given to next Sunday?

Connect the dots to find a clue

___ ___ ___ Sunday

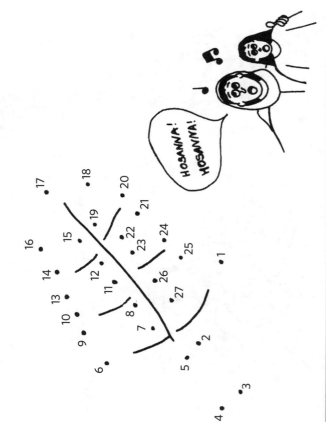

JOHN 11:22

When Jesus arrived, Lazarus had already been buried for four days. Martha ran to greet Jesus.

Write every second letter on the lines below to find Martha's words

BLLOARMDEIOKRNSOAWNTEHDAPT
QGBOLDAWEIOLULIGNRBACNFTKW
DHLAPTSERVNEEERGYOONUYAKSRK

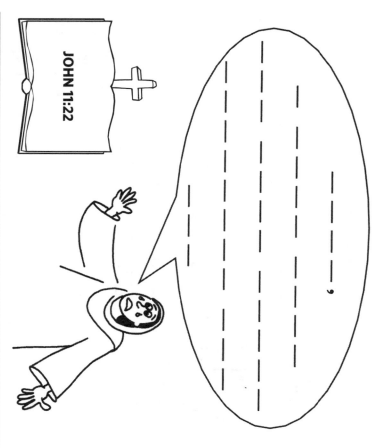

I am the resurrection and the life! Whoever believes in me will never die.
(JOHN 11:25-26)

Jesus called Lazarus from the tomb.
Connect the dots and read what happened next

DEAD • 2

MAN • 3

CAME • 4

THE • 1

12 • 11 • IN

10 • BELIEVED

5 • OUT

JESUS

SAW • 8

9 • AND

7 • MANY

6 • AND

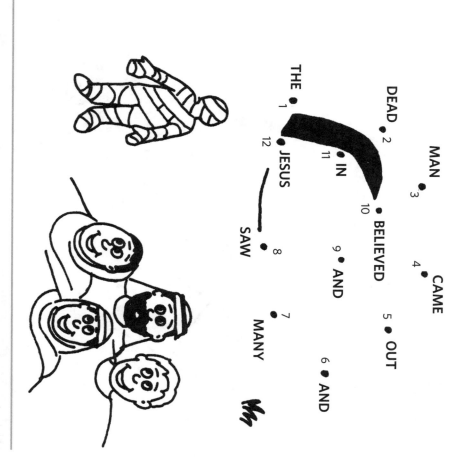

Hosanna! Hosanna!

MATTHEW 21:1-11

What did the prophecy say about Jesus riding into Jerusalem?

Use the letter code to find out

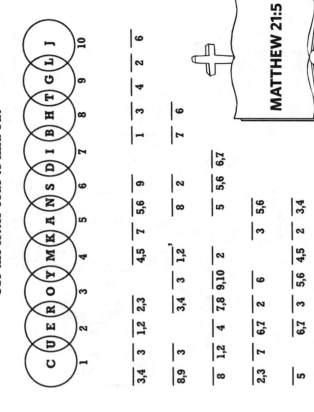

| C | U | E | R | O | Y | M | K | A | N | S | D | I | B | H | T | G | L | J |
| 1 | | 2 | | 3 | | 4 | | 5 | | 6 | | 7 | | 8 | | 9 | | 10 |

___ ___ ___   ___   ___   ___ ___   ___   ___ ___ ___
3,4 3 1,2 2,3   4,5   5,6 9   1 3 4 2 6

___ ___   ___   ___ ___   ___ ___   ___   ___ ___
8,9 3   3,4   3   1,2   7   6   8 2

___ ___ ___   ___ ___ ___   ___   ___ ___ ___
8   1,2 4   7,8 9,10 2   5   5,6 6,7

___ ___   ___   ___ ___   ___   ___ ___
2,3 7   6,7   2   6   3   5,6

___   ___ ___   ___   ___ ___   ___   ___ ___
5   6,7   3   5,6   4,5   2   3,4

MATTHEW 21:5

This woman discovers an empty tomb next Sunday.

Who is she?

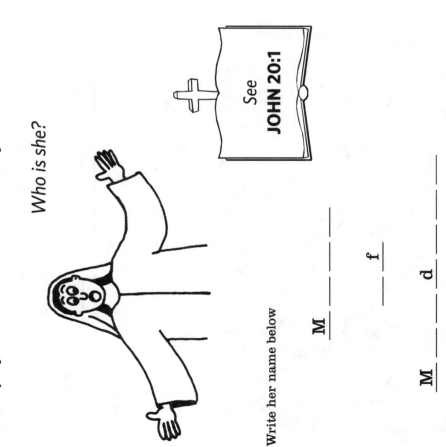

See
JOHN 20:1

Write her name below

M ___ ___ ___   ___ f ___

M ___ ___ d ___ ___ ___

Where did Jesus send his disciples to find the donkey and colt?

Follow the letters of the alphabet in order to find the route they took

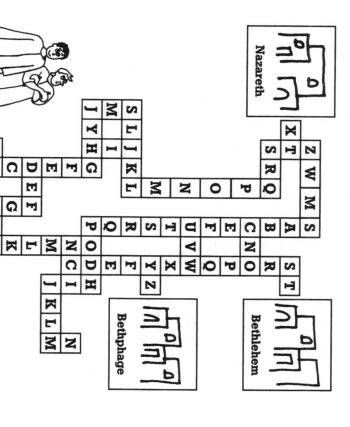

Nazareth

Bethphage

Bethlehem

The people spread cloaks and palms on the road as Jesus rode into Jerusalem.

Fill the blanks with words from the leaves to see what the crowds shouted

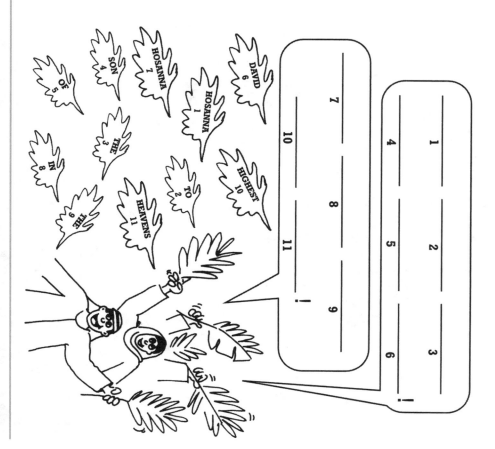

HOSANNA 7

SON 4

OF 5

HOSANNA 1

TO 2

THE 3

DAVID 6

IN 8

THE 9

HEAVENS 11

HIGHEST 10

1 ___ 2 ___ 3 ___
4 ___ 5 ___ 6 ___
7 ___ 8 ___ 9 ___
10 ___ 11 ___ !

Jesus is risen!

JOHN 20:1-9

Mary of Magdala came running to Simon Peter and John!

Choose the word in each group that does not fit and write it on the line below

(Lunch / Breakfast / Lord / 3)

(5 / Know / Rain / Fog)

(1 / Chick / They / Bunny)

(Shower / Tomb / Bath / 4)

(The / Sausage / Bacon / 2)

(6 / Eye / Where / Nose)

" _____ have taken
       1

_____ _____ from the
    2   3

_____ and we don't
    4

_____ he is!"
    5   6

JOHN 20:2

THINK and LOOK ahead

I am one of the Twelve Apostles who is filled with doubt. *Who am I?*

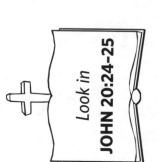

Look in
JOHN 20:24–25

The two disciples ran to the tomb! What did they see when they got there?

The two disciples went into the tomb and then they understood the words of Scripture!

Use the code cracker to find out

CODE CRACKER

D (1) E (3) I (5) B (7) S (9) O (11) H (13) G (15) R (17)
U (2) N (4) L (6) T (8) F (10) A (12) Y (14) C (16) P (18)

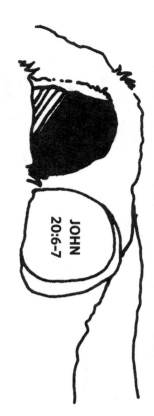

JOHN
20:6-7

$\overline{6}\ \overline{5}\ \overline{4}\ \overline{3}\ \overline{4}$ $\overline{16}\ \overline{6}\ \overline{11}\ \overline{8}\ \overline{13}\ \overline{9}$ $\overline{11}\ \overline{4}$

$\overline{8}\ \overline{13}\ \overline{3}$ $\overline{15}\ \overline{17}\ \overline{11}\ \overline{2}\ \overline{4}\ \overline{1}$; $\overline{11}\ \overline{4}\ \overline{3}$

$\overline{17}\ \overline{11}\ \overline{6}\ \overline{6}\ \overline{3}\ \overline{1}$ $\overline{2}\ \overline{18}$ $\overline{5}\ \overline{4}$ $\overline{12}$

$\overline{18}\ \overline{6}\ \overline{12}\ \overline{16}\ \overline{3}$ $\overline{7}\ \overline{14}$ $\overline{5}\ \overline{8}\ \overline{9}\ \overline{3}\ \overline{6}\ \overline{10}$.

Can you unscramble the words below?

EH TUSM
SERI
FMRO HET
EDDA

JOHN 20:9

Doubting Thomas

JOHN 20:19-31

The disciples had hidden away in a locked room when suddenly Jesus appeared to them.

Finish this picture. Imagine how the disciples felt!

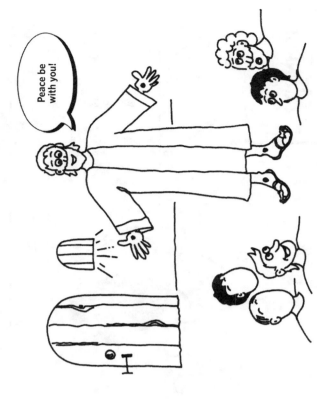

Peace be with you!

JOHN 20:19

THINK and LOOK ahead

Next week two disciples set off on a journey.

Where are they going?

_____

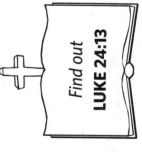

Find out
LUKE 24:13

Were you right?

Write the letter that is missing from the second word in the box

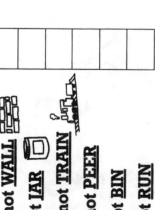

In **WELL** but not **WALL**

In **IAM** but not **IAR**

In **TRAM** but not **TRAIN**

In **PEAR** but not **PEER**

In **BUN** but not **BIN**

In **SUN** but not **RUN**

The disciple called Thomas was not there when Jesus appeared. He would not believe what the other disciples told him!

Jesus appeared to Thomas and showed him his wounds.

Use the code breaker to find his words

△	U	E	V	W	S
○	N	D	I	L	I
□	B	O	H	T	E
	1	2	3	4	5

"
△1 ○1 ○4 △2 △5 △5   ○3   △5 △2 △2

□3 ○3 △5   △4 □2 △1 ○1 ○2 △5

○3   △4 ○3 ○4 ○4

○1 □2 □4

□1 △2 ○4 ○5 □5 △3 □5 !"

JOHN 20:25

Unscramble Thomas' words

YM ____

DROL DNA ____ ____

YM ODG ____ ____

JOHN 20:28

The road to Emmaus

LUKE 24:13-35

Two disciples of Jesus were on the road to Emmaus when another traveler joined them.

Find which route will take them to Emmaus

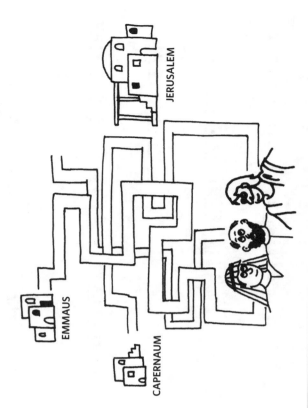

JERUSALEM

EMMAUS

CAPERNAUM

THINK and LOOK ahead

Find out who
enters the sheepfold
by the gate!

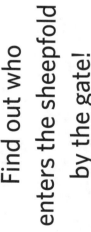

JOHN 10:2

Solve these problems to check your answer

		6	12	4
		x 2	– 8	+ 5
Numbers		___	___	___
Letters		___	___	___

16	2	7	8	10	3	3	3	10
– 8	x 2	+ 2	x 2	– 6	x 3	x 3	+ 2	x 2
___	___	___	___	___	___	___	___	___

4 = H
5 = R
8 = S
9 = E
12 = T
16 = P
20 = D

Sadly they told the traveler
all about Jesus of Nazareth, and
how he had been put to death.

Use the code to see who the traveler was
and what he talked about

A	B	C	D	E	F	G
H	I	O	R	X	E	K
J	C	A	L	N	P	D
M	T	B	U	S	F	W

H₌ E₌ J D₌ E₌   F₌ E₌ F₌ D₌ C₌ B₌ E₌ F₌ G₌
A₌ F₌ E₌ J D₌ E₌

C₌ D₌ D₌   B₌ A₌ F₌

E₌ B₌ D₌ B₌ F₌ B₌ D₌ D₌ F₌ E₌

C₌ C₌ C₌ D₌ B₌   A₌ B₌ A₌ E₌ F₌ D₌ E₌

When did they
recognize Jesus?

Fit the numbered words in place to reveal the answer

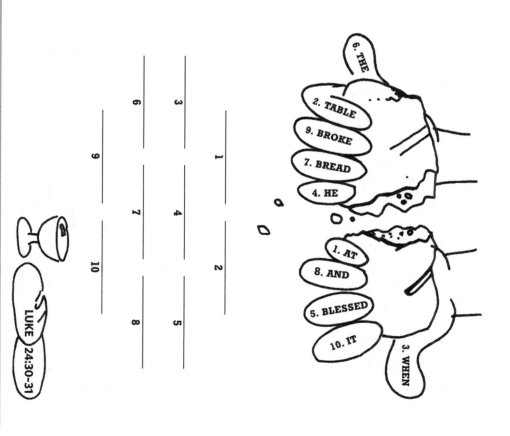

6. THE
2. TABLE
9. BROKE
7. BREAD
4. HE
1. AT
8. AND
5. BLESSED
10. IT
3. WHEN

1 _____ 2 _____
3 _____ 4 _____ 5 _____
6 _____ 7 _____ 8 _____
9 _____ 10 _____

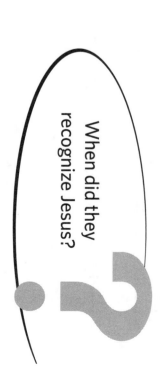

LUKE 24:30-31

The Good Shepherd

JOHN 10:1-11

Jesus told a story about a shepherd and his sheep.

How do the sheep recognize their shepherd?

Write the
first letter of
each picture
in the box

JOHN 10:4

THINK and LOOK ahead

Find out
JOHN 14:1

Who does Jesus
tell us to trust in?

Unscramble the letters to reveal the answer

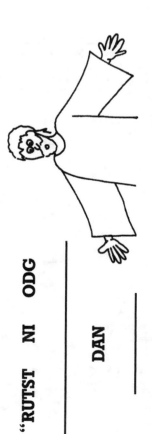

"**RUTST   NI   ODG**

_____ __ ___

DAN

___

USRTT   NI   EMI!"

_____ __ ___

JOHN 10:3-4

What does the shepherd do with his sheep?

Use the coded letters to find out!

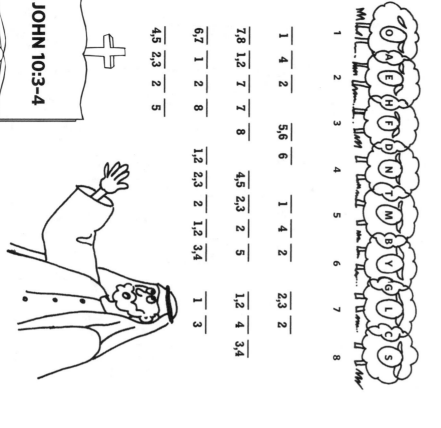

```
O  A  E  H  F  D  N  T  M  B  Y  G  L  C  S
1  2  3  4  5  6  7  8
```

1 4 2

1 4 2   5,6 6   1 4 2   2,3 2

7,8 1,2 7 7 8   4,5 2,3 2 5   1,2 4 3,4

6,7 1 2 8   1,2 2,3 2 1,2 3,4   1 3

4,5 2,3 2 5

Jesus is the Good Shepherd and we are his sheep.

Use the code to find the words of Jesus

```
A  z    H  s    O  l    V  e
B  y    I  r    P  k    W  d
C  x    J  q    Q  j    X  c
D  w    K  p    R  i    Y  b
E  v    L  o    S  h    Z  a
F  u    M  n    T  g
G  t    N  m    U  f
```

"
___ ___ ___ ___ ___
r   z   n   g   s   v

___ ___ ___ ___ ___ ___
t   l   l   w

___ ___ ___ ___ ___ ___ ___
h   s   v   k   s   v   i   w

___ ___ ___ ___ ___
d   s   l   o   z   b   h

___ ___ ___ ___ ___
w   l   d   m   s   r   h

___ ___ ___
o   r   u   v

___ ___ ___ ___
u   l   i

___ ___ ___
s   r   h

___ ___ ___ ___
h   s   v   v   k
"

JOHN 10:11

Jesus is the Way

JOHN 14:1-12

The disciples were worried because Jesus was going away.

Write the next letter of the alphabet above the letters given to see how Jesus reassured them.

For example: B will be written above A

"

___ ___ ___ ___ ___
X N T J M N V S G D

___ ___ ___ ___ ___ ___
V Z X S N S G D

___ ___ ___ ___ ___
O K Z B D H Z L

___ ___ ___ ___ ___
F N H M F
"

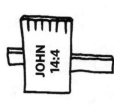

JOHN
14:4

THINK and LOOK ahead

Look in
JOHN 14:15

What must we do if we love God?

___ ___ ___ ___
10 5 5 1

___ ___ ___
2 11 7

___ ___ ___ ___ ___ ___ ___ ___ ___ ___ ___ ___
12 6 3 3 8 4 9 3 5 4 13 7

Use the code to
check your answer

P = 1   H = 2   M = 3   N = 4   E = 5
O = 6   S = 7   A = 8   D = 9   K = 10
I = 11   C = 12   T = 13

Thomas still felt worried, so he asked Jesus a question.

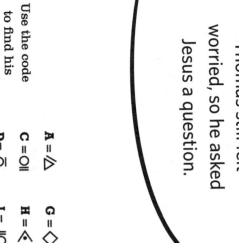

Use the code to find his words below

A = △	G = ◇	L = △	T = ∨
C = ⊙‖	H = ⟨	N = ≈	U = ⊡
D = ⍌	I = ‖⊙	O = ◇	W = ⅂
E = △	K = □	R = ⬦	Y = △

"

△◇⊠⍌ ⅂△ ⍌◇ ≈◇∨ □≈◇⅂

⅂△△⊠△ △◇⍌ △⊠△

◇⍌‖≈◇ !

⟨◇⅂ ⍓△≈ ⅂△

□≈◇⅂ ∨⟨△

▽≈△

⅂△△ ?"

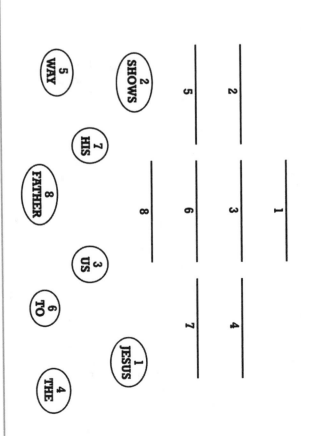

I am the Way, the Truth and the Life!

JOHN 14:6

Arrange the words in order on the lines below to see what Jesus means

1 _____

2 _____ 3 _____ 4 _____

5 _____ 6 _____ 7 _____

8 _____

(2 SHOWS) (7 HIS) (8 FATHER) (3 US) (6 TO) (1 JESUS) (4 THE)

(5 WAY)

You will not be alone

JOHN 14:15–21

If we love Jesus we will keep his commandments.

Which are the two greatest commandments?

Use the secret code pad to find out!

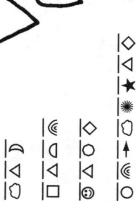

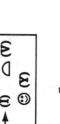

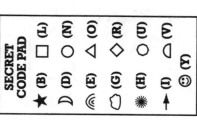

SECRET CODE PAD

★ (B)	□ (L)		
⊃ (D)	○ (N)		
⦅ (E)	△ (O)		
⬡ (G)	◇ (R)		
✳ (H)	○ (U)		
↑ (I)	⊂ (V)		
☺ (Y)			

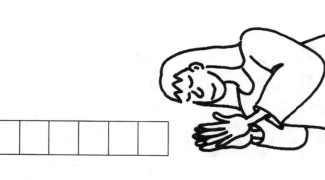

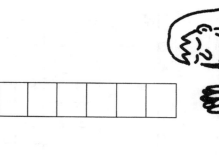

MARK 12:29–31

THINK and **LOOK** ahead

How can we keep in touch with Jesus?

Use the clues to spell out the answer

1. The first letter of
2. The fourth letter of
3. The second letter of
4. The tenth letter of
5. The fifth letter of
6. The second letter of

Jesus was going to leave the disciples and return to his heavenly Father.

What did he promise to do?

Arrange these words in correct alphabetical order to read Jesus' words

$\frac{I}{A}$

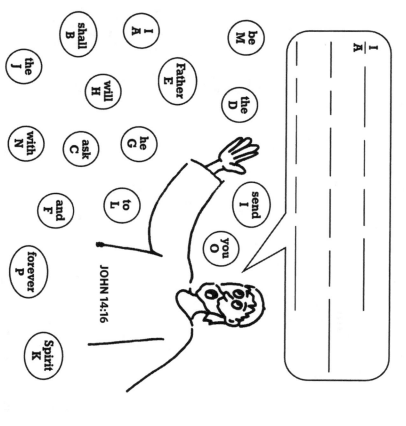

be M

the D

Father E

I A

will H

he G

the J

shall B

ask C

with N

and F

to L

send I

you O

forever P

Spirit K

JOHN 14:16

Through the Holy Spirit, Jesus stays with us in a special way.

Follow the arrows to spell out John 14:19

N	O	W	B	D	W	J	P
T	E	R	L	I	E	S	R
H	D	L	G	E	B	E	B
E	O	N	E	O	M	T	U
E	S	R	S	U	Y	S	I
E	L	A	W	U	L	L	V
L	T	H	I	T	I	E	M

Keep in touch!

JOHN 17:1-11

Before Jesus left his friends and returned to his heavenly Father, what did he do?

Use this code to find out!

A =  D = ▦ E =  F = 🐟 H = ✋ I = 🥕 N = 🔩
O = 🐔 P = 🐓 R = ☀ S = ⭐ T = ☀ V = 🐟 Y = 🪢

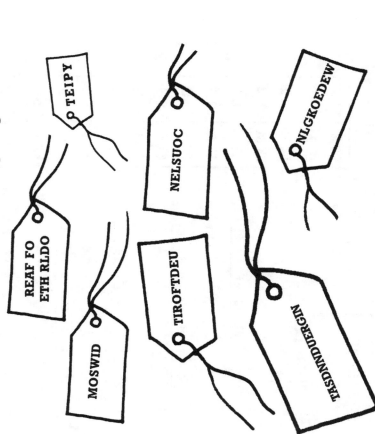

THINK and LOOK ahead

At Pentecost the disciples received the gifts of the Holy Spirit!

What are they?

Unscramble the words on each gift tag to find out

TEIPY

REAF FO ETH RLDO

MOSWID

NELSUOC

TIROFTDEU

TASDNNDUERGIN

NLGKOEDEW

ANSWERS (clockwise) fear of the Lord; piety; counsel; knowledge; understanding; fortitude; wisdom

Jesus was sending the disciples out into the world to spread his message of love.

Use the map references to find out what Jesus prayed for

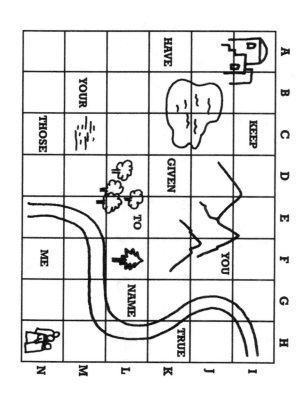

	A	B	C	D	E	F	G	H
I		KEEP				YOU		
J			GIVEN		TO		NAME	
K		HAVE					TRUE	
L			THOSE					
M		YOUR			ME			
N								

C, I ___ C, N ___ E, J ___ A, K ___

D, K ___ E, N ___ H, K ___ E, L ___

B, M ___ G, L ___

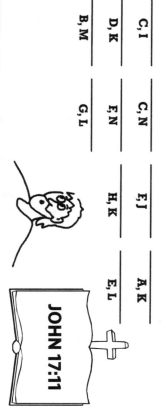

JOHN 17:11

How can we share the eternal life Jesus offers?

Use the code to find the answer given in John 17:3

A 1	N 14
B 2	O 15
C 3	P 16
D 4	Q 17
E 5	R 18
F 6	S 19
G 7	T 20
H 8	U 21
I 9	V 22
J 10	W 23
K 11	X 24
L 12	Y 25
M 13	Z 26

___ ___
2 25

___ ___ ___ ___ ___ ___ ___
11 14 15 23 9 14 7

___ ___ ___ ___ ___ ___
7 15 4 1 14 4

___ ___ ___ ___ ___ ___
8 9 19 19 15 14

___ ___ ___ ___ ___
10 5 19 21 19

JOHN 17:3

The coming of the Spirit

JOHN 20:19–23; ACTS 2:1–11

The disciples had gathered in one room.

What did they hear?

Color the squares marked with a •.
The remaining letters will reveal the answer

A•	C•	E•	A	F•	G	•H	M•	Z	Y•
•J	I	P	O	W	E	R	F	U	L•
O•	S•	L	E•	R•	W	I	N	D•	D
P•	F	R	O	M	S•	•L	O	N•	R
D•	A•	E•	H	E	A	V	E	N	S•

ACTS 2:2

THINK and LOOK ahead

What name do we give to
God the Father, Son, and Holy Spirit?

Write the missing letter in the series

R S U V W	
EFGIJ	
ABCDF	

PQRSU	
OPQST	
FGHJK	
MOPQR	
EFGHJ	
SUVWX	
WXZAB	

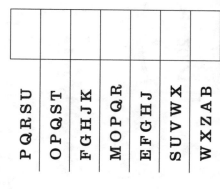

FATHER, SON, & HOLY SPIRIT

ONE GOD

What appeared as tongues of fire above their heads?

Write the letters in the "flames"

ACTS 2:3

1. The first letter of 🌥
2. The first letter of
3. The fourth letter of 🖐
4. The first letter of
5. The second letter of 🏠
6. The third letter of 🎄

7. The first letter of "
8. The fourth letter of
9. The second letter of
10. The second letter of
11. The second letter of
12. The second letter of
13. The fourth letter of

The Spirit gave them the courage to share the Word of God with everyone!

Find the words of Jesus, using the key

	1	2	3	4
★	A	S	H	E
⌒	D	G	O	N
☀	U	T	O	M

"

★1 ★2

★2 ★3 ★4   ⌒1 ★1 ☀2 ★3 ★4 ⌒2

★2)4 2   ☀4 ★4   ,   ★2 ☀3   ⌒4 ★1 ☀4

★2 ★4)4)1 ⌒4)4)2   ⌒3 ☀3 ☀1

JOHN 20:21

God's love for us

JOHN 3:16-18

Who did God send to save the world from sin?

Find the opposite below to spell out the answer

The opposite of **QUIET** is

The opposite of **LOW** is

The opposite of **DARK** is

The opposite of **QUICKLY** is

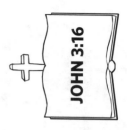

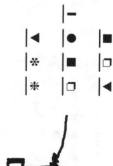

JOHN 3:16

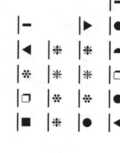

Color the letters

THE HOLY TRINITY

Jesus spoke to a Pharisee called Nicodemus about the Son of God.

Follow the instructions to find his words

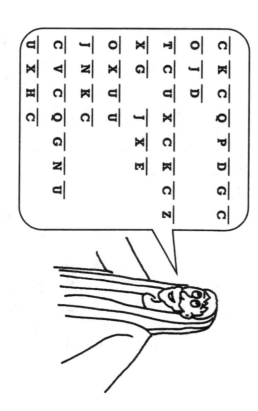

C	K	C	Q	P	D	G	C
O	J	D					
T	C	U	X	C	K	C	Z
X	G	J	X	E			
O	X	U	U				
J	N	K	C				
C	V	C	Q	G	N	U	
U	X	H	C				

1. Change the letter C to E
2. Change the letter D to O
3. Change the letter G to N
4. Change the letter J to H
5. Change the letter K to V
6. Change the letter P to Y
7. Change the letter Q to R
8. Change the letter T to B
9. Change the letter U to L
10. Change the letter X to I
11. Change the letter Z to S
12. Change the letter E to M
13. Change the letter O to W
14. Change the letter N to A
15. Change the letter H to F
16. Change the letter V to T

On Trinity Sunday who do we give glory and praise?

Fit the pieces in the puzzle

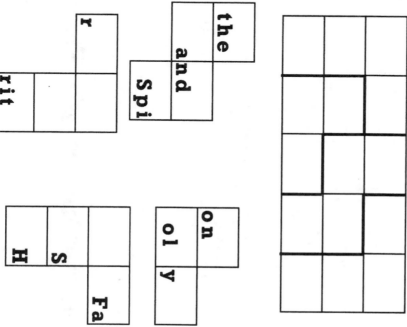

the

and

Spi

on

ol

y

r

rit

s

H

Fa

The Lamb of God

JOHN 1:29-34

In the Old Testament, lambs were often sacrificed when someone wanted to ask God's forgiveness for their sins (Leviticus 5:6).

Hidden in this puzzle are seven words connected with "lambs." See if you can find them all!

P	O	L	N	B	E	P	D
K	C	O	L	F	A	R	L
O	A	E	B	S	E	K	O
W	A	O	T	H	S	E	F
T	N	U	P	E	M	D	S
R	R	E	B	E	B	M	A
E	H	L	K	P	M	C	P
S	H	E	E	P	D	O	G

THINK and LOOK ahead

After John the Baptist's arrest, Jesus returned to Galilee.

Which lakeside town did he settle in?

Find out in **MATTHEW 4:13**

Add and subtract words or letters to spell out the name

 – GE +  – A + 🖐 – IL + ☂ – BRELLA

When John saw Jesus
what did he call him?

Why do you think
John called Jesus this?

Moving clockwise, write down every other letter.
Do this twice to find the answer

START

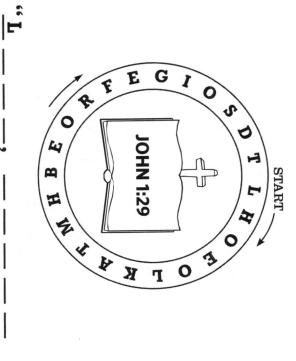

JOHN 1:29

"T _ _ _ , _ _ _ _ _"

Write the next letter of the alphabet above the given letters.
For example, B will be written above A

"
S G D   K Z L A   N E

F N C   S Z J D R

Z V Z X   S G D   R H M

N E   S G D   V N Q K C
"

JOHN 1:29

Follow me!

MATTHEW 4:12–23

Jesus chose his first disciples beside the Sea of Galilee.

Can you match the brothers?

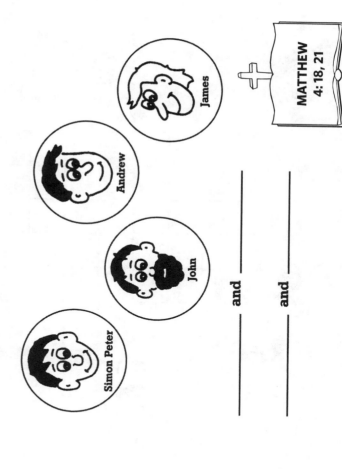

Simon Peter   John   Andrew   James

_____ and _____

_____ and _____

MATTHEW 4:18, 21

What did Jesus say that made these fishermen follow him?

Use the secret code pad to read his words!

SECRET CODE PAD

A (1) B (2) C (3) D (4) E (5) F (6) G (7) H (8) I (9) J (10)
K (11) L (12) M (13) N (14) O (15) P (16) Q (17) R (18)
S (19) T (20) U (21) V (22) W (23) X (24) Y (25) Z (26)

$\overline{(3)}\;\overline{(15)}\;\overline{(13)}\;\overline{(5)}$ $\overline{(6)}\;\overline{(15)}\;\overline{(12)}\;\overline{(12)}\;\overline{(15)}\;\overline{(23)}$ $\overline{(13)}\;\overline{(5)}$

$\overline{(1)}\;\overline{(14)}\;\overline{(4)}$ $\overline{(9)}$ $\overline{(23)}\;\overline{(9)}\;\overline{(12)}\;\overline{(12)}$

$\overline{(13)}\;\overline{(1)}\;\overline{(11)}\;\overline{(5)}$ $\overline{(25)}\;\overline{(15)}\;\overline{(21)}$

$\overline{(6)}\;\overline{(9)}\;\overline{(19)}\;\overline{(8)}\;\overline{(5)}\;\overline{(18)}\;\overline{(19)}$ $\overline{(15)}\;\overline{(6)}$

$\overline{(16)}\;\overline{(5)}\;\overline{(15)}\;\overline{(16)}\;\overline{(12)}\;\overline{(5)}$ "

MATTHEW 4:19

What did these brothers
do for a living?

Use the picture clues to complete the crossword.
The letters in the darker boxes will spell out the answer

Can you see what
James and John are trying
to untangle?

Draw a straight line between the dots with the same number

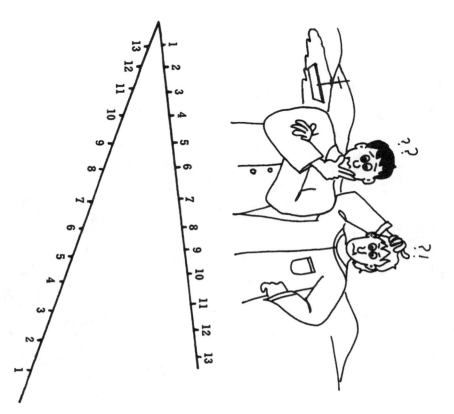

The secret of happiness

MATTHEW 5:1-12

Jesus went up a hillside and began to teach the crowds about true happiness.

Use the clues to find the name of the sermon he gave that day

What things make YOU feel happy?

Write your ideas below or draw some pictures in the spaces provided

Happiness is . . .

Can you match the items to read the words of Jesus?

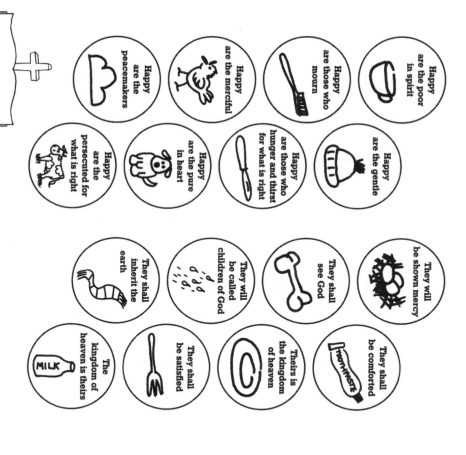

MATTHEW
5:3-10

Use the guide below to color this picture

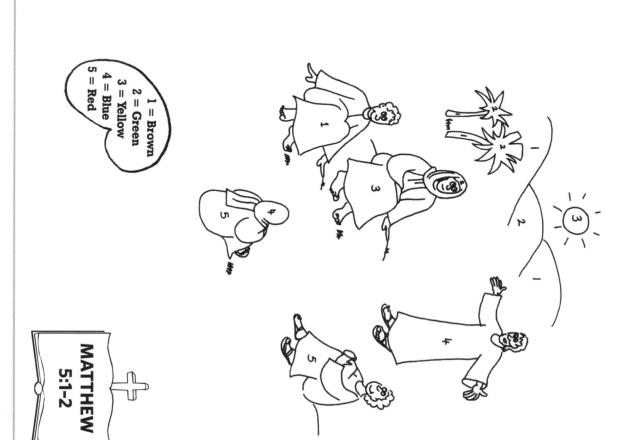

1 = Brown
2 = Green
3 = Yellow
4 = Blue
5 = Red

MATTHEW
5:1-2

Be a light for all to see

MATTHEW 5:13-16

Jesus told his disciples to let their love shine out for all to see!

Connect the dots to find Matthew 5:14

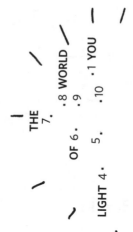

LIGHT 4·
5·
OF 6·
THE
7·
·8 WORLD
·9
·10 ·1 YOU

THE 3·
·2 ARE

Can you find the names of the objects in this puzzle?

Circle each word

P	S	M	O	O	N
H	C	T	A	M	R
T	B	A	F	L	E
M	O	I	A	L	T
K	R	R	D	E	N
E	P	N	C	M	A
L	A	M	P	H	L
C	R	S	U	N	T

Jesus said,
"No one lights a lamp
and then covers it!"

How many candles can you find hidden in this picture?
There should be ten!

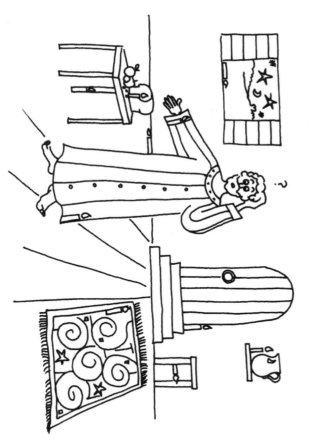

What did Jesus
tell us to do?

Use the secret code pad to spell out his words

CODE PAD

F	(a)
E	(b)
N	(c)
I	(d)
S	(e)
M	(f)
T	(g)
I	(h)
H	(i)
G	(j)
R	(k)
U	(l)
L	(m)
O	(n)
Y	(o)

o n l k   m h j i g
_____ _____
f l e g   e i d c b
_____ _____
h c   g i b
_____
e d j i g   n a
_____
f b c
_____

Rules for life

MATTHEW 5:17-37

Jesus began to teach his disciples about God's commandments.

Write the first letter of each picture to spell out the two great commandments Jesus gave us

Jesus said...

If you have disagreed with someone, go and make your peace.

MATTHEW 5:23-24

Can you write Jesus' message in code?

I F   Y O U   H A V E
     L

D I S A G R E E D   W I T H

S O M E O N E ,   G O

A N D   M A K E   Y O U R

P E A C E

Use these clues to find the missing letters
and decode the symbols below

A young goat

Whoever comes first in a race

The number of fingers on each hand

A young dog

The opposite of cold

Rain falls from these

The place where you live

The color of grass

A young sheep

**Can you use
the symbols to find
Jesus' words?**

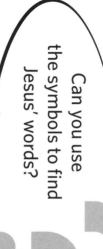

Write each letter above its symbol!

SYMBOL DECODER

◇ = **A**   ≋ = ▪⁞▪   ▽ = ⌒⁞⌒   ≈ = ⌒⁞⌒ ...

◇ = A	≋ =	∨ =	⌒ =
⊃ =	⁞ =	□ =	⌒ᴵ =
✕ =	∟ =	✳ =	⚡ =
☺ =	⋒ =	⟵ =	△ =
		✂ =	⊙ =
		⇩ =	△ =

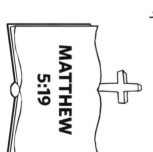

**MATTHEW
5:19**

Love your enemies

MATTHEW 5:38-48

What did the Old Testament teach about enemies?

Use the key to find out what is written on the scroll

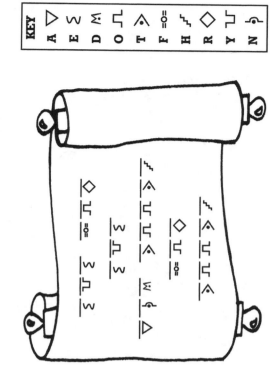

KEY

A	▷
E	∨∨
D	⋈
O	⌐∟
T	∧
F	=○=
H	↗
R	◇
Y	⊔
N	ᓂ

MATTHEW 5:38

Jesus showed us how to love our enemies by his words and actions!

Can you match each picture with its caption?

A

B

C

A and ___

Zacchaeus, come down! I want to visit your house today. 1

B and ___

A good Samaritan took care of the traveler. 2

C and ___

Father, forgive them; they know not what they do. 3

You can find these stories in the references given

Luke 19: 1-10

Luke 10: 29-37

Luke 23:34

The Old Laws had taught the people to seek

Inside this circle is a clue. Write the seven-letter answer around the outside, starting at the black arrow

1 _ 2 _ 3 _ 4 _ 5 _ 6 _ 7 _

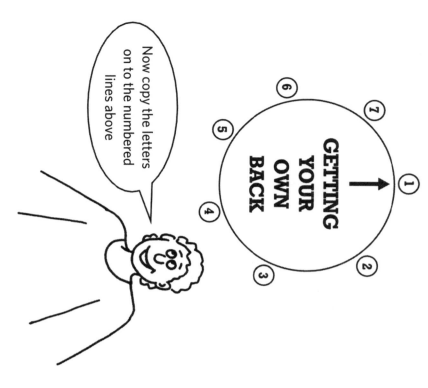

Now copy the letters on to the numbered lines above

Use this code to find his words from Matthew 5:44

Jesus came to teach the people a new law about love.

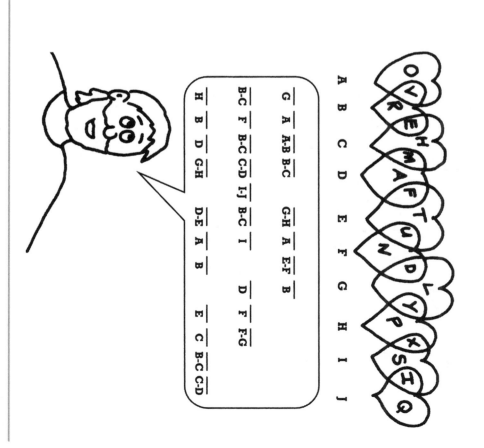

ANSWER: Revenge

Do not worry

MATTHEW 6:24-34

Jesus did not want us to worry about unimportant things.

Follow the arrows to spell out what he said

L	E	W	R	R	S
B	T	D	O	W	Y
N	O	U	B	A	C
W	T	R	O	E	G
H	A	T	A	W	E
S	O	O	R	A	F

D ___ ___ ___ ___ ___ ___ ___ ___ ___ ___ ___ ___ ___ !

___ ___ ___ ___ ___ ___

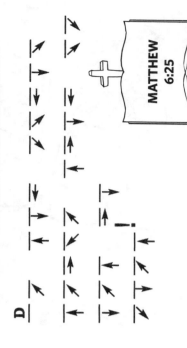

MATTHEW
6:25

God loves us most of all!

Unscramble the words of Jesus

ROUY VENHEALY

THAFER LIILW

KETA RACE OF

LAL UROY DENES

MATTHEW 6:32-33

God takes care of the birds in the sky.

How many insects can you find in this picture?
Circle them

God clothes the flowers in the fields.

Write the numbered words on the lines

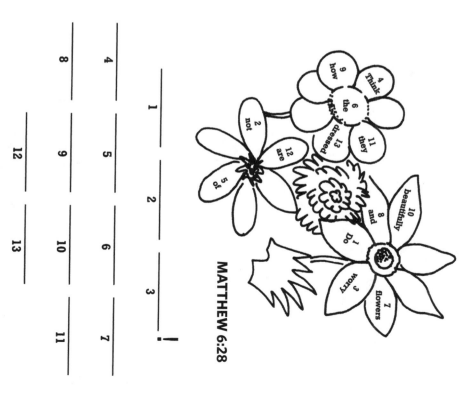

4 Think
9 how
6 the
11 they
2 not
13 dressed
12 are
5 of
8 and
10 beautifully
1 Do
3 worry
7 flowers

MATTHEW 6:28

1 _____ 2 _____ 3 _____ !

4 _____ 5 _____ 6 _____ 7 _____

8 _____ 9 _____ 10 _____ 11 _____

12 _____ 13 _____

Build your lives on me!

MATTHEW 7:21-27

Jesus told a parable about a wise man who built a house.

Can you spot eight differences between these houses?

?

What message did Jesus want to give us?

Use the code cracker to find his words

__ __ __   __ __ __ __   __ __
23 8 15   5 22 5 18   20 15

__ __ __ __ __ __ __   __ __ __ __ __
12 9 19 20 5 14 19   13 25   23 15 18 4 19

__ __ __   __ __ __ __
1 14 4   1 3 20 19

__ __   __ __ __ __   __ __ __ __   __ __
15 14   20 8 5 13   23 9 12 12   13 25

__ __ __   __ __   __ __ __ __ __
6 1 20 8   5 18   18 19

__ __ __   __ __ __
23 9 12 12

A 1	N 14
B 2	O 15
C 3	P 16
D 4	Q 17
E 5	R 18
F 6	S 19
G 7	T 20
H 8	U 21
I 9	V 22
J 10	W 23
K 11	X 24
L 12	Y 25
M 13	Z 26

MATTHEW
7:21, 24

What did the sensible man do?

Write the first letter of each picture clue to spell out the answer

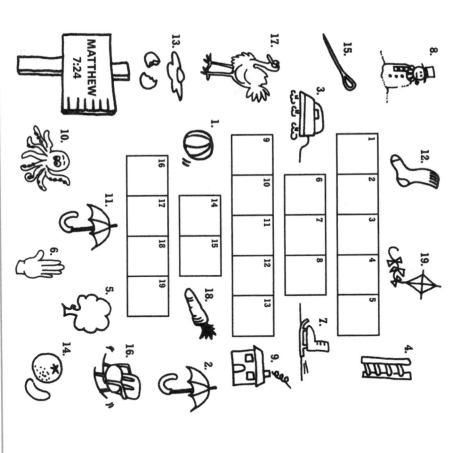

MATTHEW 7:24

The foolish man built his house on sand.

Copy these jigsaw pieces to make a picture that shows what happened next

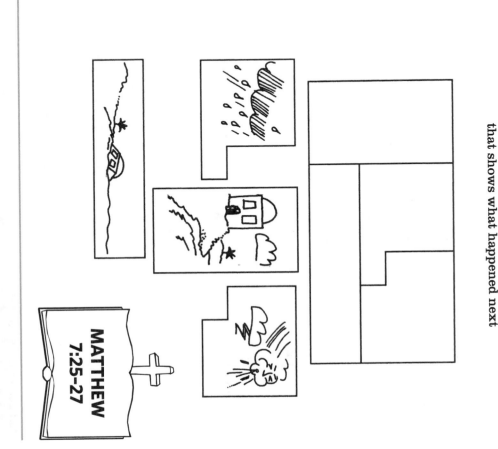

MATTHEW 7:25-27

Jesus makes a friend

MATTHEW 9:9-13

One day Jesus called a man to follow him.

Solve the clues to find the man's name.
The first letter of each word will spell out the answer

CLUES
1. The opposite of few
2. The fruit Eve shared with Adam
3. You use a watch to tell this
4. Another name for a pill
5. The place where you live
6. The name of our planet
7. A spider spins this

MATTHEW 9:9

THINK and LOOK ahead

Find out
MATTHEW 9:36

Why did Jesus
feel sorry
for the crowds?

**They
were like**

_ _ _ _ _ _

without a

_ _ _ _ _ _ _

Jesus went to Matthew's house and ate with many of his friends.

Use the code to find out what the Pharisees said about Jesus

W	N	R	T
E	D	C	L
A	C	Y	S
H	I	O	X

MATTHEW 9:11

"_____ _____ _____ _____ _____ _____ _____ _____ ?"

What was Jesus' reply to them?

Crack the code!

1	2	3	4	5	6	7	8	9	10	11	12	13
I	H	C	N	M	E	A	O	L	V	T	S	R

"__
1

__ __ __ __
2 7 10 6

__ __ __ __
3 8 5 6

__ __
11 8

__ __ __ __
3 7 9 9

__ __ __ __ __ __ __
12 1 4 4 6 13 12"

MATTHEW 9:13

The Twelve Apostles

MATTHEW 9:36—10:8

Jesus felt sorry for the people because they were like sheep without a shepherd.

Add or subtract letters to see what Jesus told his disciples

A B C D E F G H I J K L M N O P Q R S T U V W X Y Z

$\overline{X-4}$ $\overline{G+1}$ $\overline{A+4}$ $\overline{N-6}$ $\overline{D-3}$ $\overline{K+7}$ $\overline{Z-4}$ $\overline{I-4}$ $\overline{M+6}$ $\overline{U-1}$

$\overline{E+4}$ $\overline{Z-7}$ $\overline{G+11}$ $\overline{L-3}$ $\overline{B+1}$ $\overline{F+2}$

$\overline{J-8}$ $\overline{N+7}$ $\overline{E+15}$ $\overline{N-2}$ $\overline{F-5}$ $\overline{A+1}$ $\overline{K+4}$ $\overline{Q+1}$ $\overline{C+2}$ $\overline{V-4}$ $\overline{L+7}$

$\overline{F-5}$ $\overline{S-1}$ $\overline{B+3}$ $\overline{E+1}$ $\overline{B+3}$ $\overline{Z-3}$

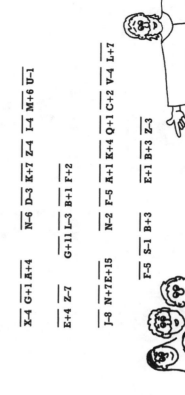

MATTHEW 9:37

What else did he tell them?

Look at these word sets.
Find the odd ones out and write them on the lines

(RABBIT RAT RECEIVED 2)

(HOUR MINUTE NOW 4)

(DOG FREELY CAT 6)

(APPLE YOU PEAR 1)

(FREELY SMALL TINY 3)

(CHOCOLATES GIVE SWEETS 5)

_____ 1

_____ 2

_____ 3

_____ 4

_____ 5

_____ 6

MATTHEW 10:8

So he called twelve of his disciples to send them out to the people.

MATTHEW
10:2

Pictured below are the twelve men Jesus chose.
Can you unscramble their names?

  TPREE _____

  WRENAD _____

   ASJME _____

  HONJ _____

 LIHPPI _____

   OOLWEMRTABH _____

SATHOM _____

  HATTWEM _____

 SAMJE _____

DDAETHAUS _____

MISON _____

DUJAS _____

Jesus told them what to say and gave them the power to do everything he asked.

Write the first letter of each object to read his instructions to them

and

 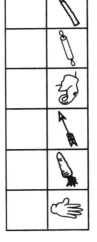 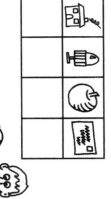 

MATTHEW 10:1, 7-8

Do not be afraid!

MATTHEW 10:26–33

The apostles were feeling worried about preaching to the people.

Cross out the letters with odd numbers and copy the remaining letters in order on to the lines below to see what Jesus told them

X̶ D O B N K O T B R E A D F R L A I E D P R F O C L E
3 4 6 9 8 7 14 10 6 13 4 12 13 2 16 19 4 8 15 18 22 10 3 6 4 12 9

A I S M F J R O M G T E H E M R O L O F T R O P J S
18 4 17 8 16 17 4 2 6 13 2 11 16 4 5 14 22 3 6 8 2 7 18 4 9 10

_ _ _ _ _ _ _ _

_ _ _ _ _ _ _

_ _ _ _ _ _ _

MATTHEW 10:26-27

God watches over every one of us.

Write the next letter of the alphabet above the given letters to read Jesus' words from Matthew 10.31

A B C D E F G H I J K L M N O P Q R S T U V W X Y Z

Y
X

_ _ _
N T

_ _ _
Z Q D

_ _
V N

_
Q

_
S G

_ _
L N

_ _
Q D

_ _
S G

_
Z

_
M

_ _
L Z

_
M

_
X

_ _
R O

_
Z

_
Q

_
Q

_
N

_
V

_
R

Jesus wanted them
to know that God would
take care of them.

MATTHEW 10:29

God even knows the
number of hairs on your head!
(Matthew 10:30)

Use the key to find the letters and spell out what he told them

1	2	3	4	5	6	7	8	9	10	11	12	13	△	□
A	C	E	G	I	K	M	O	Q	S	U	W			
B	D	F	H	J	L	N	P	R	T	V	X	Z		

7△ 8□ 10△   8□ 7△ 3□   10□ 8△ 1□ 9△ 9△ 8□ 12□

3□ 1□ 6△ 6△ 10□   10△ 8□   10△ 4△ 3□

4□ 9△ 8□ 11□ 7△ 2□   12□ 5□ 10△ 4△ 8□ 11□ 10△

13□ 8□ 11□ 9△   3△ 1□ 10△ 4△ 3□ 9△

6□ 7△ 8□ 12□ 5□ 7△ 4□

These men are losing their hair!
Which man has the most hair?
Which man has the least?

A   B   C   D   E

The man with most hair   [ ]

The man with least hair   [ ]

Make Jesus welcome

MATTHEW 10:37-42

If Jesus came to your house today
how would you make him feel welcome?

Write what you could DO and SAY

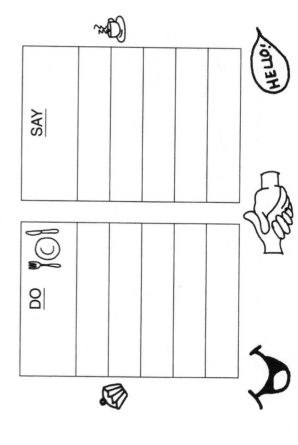

DO	SAY

THINK and LOOK ahead

Jesus mentions
this object
next week.
*What is it and
what could it
be used for?*

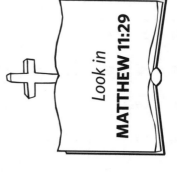

Look in
MATTHEW 11:29

CLUE

SOUNDS LIKE

A

_ _ _

Jesus wants us to welcome EVERYONE as we would welcome him!

Follow the instructions to find the words of Jesus

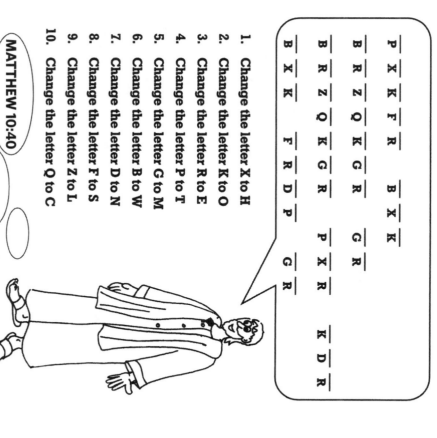

P X K F R   B X K

B R Z Q K G R   G R

B R Z Q K G R   P X R   G R

B X K   F R D P   G R

1. Change the letter X to H
2. Change the letter K to O
3. Change the letter R to E
4. Change the letter P to T
5. Change the letter G to M
6. Change the letter B to W
7. Change the letter D to N
8. Change the letter F to S
9. Change the letter Z to L
10. Change the letter Q to C

MATTHEW 10:40

There are many different ways to make someone feel welcome!

Can you find and circle these words in the puzzle below?
Some appear more than once

KISS   HANDSHAKE   HUG   WAVE   SMILE
MEAL   DRINK   PLAY   SHARE

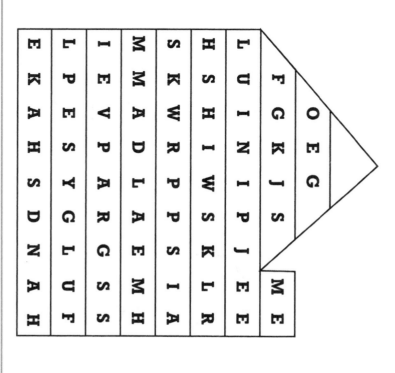

O	E	G					
F	G	K	J	S			M
L	U	I	N	I	P	J	E
H	S	H	I	W	S	K	R
S	K	W	R	P	P	S	I
M	M	A	D	L	A	E	H
I	E	V	P	A	R	G	S
L	P	E	S	Y	G	L	U	F
E	K	A	H	S	D	N	A	H

Jesus is gentle and kind

MATTHEW 11:25–30

Jesus taught us to know God the Father.

Use the key to find the words of Matthew 11:27

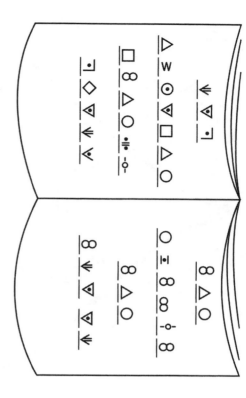

THINK and LOOK ahead

I use stories to help everyone to understand my message. What are they called?

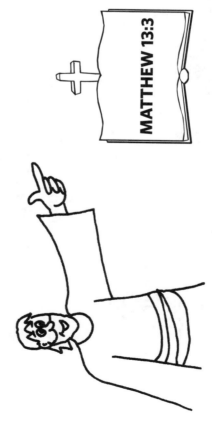

MATTHEW 13:3

Write the first letter of each picture clue in the boxes

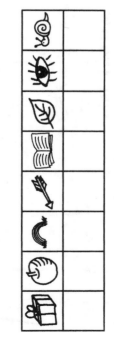

Find what Jesus said about himself using the code cracker.

Follow the instructions to find the words of Jesus

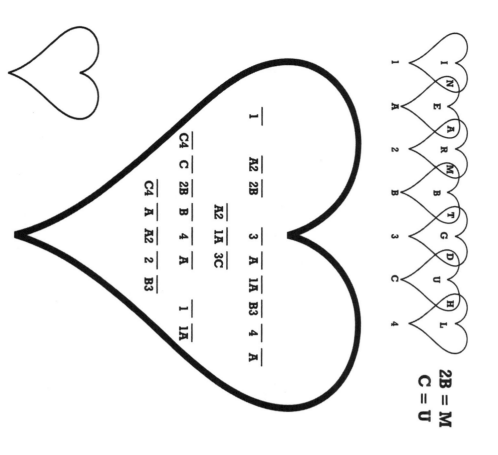

2B = M
C = U

Replace the words in the parentheses with other rhyming words so the phrase below makes sense!

(HUM) _____ _____ to (PEA) _____

(HAND) _____ _____ I (PILL) _____

give (WHO) _____ _____ (BEST) _____

MATTHEW 11:28

Yokes were used by people and animals to share a heavy load. Jesus offered to share our load or problems and worries.

The parable of the sower

MATTHEW 13:1-23

A great crowd gathered to listen to Jesus.

Where did he sit so that everyone could see and hear him?

Connect the dots to complete the picture

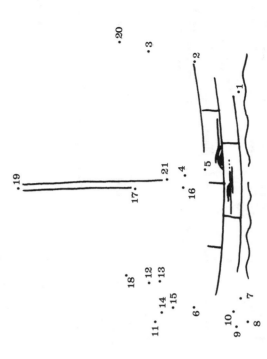

MATTHEW 13:2

THINK and LOOK ahead

Next week Jesus tells another parable about sowing seed.

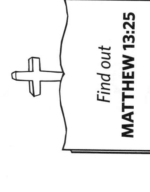

Find out
MATTHEW 13:25

Which weed is mixed with the good seed?

You can check your answer by writing the missing letters in the boxes

ABCEF				
XYZBC				
QSTUV				
JKLMO				
CDFGH				
HIJKM				

Jesus told the people a parable.

Find the words missing from this poem

A _____ went, his _____ to sow,

He did not _____ if they would grow.

Some seeds fell on _____ ground,

Some the hungry _____ soon found.

some fell among the _____ so tall.

They stood no chance to _____ at all!

But some seeds fell on fertile _____ and

soon the _____ grew all around!

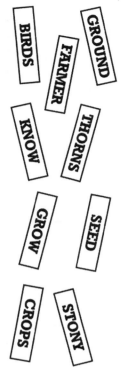

GROUND

FARMER

BIRDS

THORNS

KNOW

SEED

GROW

STONY

CROPS

Then Jesus explained what this parable meant to his disciples.

Write the first letter of each picture in the boxes below

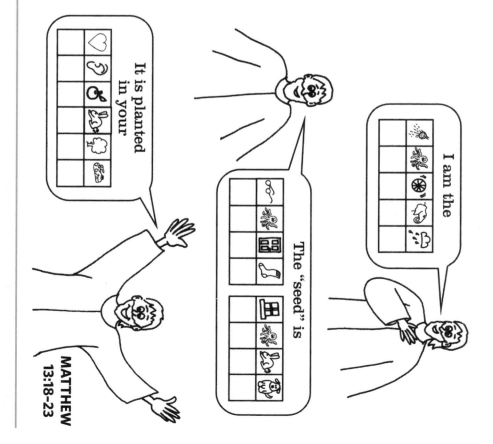

I am the

The "seed" is

It is planted in your

MATTHEW 13:18-23

The wheat and the weeds

MATTHEW 13:24-43

Jesus told a parable about a farmer who sowed some wheat. An enemy came and scattered weed seeds amongst the crop.

How many weeds can you find hidden in the picture below? Circle and count them

MATTHEW 13:25

THINK and LOOK ahead

Why is this man so happy to have sold everything to buy a field?

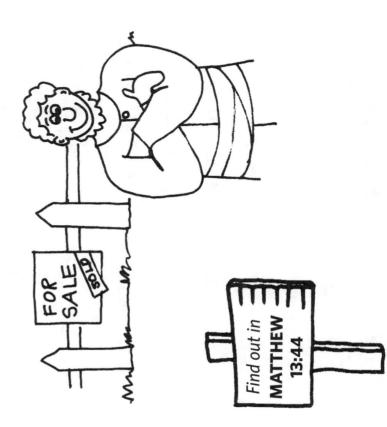

Find out in **MATTHEW 13:44**

The farmer waited until harvest time to separate the weeds from the wheat.
He burnt the weeds and stored the wheat in his barn.

Help these servants to take the weeds and wheat to the right place

Jesus explained this parable to his disciples.

Use the code to read the words of Jesus

T	V	E	I
N	H	G	W
B	O	F	P
S	D	L	U	K

MATTHEW 13:41-43

Priceless treasure!

MATTHEW 13:44-52

Jesus told three parables all about the same thing!

What was it?

Each number equals a letter in this code.
Solve the math problems to crack the code

3 = A	4 = E	5 = V	8 = D	9 = F	10 = K	11 = T
12 = G	13 = O	14 = H	16 = N	18 = I	20 = M	

6	7	16	6	9	8	4	16	7	16
+5	x2	÷4	+4	x2	+8	x3	÷2	+6	+4
—	—	—	—	—	—	—	—	—	—

9	3	20	2	13	25	11	13
+4	x3	−6	x2	−10	÷5	−7	+3
—	—	—	—	—	—	—	—

MATTHEW 13:44, 45, 47

There are all kinds of fish in a fishing net and all kinds of people in the kingdom of heaven.

The good will be saved and the bad thrown away!

Complete this picture by drawing a straight line to connect the dots with the same numbers or letters

MATTHEW 13:47

The first parable compared the kingdom of heaven to treasure.

Then Jesus compared the kingdom of heaven to a precious pearl worth selling everything to own.

Use the code to read what Jesus says in Matthew 13:44

S	A	F	L	H	T	E	N	O	B	D	Y	U	M	I	G	V	R

"

How many pearls can you count in this jumbled picture?

MATTHEW 13:44

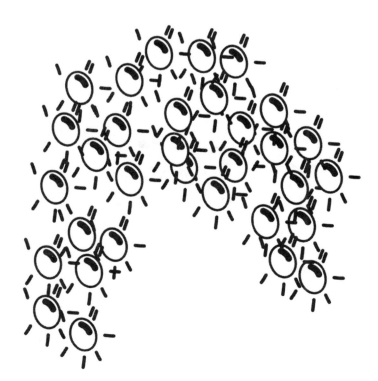

Number of pearls: _____

MATTHEW 13:46

The miracle of the loaves and fish

MATTHEW 14:13–21

A large crowd of people followed Jesus to a lonely place. *When he saw them what did he do?*

Match the puzzle pieces to find out

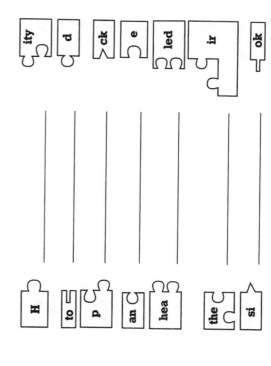

The crowd did not go hungry! There was plenty left over.

How many baskets of scraps did they collect? Find the answer to the problem below to see!

$$(7 \times 2) + 6 + (3 \times 2) - 12 - (2 \times 1)$$

= ☐ baskets

Jesus told his disciples to give the people some food.

Why do they look so worried?

They need not have worried!
What did Jesus do next?

Their words have been written backward.
Rewrite them to see what they said

DORL → LORD

LLA EW EVAH ___ ___

ERA OWT SEVAOL ___ ___

DNA EVIF HSIF ___ ___ !

Add or subtract letters to find the answer

A B C D E F G H I J K L M N O P Q R S T U V W X Y Z

B+6 N-9   Q+2 Y+2 L-3 A+3   H-7

A+1 F+6 F-1 P+3 Z-7 O-6 M+1 J-3 ,

E-3 I+9 S-4 G+4 F-1   U-1 D+4 A+4

K-9 Q+1 B+3 L-11 E-1   W+4 P-2 F-2

H+11 K-3 E-4 O+3 K-6 H-4   H+1 V-2

MATTHEW 14:17

Have faith!

MATTHEW 14:22–33

The disciples set off by boat to the other side of the Sea of Galilee.

Can you help them to steer a safe passage across the sea by completing the directions below?

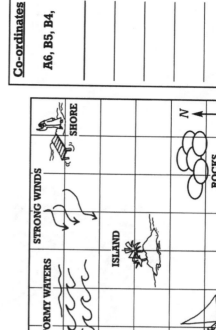

Co-ordinates
A6, B5, B4,
_____
_____
_____
_____
_____
_____

Jesus reached out and saved him, and the disciples were amazed by everything they had seen!

Follow the arrows to find their words in Matthew 14:33

H	Z	G	L	M	E	R	I	T	L
P	E	G	S	A	B	J	E	R	B
R	F	Y	T	H	S	O	D	A	G
W	L	Y	O	E	P	N	R	L	Z
G	M	U	C	R	(D)	E	O	F	P
(T)	R	B	A	D	J	O	G	S	U

The wind grew stronger
and the disciples felt afraid.
*What sight frightened
them even more?*

One of the disciples
walked across the water to
meet Jesus, but he grew
afraid and began to sink.

Use the code to find the missing letters

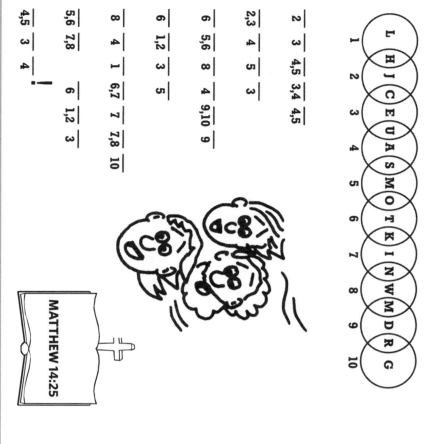

| L | H | J | C | E | U | A | S | M | O | T | K | I | N | W | M | D | R | G |
| 1 | 2 | 3 | 4 | 5 | 6 | 7 | 8 | 9 | 10 |

$\overline{2}$ $\overline{3}$ $\overline{4,5}$ $\overline{3,4}$ $\overline{4,5}$

$\overline{2,3}$ $\overline{4}$ $\overline{5}$ $\overline{3}$

$\overline{6}$ $\overline{5,6}$ $\overline{8}$ $\overline{4}$ $\overline{9,10}$ $\overline{9}$

$\overline{6}$ $\overline{1,2}$ $\overline{3}$ $\overline{5}$

$\overline{8}$ $\overline{4}$ $\overline{1}$ $\overline{6,7}$ $\overline{7}$ $\overline{7,8}$ $\overline{10}$

$\overline{5,6}$ $\overline{7,8}$ $\overline{6}$ $\overline{1,2}$ $\overline{3}$

$\overline{4,5}$ $\overline{3}$ $\overline{4}$!

MATTHEW 14:25

Write the first letter of each picture clue to complete the puzzle
and find out who lost faith and what he said to Jesus

MATTHEW 14:30

The Canaanite woman

MATTHEW 15:21-28

Jesus went to a region where few people knew him.

Where did he go?

Write the letter that is missing from the second word
in the boxes to spell out the answer

AND

In **BAT** but not **BALL**

In **YES** but not **SET**

In **REST** but not **NEST**

In **HEN** but not **HAND**

In **SOCK** but not **LOCK**

In **SAIL** but not **SALE**

In **DOG** but not **LOG**

In **OPEN** but not **PEN**

In **NOSE** but not **HOSE**

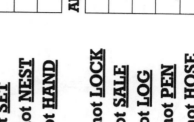

THINK and LOOK ahead

Next week Jesus goes to another region
to preach to the people. *Where does he go?*

Add or subtract letters to find out

A B C D E F G H I J K L M N O P Q R S T U V W X Y Z

A+2	F−5	B+3	K+8	P−15	M+5	C+2	C−2

L+4	B+6	M−4	G+5	R−9	O+1	V−6	E+4

*Check your
answer in*
MATTHEW 16:13

A woman came to Jesus
and cried out for help

Fit these words into the boxes.
Then write them in the correct lines below

HELP   ILL   MY   LORD   DAUGHTER   ME
IS

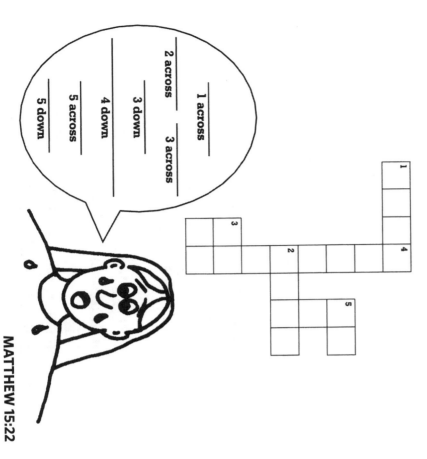

1 across _____

2 across _____   3 across _____

3 down _____

4 down _____

5 across _____

5 down _____

MATTHEW 15:22

She would not go away
and kept on pleading!

Use the code cracker to find Jesus' words to the woman

1 A	14 N
2 B	15 O
3 C	16 P
4 D	17 Q
5 E	18 R
6 F	19 S
7 G	20 T
8 H	21 U
9 I	22 V
10 J	23 W
11 K	24 X
12 L	25 Y
13 M	26 Z

"

$\overline{23}\ \overline{15}\ \overline{13}\ \overline{1}\ \overline{14}$

$\overline{2}\ \overline{5}\ \overline{3}\ \overline{1}\ \overline{21}\ \overline{19}\ \overline{5}$

$\overline{15}\ \overline{6}$ $\overline{25}\ \overline{15}\ \overline{21}\ \overline{18}$

$\overline{7}\ \overline{18}\ \overline{5}\ \overline{1}\ \overline{20}$ $\overline{6}\ \overline{1}\ \overline{9}\ \overline{20}\ \overline{8}$

$\overline{25}\ \overline{15}\ \overline{21}\ \overline{18}$ $\overline{23}\ \overline{9}\ \overline{19}\ \overline{8}$

$\overline{9}\ \overline{19}$ $\overline{7}\ \overline{18}\ \overline{1}\ \overline{14}\ \overline{20}\ \overline{5}\ \overline{4}$ "

MATTHEW 15:28

Who am I?

MATTHEW 16:13-20

One day Jesus asked his disciples a difficult question. Only Peter knew the right answer.

Fit the shapes into the puzzle below to find his words

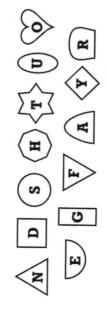

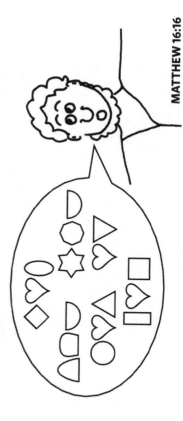

MATTHEW 16:16

THINK and LOOK ahead

Next week the disciples are sad and worried about Jesus.

Can you find out why?

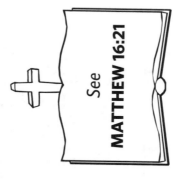

See **MATTHEW 16:21**

Because...

Jesus was delighted that Peter knew the answer!

Use the code to find out what Jesus said in Matthew 16:17

SECRET CODE PAD

5 = YOU   4 = REVEALED   3 = THIS
8 = HEAVENLY   9 = FATHER   14 = HAS
12 = MY   6 = TO

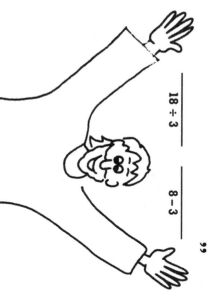

"

4×3 ___ $16 \div 2$ ___ $6 + 3$ ___

$(3 + 4) \times 2$ ___ $11 - 7$ ___ $9 \div 3$ ___

$18 \div 3$ ___ $8 - 3$ ___

"

Jesus told Peter that he would be given the "keys to the kingdom of heaven" (Matthew 16:19).

Use the key code to see what Jesus said

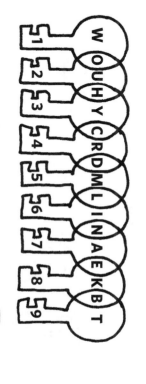

Key code: W O U H Y C R D M L I N A E K B T (1–9)

"

___ ___ ___   ___   ___ ___
3 1,2 2   7   4 7,8

___ ___ ___   ___ ___ ___ ___
9 2,3 7,8   4 1,2 3,4 8

___ ___ ___ ___ ___   ___   ___ ___ ___
1 2,3 6 3,4 2,3   6   1 5,6 5,6

___ ___ ___ ___ ___   ___ ___
8,9 2   6 5,6 4,5   5 3

___ ___ ___ ___ ___ ___
3,4 2,3 2   4 3,4 2,3

"

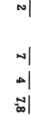

MATTHEW 16:18

God's way!

MATTHEW 16:21-27

Jesus had told his disciples that he would have to suffer and die before rising again. Peter loved Jesus and wanted to stop such a thing from happening.

Write the first letter of each picture to find Peter's words

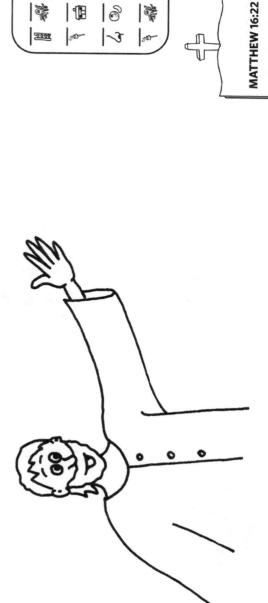

MATTHEW 16:22

THINK and LOOK ahead

Look up Matthew 18:20 to find the missing words.

When _____ or _____ meet in my name, I am there with them.

Jesus scolded Peter for his words.

Use the code to find out what Jesus said

CODE BREAKER

	□	○	△	◇
1	D	T	O	N
2	W	K	P	S
3	G	Y	A	U
4	H	E	I	R

" 2△ 4○ 1○ 4○ 4◇ '

1○ 4□ 4○   2□ 3△ 3○   3○ 1△ 3○

1○ 4□ 4△ 1○ 2○   4△ 4 2○   1○ 1△ 3◇

3□ 1△ 1□ 2◇ ,   2□ 3△ 3○ __ !"

MATTHEW 16:23

Sometimes God's way is not how we would like it to be, and, like Peter, we can find it hard to follow.

Jesus told us what we must do if we are to follow him.
Color each square with a * and cross out each square with a •.
Write the remaining letters in order on the lines below

	START ↓			
*M	*T	*K		
R	•O	•O		
*L	*A	•P	•K	
*Y	E	•s	•P	
*M	U	*E	•P	
*K	•J	*O	•E	•R
E	•C	•B	•U	*R
•J	S	S	*R	*L
*A	*O	N		O
*K	D	F		
O	*E	L		
L	•O	•J		
*U	•W	•O		
M	*R	E		

"

___ ___ ___

___ ___

___ ___

___ ___ ___ , ___

___ ___ ___ "

MATTHEW 16:24

I am with you

MATTHEW 18:15–20

When someone has a problem
what can we do to help?

Fill in the first letters of the picture clues
to find the answers in the crossword

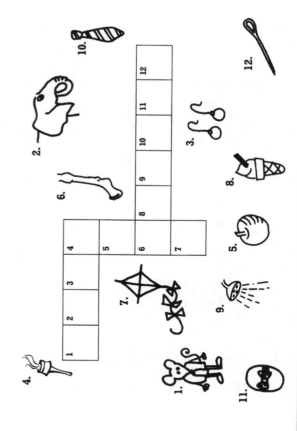

Write the names of some of the people
who join you on Sunday to pray

Jesus wanted us to know that he is always with us.

Write the name of your best friend and draw a picture of you both making up after a quarrel.

Write the PREVIOUS letter of the alphabet on the lines to find Jesus' words in Matthew 18:20.
For example, C will be written above D

A B C D E F G H I J K L M N O P Q R S T U V W X Y Z

"

X I F O   U X P   P S

U I S F   N F F U   J O

N Z   O B N F '   J   B N

U I F S F   X J U I   U I F N

"

My best friend is _____

Be forgiving

MATTHEW 18:21-35

Jesus told a parable about a king who took pity on his servant and canceled the servant's many debts.

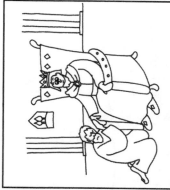

These two pictures might look the same but can you find six differences in the picture on the right?

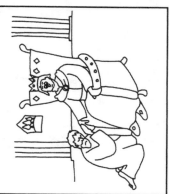

THINK and LOOK ahead

Find out how much the landowner paid his workers in the vineyard.

MATTHEW 20:2

Check your answer by writing down every second letter, starting at the arrow

o _ _ _ _ _

This servant, who had been forgiven so much, showed no mercy to another man who owed him only a small amount!

Jesus wants us to forgive each other just as we are forgiven ourselves.

Write the letter that is missing from the sequence in the box to spell out where the servant had the man sent

LMNOQ	
OPQST	
FGHJK	
PQRTU	
MNPQR	
KLMOP	

MATTHEW 18:30

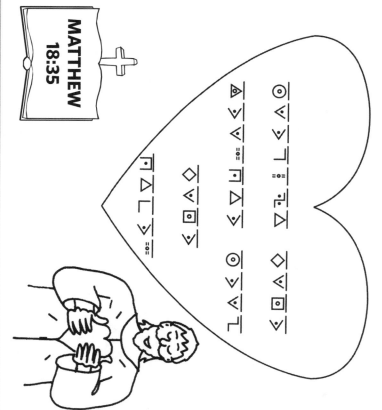

Use the secret code pad to find Jesus' words below

SECRET CODE PAD

O = ∀	A = ∟	R = ⟩	F = ⊙	T = ⚌
U = ⊡	H = ⌐	B = △	G = ⅂	M = ⌐
		Y = ◇	I = ⁞	V = ⅃

MATTHEW 18:35

Workers in the vineyard

MATTHEW 20:1-16

Jesus told his disciples another parable.

Use the numbered letters to help you to find what Jesus said in Matthew 20:1

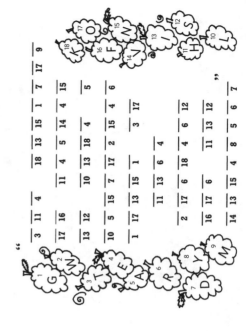

THINK and LOOK ahead

Look in
MATTHEW 21:23, 28

Jesus is telling these people a parable.
Who are they?

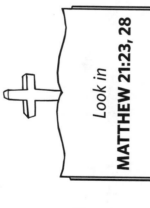

All day long he hired more workers and when evening came he paid each of them one denarius.

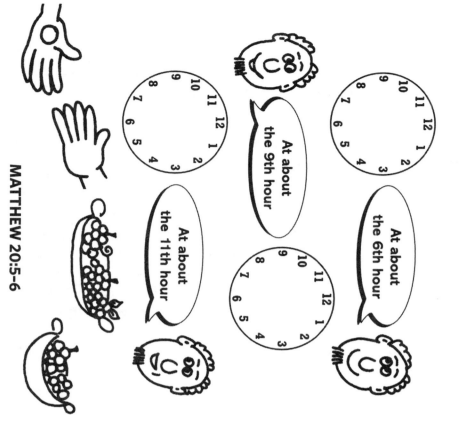

Draw hands on the clock faces to show what times he had hired the men

At about the 9th hour

At about the 11th hour

At about the 6th hour

MATTHEW 20:5-6

Like the landowner, Jesus invites us to come and work in his kingdom, where everyone will be offered the same reward of everlasting life!

Find and circle the words below in the puzzle

VINEYARD   GRAPES   WORKERS   DENARIUS
REWARD   LANDOWNER   KINGDOM

L	K	D	I	N	S	G	D
A	I	R	O	G	E	D	D
N	N	A	E	R	E	I	R
D	G	W	B	A	N	K	A
O	D	E	R	P	A	D	Y
W	O	R	K	E	R	S	E
N	M	W	L	S	I	R	N
E	A	W	F	K	U	A	I
R	E	F	J	N	S	M	V

Making choices

MATTHEW 21:28-32

One day Jesus told a parable to the chief priests and elders.

What was the story about?

Solve the clues to find the missing letters and reveal the answer

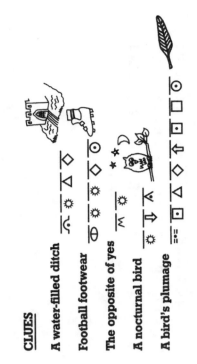

CLUES

A water-filled ditch

Football footwear

The opposite of yes

A nocturnal bird

A bird's plumage

AND

THINK and LOOK ahead

Next week Jesus tells another story about a landowner and his vineyard.

Can you find out what happened to the first three servants he sent?

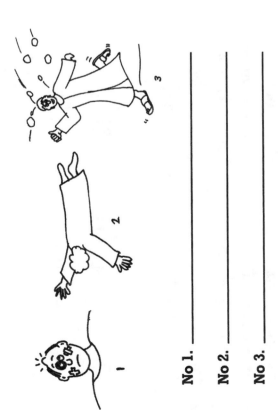

No 1. _____

No 2. _____

No 3. _____

Look in **MATTHEW 21:35**

Fill in the blanks to read the story.
Use every other letter in the order given

A f __ ther as __ e __ h __ s __ on
t __ __ o an __ __ w __ k in __ __ he
vin __ __ ard.

At f __ st t __ __ so __ sa __
" __ __ " bu __ h __ c __ __ nged hi __
__ __ nd an __ __ __ nt a __ yw __ __ __ .

T __ __ e fat __ __ as __ ed the
__ __ cond s __ n to __ o __ __ e
sa __ __ e, "Y __ __ " he s __ __ d, b __ __ t
__ __ d __ d n __ t go a __ __ er a __ l.

START →Xbackrdbijsroeg1dfomrst
zebylisrhmefnpirdensoftkemhz
apsemrisdewgeknlasymhbhrecr
jkmsqefondmtehfmpehsb
acikujhcemilopfotpl

Jesus said to them...

You did not believe him
and would not change
your minds.

Who was Jesus talking about?

Use the clues to find the answer

1	2	3	4	5	6	7	8	9	10	11	12	13	14

1. The first letter of
2. The second letter of
3. The first letter of
4. The third letter of
5. The sixth letter of
6. The first letter of
7. The fifth letter of

8. The first letter of
9. The third letter of
10. The second letter of
11. The fourth letter of
12. The second letter of
13. The fourth letter of
14. The first letter of

Listen to God's message

MATTHEW 21:33–43

A man planted a vineyard and rented it to some farmers. At harvest time he sent some servants to collect what belonged to him.

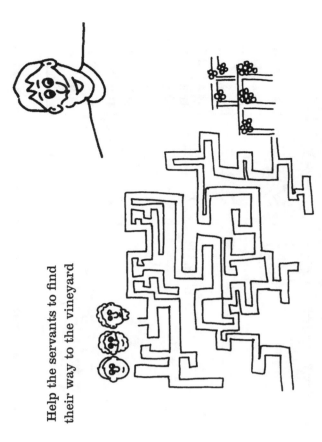

Help the servants to find their way to the vineyard

THINK and LOOK ahead

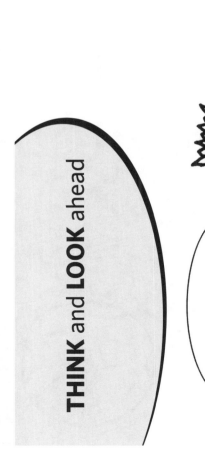

I am sending invitations for what?

Look in Matthew 22:2 and check your answer by writing the first letter of each object

The first servants were killed or beaten, and the second group of servants were treated in the same way!

So finally he sent his own son.

GOOD LUCK!

Unscramble the jumbled words to find what Jesus meant by this story

"The _____ of _____
      INGKMOD   VEANEH

will be _____ to _____
         NEGIV   NYOAEN

who _____ and _____
     RSAEH   HSRASE

the _____ of God!"
     RDOW

MATTHEW 21:43

Use the code cracker to find out what the farmers are plotting

A 1	N 14	
B 2	O 15	
C 3	P 16	
D 4	Q 17	
E 5	R 18	
F 6	S 19	
G 7	T 20	
H 8	U 21	
I 9	V 22	
J 10	W 23	
K 11	X 24	
L 12	Y 25	
M 13	Z 26	

" __ __ __ __ ,
  12 5 20 19

__ __ __ __ __
11 9 12 12

__ __ __ __
8 9 13

__ __ __
1 14 4

__ __ __ __
20 1 11 5

__ __ __ __
8 9 19

__ __ __ __ __ __ __ __ __ __ __ __ __ !"
9 14 8 5 18 9 20 1 14 3 5

MATTHEW 21:38

The wedding party

MATTHEW 22:1-14

A king sent out some invitations for his son's wedding party but many people did not bother to go!

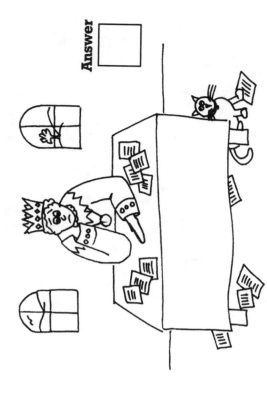

How many invitations can you spot? Write the answer in the box below

Answer

THINK and LOOK ahead

Find out in **MATTHEW 22:19–21**

Next week the Pharisees try to trick Jesus with a question about paying taxes to which Roman emperor?

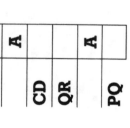

CHECK

Write the next letter in the series

AB	
CD	A
QR	
PQ	A

So he invited
EVERYONE to the party
and filled the wedding
hall with guests.

Which objects do not belong in the picture? Circle them

God invites everyone to be
part of his kingdom!

Use the code breaker to find the
words Jesus said in Matthew 22:14

CODE BREAKER

	AB	IJ	KL	MN	⌐ = L
GH		OP	QR	ST	□ = Q
EF	CD	UV	WX	YZ	∨ = G

GOD'S INVITATION

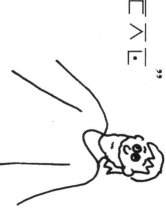
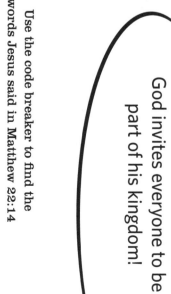

Give to God what belongs to God

MATTHEW 22:15–21

The Pharisees asked Jesus a difficult question.

Use the code to find their words

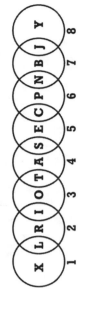

X	L	R	I	O	T	A	S	E	C	P	N	B	J	Y
1	2	3	4	5	6	7	8

"

___ ___   ___ ___   ___   ___ ___ ___ ___ ___ ___   ___ ___ ___ ___
2,3 4,5   3,4 3   2,3 3,4   4 5,6 5,6 5 6 3,4   4   7 1,2 5

___   ___ ___ ___   ___ ___ ___ ___   ___ ___ ___
3,4 3   6 4   8   5,6 4   5   3,4   4   1   5

___ ___   ___
3,4 4   4,5

___ ___   ___   ___
5,6 4,5   4   2

___   ___   ___ ___   ___ ___
3   2   6,7 3   3,4

?"

MATTHEW 22:17

Here is a tricky question for you to answer!

Can you match each coin with the country where it is used?

 Greece

 United States of America

France

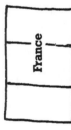 United Kingdom

 Spain

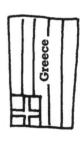 Dime

Pound

Peseta

Franc

Drachma

The Pharisees wanted
Jesus to say something that
would make everyone
mad at him!

Jesus answered the
trick question wisely

Find Jesus' question to the Pharisees by following the arrows

L	A	C	S	W	H	E	H	P
P	T	Y	S	E	I	W	S	O
U	R	A	E	A	T	H	D	N
O	Y	X	J	D	X	N	A	M
O	H	N	I	C	A	E	R	E
Ⓢ	W	M	B	O	M	S	I	M
N	Q	K	G	C	E	S	O	N

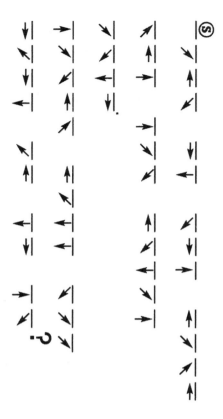

Ⓢ

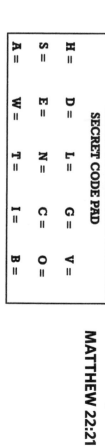

Give to Caesar
what belongs to Caesar,
and to God what belongs
to God!

MATTHEW 22:21

Make your own secret code pad
and write Jesus' words in code

SECRET CODE PAD

H =	D =	L =	G =	V =
S =	E =	N =	C =	O =
A =	W =	T =	I =	B =

The greatest commandment

MATTHEW 22:34-40

The Pharisees asked Jesus another question.

Add or subtract letters to find what the
Pharisees asked in Matthew 22:36

A B C D E F G H I J K L M N O P Q R S T U V W X Y Z

"

__ __ __ __ __ __ , __ __ __ __ __ __
K+2 F-5 L+7 P+4 B+3 W-5   Q+6 G+1 R-9 B+1 B+6

__ __ __   __ __ __ __ __ __   __ __ __ __ __ __ __
K-2 V-3   J+10 C+5 O-10   F+1 Q+1 Z-21 D-3 N+6 I-4 O+4 U-1

__ __ __ __ __ __ __ __ __ ?"
B+1 K+4 N-1 P-3 J-9 H+6 C+1 I+4 F-1 H+6 S+1

In the Old Testament,
God gave us the Ten Commandments.

To whom did God give them and where?

Write the first letter of each picture clue to
complete the puzzle and find out!

1	2	3	4	5

ON

6	7	8	9	10

11	12	13	14	15

EXODUS
19:20; 20:1-17

Use the code to find Jesus' answer

1	R	U	T	O
2	E	S	A	H
3	G	N	D	M
4	L	I	Y	G
5	V	S	W	R
	♡	☀	↪	☺

"

1☺ 4♡ 1☺ 5↪ 2♡ 4☺ 1☺ 3↪

5↪ 4☀ 1☺ 2↪ 2↪ 4♡ 4♡ 4↪ 1☺ 1☀ 4♡

2↪ 2♡ 2↪ 5↪ 1↪ ' 2☀ 1☺ 1↪ 4♡ '

2↪ 3↪ 3☀ 3↪ 3☺ 4☀ 3☀ 3↪

"

✝ MATTHEW 22:37

Which is the second greatest commandment?

Unscramble the words

OT   OLEV   RYUO

BNEORGHI   SA

ORUYSLEF

MATTHEW 22:39

Practice what you preach

MATTHEW 23:1-12

Jesus warned the people about the Pharisees, who boasted about their holiness and drew attention to themselves.

Use the code cracker to see what Jesus said in Matthew 23:3

z y x w v u t s r q p o n m l k j i h g f e d c b a
A B C D E F G H I J K L M N O P Q R S T U V W X Y Z

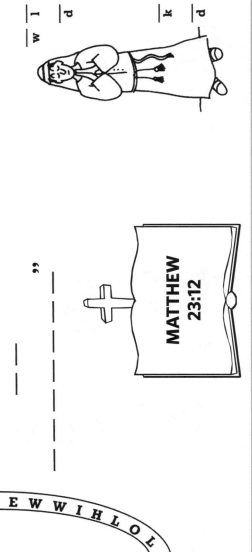

w l ___ m l g ___ x l k b

___ d s z g ___ g s v b

l ___ w ___ g ___ v b

___ w l m l g ___ g

k i z x g r x v

___ k i x z z g ___ r v

d s z g ___ g s v b

k i v z x s

We need to practice what we preach and put our words into action, without drawing attention to ourselves like the Pharisees!

Start at the arrow and write every second letter to spell out the words of Jesus

Start

"A ___ ___ ___ ___

___ ___ ___ ___

___ ___ ___ ___

___ ___ ___ ___

___ ___ ___ ___ ,"

A E N L Y F O U N P E W W I H L O L R B A E H I S U E M S B H L I T E M D S

Finish

MATTHEW 23:12

What did the Pharisees
wear to draw attention
to themselves?

Phylacteries were leather boxes that the
Pharisees wore on their heads and arms.
They contained Scripture verses to
remind them of God's laws.

Tassels were worn as a
sign of devotion to God.

Look at these Pharisees and decide which one
believes himself to be the holiest!

Use the numbered letters to spell out the answer

| 1 | 2 | 3 | 4 | 5 | 6 | 2 |

| 7 | 8 | 9 | 10 | 4 | 11 | 12 | 6 | 2 | 13 | 6 | 14 |

AND

| 10 | 3 | 15 | 16 | 6 | 2 |

| 12 | 4 | 14 | 14 | 6 | 10 | 14 |

R² B¹ A⁴ O³ E⁶ Z M D⁵ Y I¹⁰ C¹¹ P⁷ T¹² J S¹⁴ Y⁹ G¹⁶ C I¹³ H⁸ N¹⁵

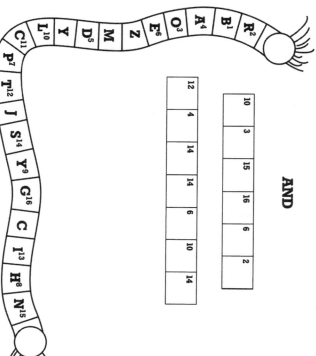

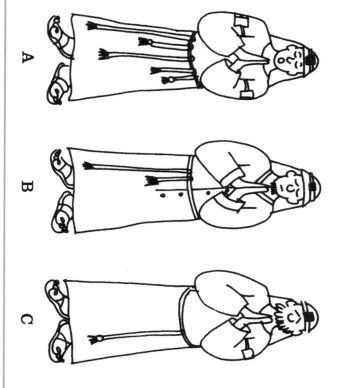

A   B   C

Be ready

MATTHEW 25:1-13

In another parable, with whom did Jesus compare the kingdom of heaven?

Write the first letter of each picture in the boxes

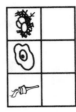
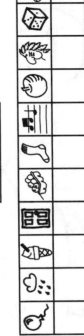

THINK and LOOK ahead

This man is giving something to each of his servants.

What are they being given?

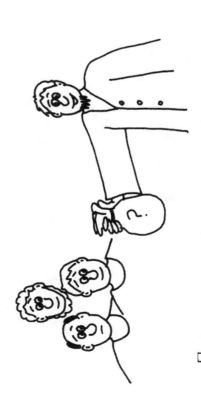

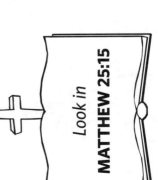

Look in
MATTHEW 25:15

Write the answer below

_ _ _ _ _ _ _ _

Fit the rhyming words on the lines to finish the story

OIL   LOW   SO   WAIT   SLEEP   WOE

SPOIL   KNOW   GO   LATE   GREET   GO

Ten bridesmaids took their lamps to _____

They hoped the groom would not be _____

Five were wise and brought more _____

The wedding plans they would not _____

As it grew late the lamps burned _____

When he would come they did not _____

"Get up, girls, do not _____

At last the groom is here to _____!"

The foolish five cried out with _____

"Our lamps are out, we cannot _____!"

The wise girls filled their lamps and _____

to the wedding they could _____!

Like the wise bridesmaids,
Jesus wants us to be prepared
for his coming!

Use the secret code pad to find the
words of Jesus in Matthew 25:13

U	▷
A	ΙΟΙ
S	☐
E	✎
O	⇐
Y	⌄
R	≈
T	⊡
H	◎
D	ΙΟΙ
W	▽
K	⇒
N	⬤

" ☐ ⊡ ΙΟΙ ⌄   ΙΟΙ △ ΙΟΙ ⇒ ✎

⌄ ⇐ △   ΙΟΙ ⇐

⬤ ⇐ ⊡   ⇒ ⬤ ⇐ ▷

⊡ ◎ ⇐ ✎   ΙΟΙ ΙΟΙ ⌄

⇐   ≈

▽ ⇐ ◎ ▷ ≈ ⬤ !"

THIRTY-THIRD SUNDAY OF THE YEAR, YEAR A

Gifts from God

MATTHEW 25:14-30

Before going on a long journey, a man gave each of his servants some money called "talents."

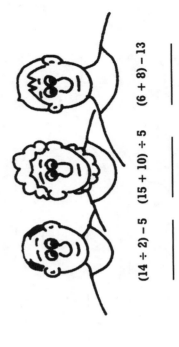

Solve the math problems to find how much each servant received

$(14 \div 2) - 5$ $(15 + 10) \div 5$ $(6 + 8) - 13$

_____   _____   _____

MATTHEW 25:15

THINK and LOOK ahead

Next week is the Feast of Christ the King!

In the gospel, what does the shepherd have to separate?

MATTHEW 25:32

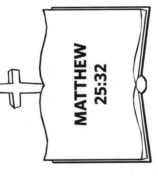

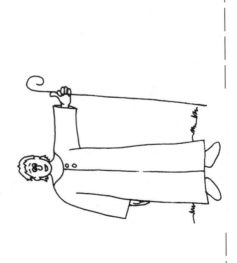

CLUES

What did each servant do with the money they were given?

Use the numbered coins to find their words below

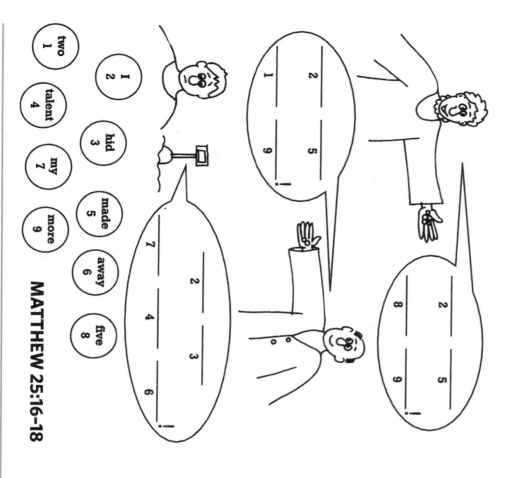

2 __ 5 __ !
2 __ 5 __ !

2 __ 5 __ 1 __ 9 __ !

8 __ 9

2 __ 3
7 __ 4 __ 6 __ !

two 1	I 2	hid 3	talent 4
made 5	away 6	my 7	five 8	more 9

The master returned and was very pleased with the two servants who had used their talents wisely.

God wants us to use the gifts he gives us and make them grow!

Write some of your gifts or "talents" below.
How do you use them?

_____
_____
_____
_____
_____

Christ is King!

MATTHEW 25:31–46

At the end of time Jesus will gather all the people before him and separate the good from the bad

Use every other letter in the order given to read Jesus' words

k l k e r p j n l e s f d o b o a r m h
m e k h k d g o b s j h r p c m e g x a

"I wi__ l s__ __arate o __ __

__ r__ m an __ the __ __ as __ a

s __ __ p __ erd __ __ es __ __ __ m __

fro __ __ __ o __ ts ''

MATTHEW 25:32

THINK and LOOK ahead

Which church season starts next week as our preparation for Christmas begins?

Write the first letter of each picture in the boxes to spell out the answer

The Season of

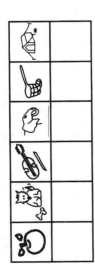

Which means

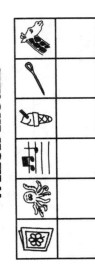

The "shepherd" rewards his "sheep" for their goodness with the gift of eternal life.

Whenever we care for others we care for Jesus too!

Follow the arrows to find the words missing from Matthew 25:35–36

A	M	S	S	R	N	E	O	R
B	T	A	I	N	E	A	P	N
I	R	R	N	G	K	D	O	R
H	S	Y	D	L	C	I	S	D
A	T	D	T	O	K	C	R	J
(H)	R	G	E	H	I	P	J	E
U	N	Y	F	D	S	E	M	B

I was (H) ___ ___ and you ___ ___ me;

and you gave me ___ ___ ___ ___ ___ . A ___ ___ ___ and

you welcomed me in, ___ ___ ___ ___ , and you

me, ___ ___ ___ and you visited me. A ___ ___ ___ and

___ ___ ___ came to see ___ ___ ___ .

Use the code to find the words of Jesus

	W	H	T
△	M	E	Y
○	O	I	D
□	R	S	U
◇	N	U	A
✂	R	F	B

MATTHEW 25:40

Year B

Stay awake!

MARK 13:33-37

Jesus told us that he will come again, but only God knows when!

Follow the instructions below to find the warnings given in Mark 13:33, 35

1. **Cross out the "sleepy" letters**
   B Z Z E Z O Z Z N Z

2. **Cross out the letters that sound like a snake**
   S S G S U S S A R S S D S

3. **Cross out the following letters: G F D L J**
   G F S D T J A G Y L D A F W G A J K F E D

Fill in the blanks with the remaining letters

1. _ _ _ _

2. _ _ _ _

3. _ _ _

THINK and LOOK ahead

Find out which Old Testament prophet spoke about "a voice crying in the wilderness."

Look in
MARK 1:2-3

Write his name below

The Prophet

_ _ _ _ _ _ _

Jesus spoke of a master and his servants. When might the master return?

Solve the clues to find the missing letters

A cupboard for clothes
14 15 13 7 13 11 16 1

Opposite of woman
6 15 3

False hair
14 4 5

Ruler who wears a crown
12 4 3 5

Used for talking or singing
2 11 4 10 1

Clothing worn on your head
8 15 9

___ ___ ___ ___ ___ ___ ___
1 2 1 3 4 3 5 ,

___ ___ ___ ___ ___ ___ ___ ___
6 4 7 3 4 5 8 9 ,

___ ___ ___ ___ ___ ___ ___ ___
10 11 10 12 10 13 11 14 , OR

___ ___ ___ ___
7 15 14 3

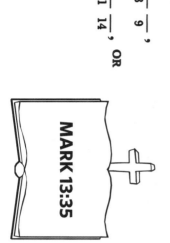

MARK 13:35

Like the master of the house, Jesus could return at any time!

Use the code to find the letters and see what Jesus is saying

For example: 5C = U

	1	2	3	4	5	6
A	I	X	Y	B	H	R
B	Z	L	F	G	S	O
C	N	D	P	G	U	D
D	C	Z	Y	E	X	L
E	J	S	O	B	P	R
F	T	B	K	N	I	M

1A 3B ___   5A 4D ___   1D 6B 6F 4D 2E ___

2E 5C 2C 2C 4D 4F 6D 3A ___ ,   5A 4D ___

6F 5C 2E 1F ___   4F 6B 1F ___

3B 1A 4F 2C ___   3A 6B 5C ___

2E 6D 4D 4D 5E 1A 4F 4B ___

MARK 13:36

Prepare for Jesus

MARK 1:1–8

Today is the Second Sunday of Advent.
We light two candles on the Advent wreath
as we prepare for Christmas.

Draw two flames and color the picture

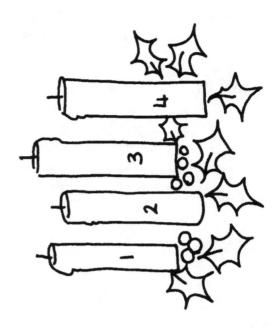

THINK and LOOK ahead

Next week the priests and Levites
ask John, "Who are you?"

What does he tell them in John 1:23?

Find the verse and then check
your answer using the code breaker

CODE BREAKER

	I	M	E	A	S	T
○	N	O	H	R	L	Y
△	G	W	D	F	V	C
	1	2	3	4	5	6

$\overline{1\square}$ $\overline{4\square}$ $\overline{2\square}$ $\overline{6\square}$ $\overline{3\bigcirc}$ $\overline{3\square}$ $\overline{5\triangle}$ $\overline{2\bigcirc}$ $\overline{1\square}$ $\overline{6\triangle}$ $\overline{3\square}$

$\overline{2\bigcirc}$ $\overline{4\triangle}$ $\overline{2\bigcirc}$ $\overline{1\bigcirc}$ $\overline{3\square}$ $\overline{6\triangle}$ $\overline{4\bigcirc}$ $\overline{6\bigcirc}$ $\overline{1\square}$ $\overline{1\bigcirc}$ $\overline{1\triangle}$

$\overline{1\square}$ $\overline{1\bigcirc}$ $\overline{6\square}$ $\overline{3\bigcirc}$ $\overline{3\square}$

$\overline{2\triangle}$ $\overline{1\square}$ $\overline{5\bigcirc}$ $\overline{3\triangle}$ $\overline{3\square}$ $\overline{4\bigcirc}$ $\overline{1\bigcirc}$ $\overline{3\square}$ $\overline{5\square}$ $\overline{5\square}$ $\overline{\square}$

Who was sent to prepare the way for Jesus?

Use the picture clues to find the missing letters. The answer is hidden in the bold squares!

Use clues in this picture to help you unscramble the words that are jumbled

John lived in the ___ ___ ___ ___ ___ ___ .
SERDET

He wore ___ ___ ___ ___ ___ skin and lived on ___ ___ ___ ___ ___ ___ ___
MACLE COLUSTS

and ___ ___ ___ ___ ___ .
NOHYE

A witness for Christ

JOHN 1:6–8, 19–28

John came to prepare the people to listen to Jesus.

He came as a

_ _ _ _ _ _ _

Write the letter that is missing from the second word in the box.
Read down to find the answer from John 1:7

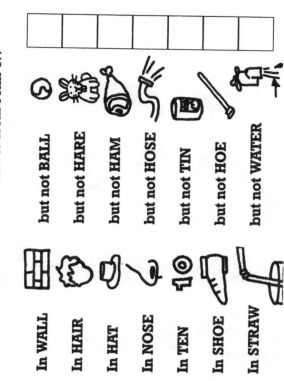

In WALL   but not BALL

In HAIR   but not HARE

In HAT   but not HAM

In NOSE   but not HOSE

In TEN   but not TIN

In SHOE   but not HOE

In STRAW   but not WATER

THINK and LOOK ahead

Next Sunday
God sends a messenger
to a town in Galilee
called Nazareth.

Who is it?

Find out
LUKE 1:26

Solve the math problems to check your answer

2 = H   4 = B   5 = N   6 = E   8 = A   9 = I

12 = G   14 = R   15 = T   16 = L

```
  5     10     18       4       8       4      10      4
 x 3   - 8    -12      + 4     - 3     + 8     - 4    x 4
 ___   ___    ___      ___     ___     ___     ___    ___


  9      4     20       7       3      12       8
 + 3   x 2    -16      x 2     x 3     - 6     x 2
 ___   ___    ___      ___     ___     ___     ___
```

The people wondered if John was the messiah promised by God.
What did he tell them?

Cross out every second letter.
Copy the remaining letters in order on to the spaces below

I M̶ A J M P N L O R T B T E H S E C C J H R R K I M S J T

___ ___ ___ ___ ___ ___

JOHN 1:20

What did John tell the people about Jesus?

Add or subtract letters to find out

A B C D E F G H I J K L M N O P Q R S T U V W X Y Z

___ ___ ___   ___ ___ ___   ___ ___ ___
W−3 E+3 N−9   K+4 Q−3 A+4   O+8 P−8 P−1

___ ___ ___ ___ ___ ___   ___ ___ ___ ___ ___
A+2 V−7 K+2 D+5 I+5 L−5   H−7 E+1 Q+3 I−4 P+2

___ ___   ___ ___   ___ ___ ___ ___ ___ ___
G+2 M+6   U−8 C+2   Y−6 G+13 H−7 J+4 A+3 U−2

___ ___ ___ ___ ___   ___ ___ ___ !
J−9 H+5 P−1 R−4 E+2   W+2 K+4 T+1

JOHN 1:26–27

God's messenger!

LUKE 1:26-38

The angel Gabriel appeared to
Mary with a message from God.

Use the code to find Gabriel's words in Luke 1:30-31

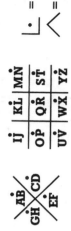

THINK and LOOK ahead

Now four candles are lit
on the Advent wreath!

What are we ready to celebrate?

_____ _____

Unscramble the letters on the gift tags to see the answer

Gabriel told Mary even more...

Mary agreed to everything the angel had told her!

Use the code cracker to break the coded words

CODE CRACKER

A 1	N 14		
B 2	O 15		
C 3	P 16		
D 4	Q 17		
E 5	R 18		
F 6	S 19		
G 7	T 20		
H 8	U 21		
I 9	V 22		
J 10	W 23		
K 11	X 24		
L 12	Y 25		
M 13	Z 26		

20 __ 8 __ 5 __   3 __ 8 __ 9 __ 12 __ 4 __

23 __ 9 __ 12 __ 12 __   2 __ 5 __

8 __ 15 __ 12 __ 25 __   1 __ 14 __ 4 __

3 __ 1 __ 12 __ 12 __ 5 __ 4 __   20 __ 8 __ 5 __

19 __ 15 __ 14 __   15 __ 6 __   7 __ 15 __ 4 __

LUKE 1:35

Write the next letter of the alphabet on the lines above the letter given

A B C D E F G H I J K L M N O P Q R S T U V W X Y Z A

__ __ __ __ __ __ __
H Z L S G D

__ __ __ __ __ __ __ __
G Z M C L Z H C

__ __ __ __ __ __ __ __
N E S G D K N Q C

__ __ __ __ __ __ __ __
C N M D Z R X N T

__ __ __ __ __ __ __ __
K D S H S A D

__ __ __ __ __ __ __ __
G Z U D R Z H C

A Savior is born!

LUKE 2:1-14

The Emperor Caesar Augustus had ordered a census. Everyone had to return to their hometown.

Using the directions below follow the route that Joseph and Mary took

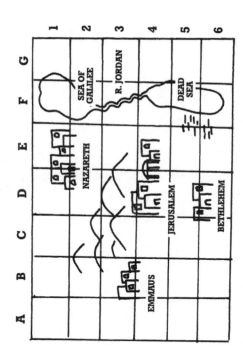

Directions

1E, 1D, 2D, 2E, 3E, 3F, 4F, 4E, 5D, 5C, 6C, 6D

THINK and LOOK ahead

I am a woman who sees baby Jesus in the Temple at Jerusalem.

Who am I and what is my age?

LUKE 2:36-37

Name: _____

Age: _____ **years old**

The time came for Mary to have her baby, but there was no room at the inn.

What did she do?

Use the Christmas code to find out

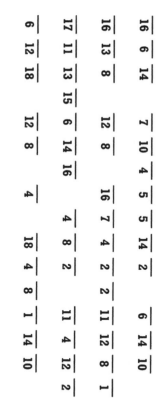

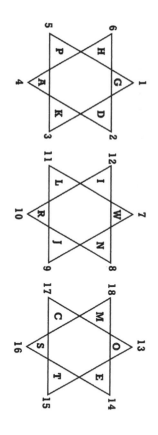

16 6 14   7 10 4 5 5 14 2   6 14 10

16 13 8   12 8   16 7 4 2 2 11 12 8 1

17 11 13 15 6 14 16   4 8 2   11 4 12 2

6 12 18   12 8   4   18 4 8 1 14 10

LUKE 2:7

A host of angels appeared to some shepherds and told them where to find Jesus.

Use the musical code to find out what the angels sang

CODE

Glory to Go__ in th__ hi__h__st

__n p_____ to __ll m__n

__or __ S__vior h__s _____n __orn

LUKE 2:11, 14

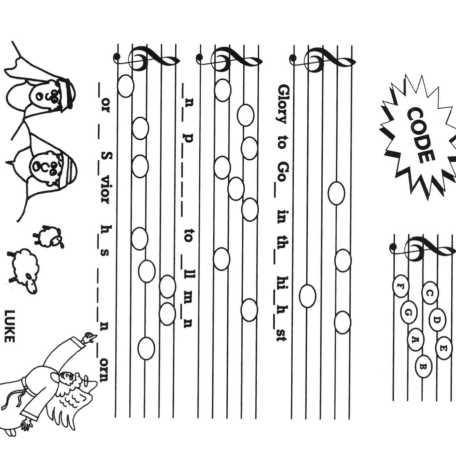

Jesus is presented in the Temple

LUKE 2:22-40

Mary and Joseph presented Jesus to the Lord according to Jewish law.

What sacrifice did they have to offer?

Fit the shapes into the puzzle below to find out

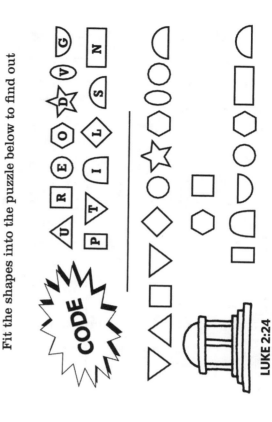

CODE

LUKE 2:24

Simeon had a warning for Mary the mother of God.

Can you remember what it was?

Use the code to see if you were right!
Example: 2 = O, 3C = W

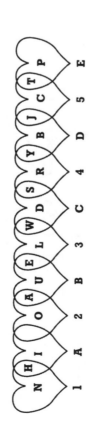

"

$\overline{1A}$ $\overline{B3}$ $\overline{3C}$ $\overline{A}$ $\overline{3}$ $\overline{3}$ $\overline{D}$ $\overline{B3}$

$\overline{4}$ $\overline{B3}$ $\overline{D5}$ $\overline{B3}$ $\overline{5}$ $\overline{5E}$ $\overline{B3}$ $\overline{C}$ $\overline{2B}$ $\overline{I}$ $\overline{C}$ $\overline{2B}$

$\overline{C4}$ $\overline{3C}$ $\overline{2}$ $\overline{4}$ $\overline{C}$ $\overline{3C}$ $\overline{A}$ $\overline{3}$ $\overline{3}$

$\overline{E}$ $\overline{A}$ $\overline{B3}$ $\overline{4}$ $\overline{5}$ $\overline{B3}$ $\overline{4D}$ $\overline{2}$ $\overline{B}$ $\overline{4}$ $\overline{2}$ $\overline{3C}$ $\overline{I}$

$\overline{C4}$ $\overline{2}$ $\overline{B}$ $\overline{3}$ $\overline{5E}$ $\overline{2}$ $\overline{2}$!"

LUKE 2:34-35

God had promised Simeon that
he would live to see Christ.

What did Simeon say when he saw Jesus?

Follow the arrows to spell out Simeon's words in Luke 2:30, 32

M	A	V	E	I	P	Y	E	R
J	A	E	O	S	R	O	A	C
D	H	T	N	L	O	F	E	G
Ⓘ	E	F	H	J	G	I	Y	M
S	A	O	Q	D	P	O	U	L
L	I	N	A	N	J	S	A	R
R	V	T	E	L	P	E	P	D
P	A	L	M	L	F	O	A	E

I

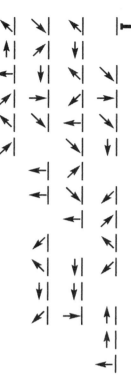

The prophetess Anna was also
in the Temple. When she saw Jesus
she began to praise God!

Can you spot ten differences in the bottom picture?

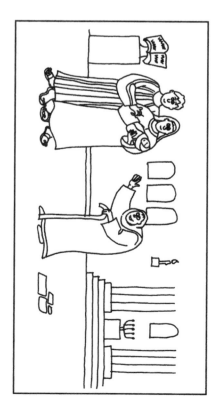

John baptizes Jesus

MARK 1:7-11

John the Baptist spoke to the people
about the person who would follow him.

What did he say?

Find the odd word out in each set and write it on the numbered line

Rock Stone With	Dog Holy Cat	Hat Will Scarf	Rose Lily He	The Star Moon	Fork Knife Spirit
5	7	2	1	6	8

	Baptize Sparrow Thrush	Apple You Pear
	3	4

___ ___ ___ ___ ___ ___ ___ ___
1   2   3   4   5   6   7   8

MARK 1:8

THINK and LOOK ahead

Find out what the
word "**rabbi**" means
for next time!

It means

_____

Look in
JOHN 1:38

Jesus came to be baptized by John in which river?

Use the clues to find the answer

1. First letter of
2. Fourth letter of
3. Second letter of
4. Third letter of
5. Second letter of
6. First letter of
7. Fifth letter of
8. Sixth letter of
9. First letter of
10. Second letter of
11. Second letter of
12. First letter of
13. Third letter of
14. Third letter of

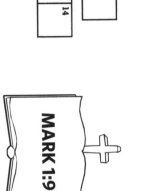

MARK 1:9

A voice spoke from the heavens as what descended on Jesus?

These words have been written backward.
Write the letters in reverse order

E H T _____

T I R I P S _____

E K I L _____

A _____

E V O D _____

MARK 1:10

Jesus in the wilderness

MARK 1:12-15

Today is the First Sunday of Lent.
For forty days before Easter we think about the life of Jesus—and also our own lives.

Use the clues below to help you to answer the questions

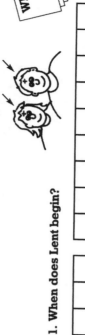
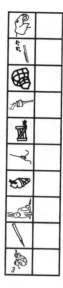

1. When does Lent begin?

2. What does "Lent" mean? (Write the first letter of each picture)

THINK and LOOK ahead

Next Sunday Jesus is transfigured on the mountain.

Which two people appear next to Jesus?

Write in the box the letter that is missing from the sequence

J K L N O

M N P Q R

R T U V W

C D F G H

P Q R T U

and

A B C D F

I J K M N

H J K L M

G H I K L

X Y Z B C

E F G I J

MARK 9:4

Jesus went into the wilderness for forty days.

What happened to him there?

Use the code cracker to find out

1	2	3	4	5	6	7	8	9	10	11	12	13
Z	Y	X	W	V	U	T	S	R	Q	P	O	N

14	15	16	17	18	19	20	21	22	23	24	25	26
M	L	K	J	I	H	G	F	E	D	C	B	A

19 22   4 26 8

7 22 14 11 7 22 23   25 2

7 19 22   23 22 5 18 15

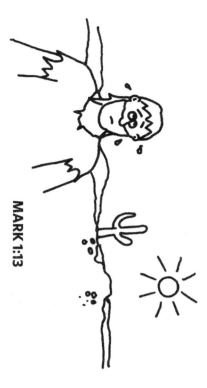

MARK 1:13

After John the Baptist was arrested, Jesus began to preach to the people.

Find and circle his words in the word search

Repent and believe the Good News!

D	N	A	B	U	R	R
S	D	L	G	S	P	E
E	E	O	Q	W	V	P
O	O	M	S	E	R	E
D	G	J	I	N	K	N
A	F	L	P	Q	R	T
C	E	S	J	D	H	B
B	A	S	P	E	K	E

REPENT
AND
BELIEVE
THE
GOOD
NEWS

"This is my beloved Son"

MARK 9:2-10

Peter, James, and John went up a high mountain with Jesus.

How did Jesus' appearance change?

Use the code to reveal the answer

	H	I	E	T	L	D
♭						
S	W	B	A	N	K	
✳	M	C	O	Z	G	Y
	1	2	3	4	5	6

MARK 9:3

THINK and LOOK ahead

See
JOHN 2:14

Next Sunday which animals are being sold in the Temple?

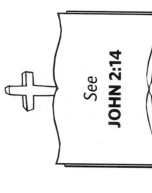

_ _ _ _

_ _ _ and _ _ _

Moses and Elijah appeared and spoke to Jesus! Then something even more amazing happened!

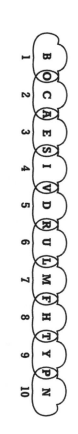

Use the numbers to find out what it was

B	(O)	C	(A)	E	(S)	I	(V)	D	(R)	U	(L)	M	(F)	H	(T)	Y	(P)	N
1		2		3		4		5		6		7		8		9		10

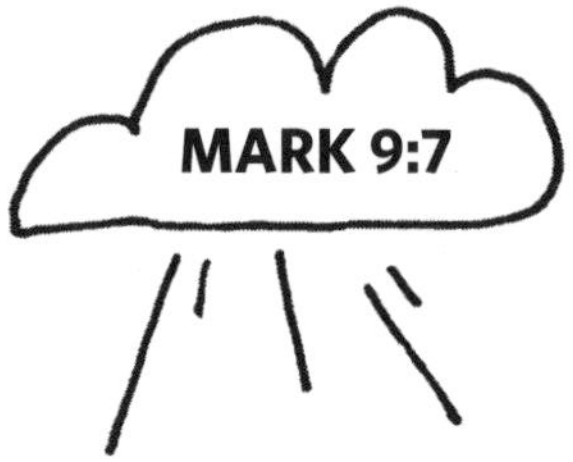

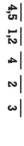

2,3

4,5 1,2 4 2 3

7,8 5,6 1,2 7   2,3   2 6,7 1,2 6 5

3,4 2,3 4 5 :

8,9 8 4 3,4   4 3,4   7 9

1 3 6,7 1,2 4,5 3 5   3,4 1,2 10 !

Jesus told them...

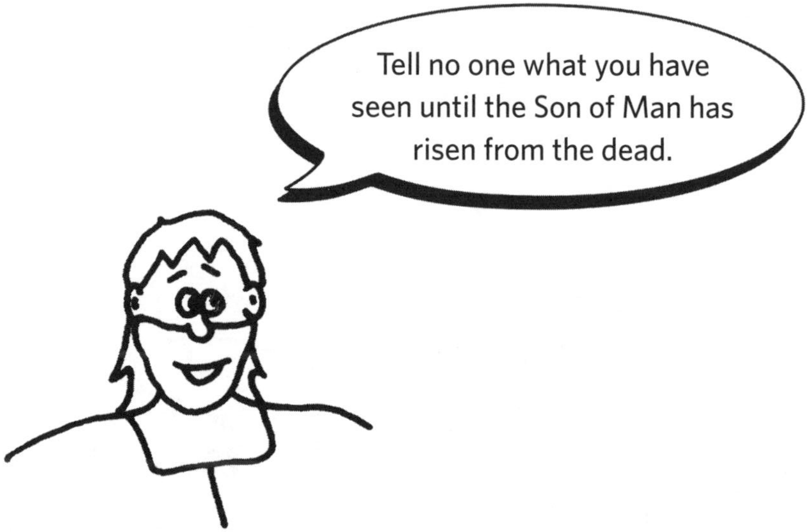

Give Peter, James, and John puzzled expressions!

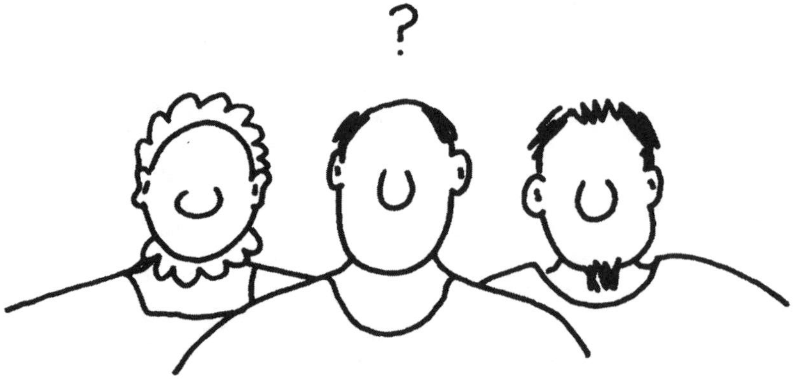

Anger in the Temple!

JOHN 2:13-25

Jesus was furious when he saw what was happening inside the Temple!

Write the PREVIOUS letter of the alphabet on each line to spell out his words

A B C D E F G H I J K L M N O P Q R S T U V W X Y Z A

S
___ ___ ___ ___   ___ ___ ___ ___ ___ ___ ___ ,
 T   U   P   Q   U   V   S   O   J   O   H

___ ___ ___ ___ ___ ___   ___
 G   B   U   I   F   S   T

___ ___ ___ ___ ___
 I   P   V   T   F

___ ___ ___ ___   ___
 J   O   U   P   B

___ ___ ___ ___ ___ ___ !
 N   B   S   L   F   U

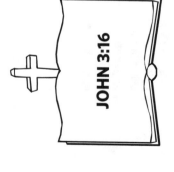

JOHN 2:16

THINK and LOOK ahead

When we believe in God what may we have?

JOHN 3:16

ANSWER

_ _ _ _ LIFE

He drove the
animals and traders
out of the Temple.

How many differences can you find in the bottom picture?
Circle the number

6   8   10   12

Jesus said...

Destroy this Temple,
and in three days I will
raise it up again.

JOHN 2:21

Which Temple
did Jesus mean?

Follow the instructions to find out

1. Change A to T
2. Change B to E
3. Change C to H
4. Change D to M
5. Change E to A
6. Change F to W
7. Change G to L
8. Change H to S
9. Change I to P
10. Change J to B
11. Change I to B
12. Change K to Y
13. Change M to I
14. Change N to D

<u> </u> <u>A</u> <u>C</u> <u>B</u>   <u> </u> <u>A</u> <u>B</u> <u>D</u> <u>I</u> <u>G</u> <u>B</u>

<u> </u> <u>A</u> <u>C</u> <u>E</u> <u>A</u>   <u> </u> <u>F</u> <u>E</u> <u>H</u>

<u> </u> <u>C</u> <u>M</u> <u>H</u>

<u> </u> <u>J</u> <u>L</u> <u>N</u> <u>K</u>

God loves the world

JOHN 3:14–21

How much do you know about our world?

Are the statements below true or false?

Check the True or False box

1. The longest river is the Nile.

2. The largest ocean is the Indian.

3. Earth is approximately 4.5 billion years old.

4. The largest desert is the Sahara.

5. Earth is bigger than Jupiter.

6. Ice covers more than one-tenth of our planet at any one time.

(Answers on back page)

THINK and LOOK ahead

We ask Philip to take us to meet Jesus.

Who are we?

JOHN 12:20–21

ANSWER CHECK

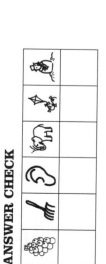

True/False Answer key (page 1)

1. True   2. False   3. True   4. True   5. False   6. True

God sent his only
Son Jesus to be our

7   15   13   11   12   8

Solve the math problems to find the missing letters

$(6 \times 3) - 6 =$ ☐ $=$ O

$(25 \div 5) \times 3 =$ ☐ $=$ A

$(17 + 4) \div 3 =$ ☐ $=$ S

$(8 \times 5) \div 5 =$ ☐ $=$ R

$(15 \div 3) + 6 =$ ☐ $=$ I

$(13 + 4) - 4 =$ ☐ $=$ V

Why does a
good person come out
into the light?

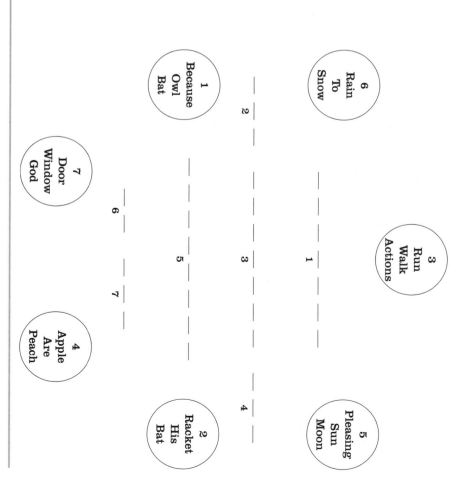

Find the odd word in each set and write it on the numbered line

6
Rain
To
Snow

3
Run
Walk
Actions

5
Pleasing
Sun
Moon

1
Because
Owl
Bat

2
Racket
His
Bat

7
Door
Window
God

4
Apple
Are
Peach

2   1   3   4   5   6   7

A grain of wheat

JOHN 12:20–30

Jesus knew that the time was coming for him to suffer and die.

Cross out the letters with odd numbers.
Write the remaining letters in order on the lines

K T L H S E M N T O I M R E P H S A G S D F C H O H M E
3 2 9 8 7 10 1 9 14 11 6 2 13 12 3 8 5 10 9 2 13 11 14 7 16 5 20 2

P L F Q O R B S T O H A E G F S O E N O J F K G G O D R
9 17 10 21 4 6 13 5 2 11 6 13 8 17 9 4 12 5 10 2 7 8 3 4 1 6 10 5

S T O P B F E D G L O P R F I F I J E D Q
7 12 16 13 2 11 8 6 2 18 1 10 7 2 6 8 9 6 8 11

66 _ _ _ _ _ _ _ _ _ _ _

_ _ _ _ _ _ _ _ _ _ _ 99

JOHN 12:23

Why is this crowd so excited?

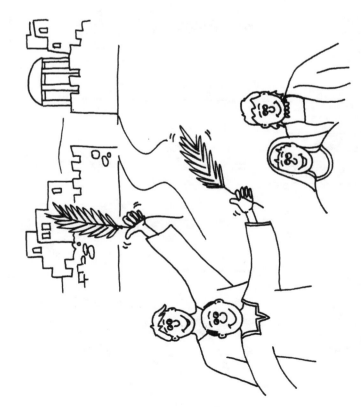

Find out by reading
MARK 11:8–10

What did Jesus say about the grain of wheat?

Find his words and read them in order 1 to 10

Jesus said...

HARVEST 10.

RICH 9.

GRAIN 4.

A 2.

IT 6.

1 8.

IF 1.

SINGLE 3.

YIELDS 7.

DIES 5.

JOHN 12:24

What does Jesus call EVERYONE to do?

Write the first letter of each word in the boxes to spell out the answer

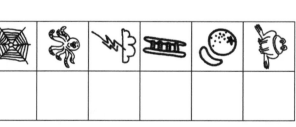

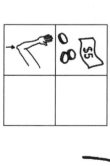

JOHN 12:26

Hosanna! Hosanna!

MARK 11:1-10

Jesus rode into Jerusalem as a "Prince of Peace."

What form of transport did he use?

Circle the answer

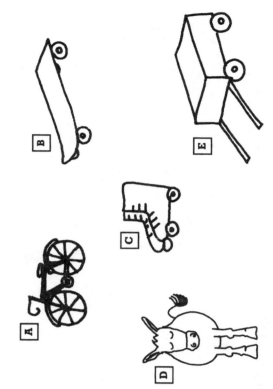

THINK and LOOK ahead

What do we call the week between Palm Sunday and Easter Sunday?

Write the first letter of each clue in the numbered boxes

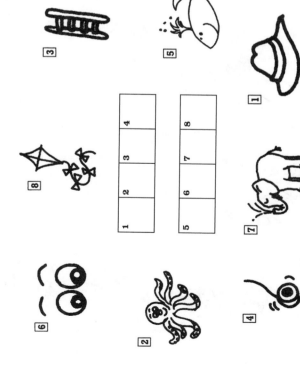

1	2	3	4
5	6	7	8

?

A great crowd had gathered to welcome him!

What did they do?

Follow the arrow to find out

L	O	M	B	E	Y	H
D	A	R	E	S	R	E	S
N	O	H	F	P	C	D	A
D	G	E	T	L	O	K	R
R	E	N	T	N	S	A	G
Y	F	M	H	I	M	D	B
R	O	E	F	E	L	P	S

(T)

" T _____ "

They shouted at the tops of their voices!

Use the code cracker to read their words from
Mark 11:9

A·B	C·D	E·F		S·T
G·H	I·J	K·L		U·V
M·N	O·P	Q·R		Y·Z / W·X

"

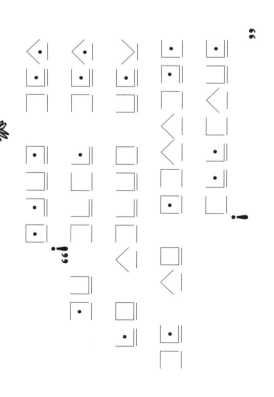

EASTER SUNDAY, YEAR B

Jesus is alive!

JOHN 20:1-9

Today we celebrate Easter Sunday when Jesus rose from the dead!

Write the word that fits the clue. The first letter of each answer will spell out a word that means "rising from the dead"

	E	U	R	C	T	O
1	2	3	4	5	6

CLUES

1. Water falling from clouds
2. Bright object in the sky
3. Red-breasted bird
4. Birds lay these
5. Frozen water
6. You use this to smell with

THINK and LOOK ahead

Next Sunday

Jesus appears to the disciples, but which one is missing?

JOHN 20:24

Look in

Easter is a time for celebrating new life!

Can you find these Easter symbols hidden in the word search puzzle?

LAMBS   EGGS   FLOWERS   BUNNIES   CHICKS

```
J  C  H  I  C  K  S
C  L  M  N  P  R  E
H  S  G  G  E  A  I
B  R  P  W  B  S  N
E  E  O  S  E  G  N
I  L  A  M  B  S  U
F  L  B  M  S  E  B
```

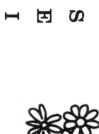

What happened when Peter and the other disciple saw the empty tomb?

Use this Easter code to find out what happened

Code key (circled letters and numbers):

- E A H (12, 13)
- D I R (4, 5)
- S (2)
- W (11)
- Y (1)
- F (10)
- T (7)
- O (6)
- P (14)
- M (3)
- N C U (8, 9)

Decode blanks:

```
__ __        __ __ __ __ __
12 13        7  13 12,13 1

__ __ __ __ __ __ __ __
7  13 12  2  8,9 5  4,5 14

__ __ __ __ __ __        __ __ __
13 12,13 1   9  8  4  12  5  2

__ __ __ __ __        __ __ __ __
11 13 4,5  8,9 13   2  12,13 4,5 4

__ __ __        __ __ __        __ __
7  13 12,13 7    13 12    3  9  2

__ __        __ __ __ __
5  4,5 2 12   10 5  6  3

__ __ __        __ __ __ __
7  13 12    4   12 12,13 4
```

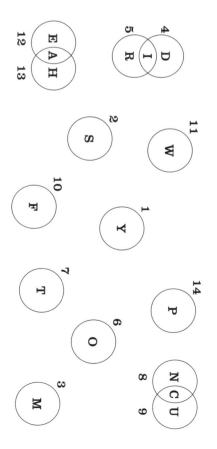

Thomas has doubts!

JOHN 20:19-31

The door was locked and bolted because the disciples were afraid!

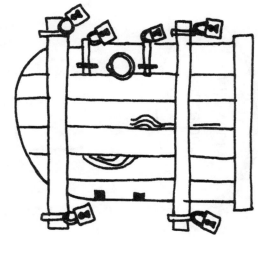

How many padlocks can you see?

Write the number in the box

THINK and LOOK ahead

What do the disciples offer Jesus to eat in next Sunday's gospel?

LUKE 24:42

Answer

Unscramble the letters to check your answer

LIRGEDL   HFSI

The disciples
were filled with joy
to see Jesus!

Complete the joyful faces in the picture

Peace be
with you!

JOHN 20:20-21

At first Thomas would not believe
that Jesus was alive.

*What did he say when
Jesus showed him his wounds?*

Use the code to find Thomas' words

1 = **O** 2 = **M** 3 = **N** 4 = **G** 5 = **Y**

6 = **D** 7 = **A** 8 = **R** 9 = **L**

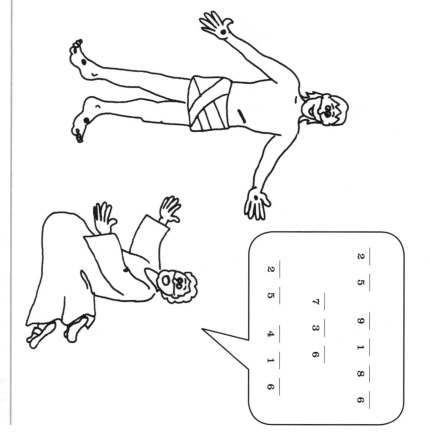

$\overline{2}$ $\overline{5}$ $\overline{9}$ $\overline{1}$ $\overline{8}$ $\overline{6}$

$\overline{2}$ $\overline{5}$ $\overline{7}$ $\overline{3}$ $\overline{4}$ $\overline{1}$ $\overline{6}$

Christ's witnesses

LUKE 24:35-48

The disciples thought that they had seen a ghost!

What did Jesus say to them?

Fit the pieces in the puzzle to find what Jesus said in Luke 24:39

THINK and LOOK ahead

How does Jesus describe himself in next week's gospel?

Look in **JOHN 10:11**

Jesus opened their minds to understand what?

Use the code symbols to find what they understood!

★

| C | D | E | F | G | H | I | O | P | R | S | T | U | W |

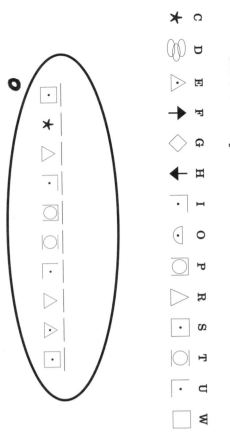

LUKE 24:45

Jesus sent his disciples to share God's message with all nations!

What did he send them to be?

Write the word that fits the clue.
The first letters of the words will spell out the answer

CLUES

1. Colorless liquid essential for life
2. Frozen water
3. Number of fingers or toes
4. A bird's home
5. World's highest mountain
6. Large graceful white bird
7. Star closest to earth
8. Large mammal with a trunk
9. Creature that carries its home

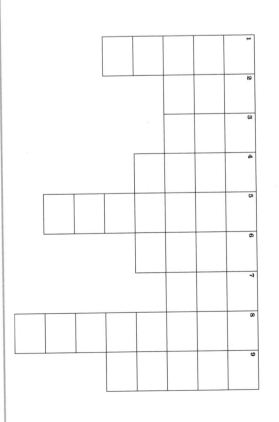

The Good Shepherd

JOHN 10:11-18

What is a good shepherd ready to do?

Use the code to find out!

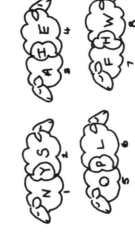

__ __ __
6 3 1,2

__ __ __
9 5 8 1

__ __ __
7,8 3,4 2

__ __ __ __ __
6 3,4 7 4

__ __ __ __ __
7 5 9,10

__ __ __ __ __ __
2 7,8 4 4 5,6

__ __ __
7,8 3,4 2

JOHN
10:11

THINK and LOOK ahead

If Jesus is "the Vine,"
what is his Father?

JOHN 15:1

Answer

N __ D __ __ E __ S __ R

What do WE belong to?

What did Jesus say about the Good Shepherd's flock?

Solve the math problems below.
Then use the answers to break the code!

$$\begin{array}{c} 5 \\ +6 \\ \hline S \end{array} \quad \begin{array}{c} 3 \\ \times 3 \\ \hline F \end{array} \quad \begin{array}{c} 8 \\ \times 3 \\ \hline C \end{array} \quad \begin{array}{c} 9 \\ \div 3 \\ \hline G \end{array} \quad \begin{array}{c} 22 \\ \div 11 \\ \hline O \end{array} \quad \begin{array}{c} 8 \\ +9 \\ \hline K \end{array} \quad \begin{array}{c} 7 \\ \times 3 \\ \hline D \end{array} \quad \begin{array}{c} 17 \\ -3 \\ \hline L \end{array}$$

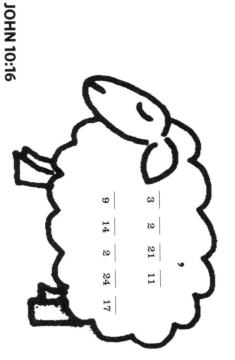

3 2 21 11

9 14 2 24 17

Fit the words into the spaces

" ☐☐☐☐ | Y

☐ N | ☐ N | ☐

☐ N | ☐ N | ☐ | ☐

☐ E "

MY   AND   KNOW

ME   I   OWN

JOHN 10:14

Jesus is the true Vine

JOHN 15:1-8

Find the words of Jesus using the grid below

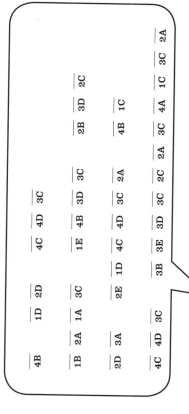

4B 1D 2D 4C 4D 3C

1B 2A 1A 3C 1E 4B 3D 3C 2B 3D 2C

2D 3A 2E 1D 4C 4D 3C 2A 4B 1C

4C 4D 3C 3B 3E 3D 3C 2C 2A 3C 4A 1C 3C 2A

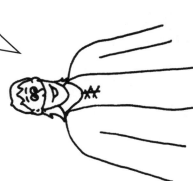

	1	2	3	4
A	U	R	Y	S
B	T	A	D	I
C	S	D	E	T
D	A	M	N	H
E	V	F	I	Y

JOHN 15:1

THINK and LOOK ahead

Next Sunday what does
Jesus command his disciples to do?

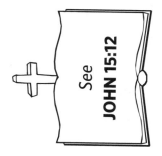

See
JOHN 15:12

" ♥3 ☺1 ☺3 ♥2   ☺1 ♥4 ♥2

☺4 ♥4 ☺1 ♥7 ♥6 ♥2 ☺7   ☺4 ♥1

♥6 ☺4 ☺3 ♥2   ♥3 ☺1 ☺3 ♥2 ♥5

☺5 ☺1 ☺2   "   ☺6

ANSWER CHECK

♥	S	E	L	N	D	H	T
☺	O	U	V	A	Y	I	R
	1	2	3	4	5	6	7

Choose a rhyming word to complete each sentence

Jesus is the vine, growing strong and _____

We are the branches, that's me and you!

God is the gardener who tends the _____.

With his love and care the harvest is fine.

Wood that is fruitless he cuts _____.

Useless branches do not stay.

With careful pruning each branch bears _____.

The harvest grows bigger and better than before!

Word list: **AWAY**   **VINE**   **TRUE**   **MORE**

JOHN 15:8

What will disciples
of Jesus do?

Find the letters amongst the grapes!

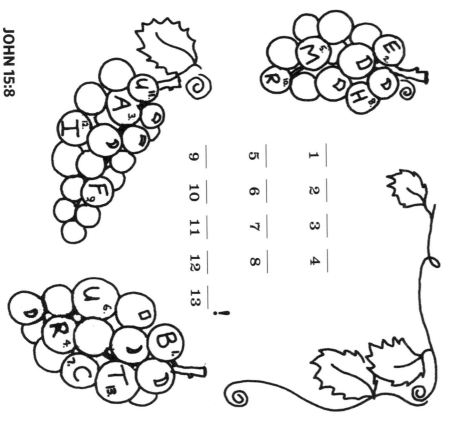

___ ___ ___ ___
1   2   3   4

___ ___ ___ ___
5   6   7   8

___ ___ ___ ___ ___ !
9 10 11 12 13

Love each other

JOHN 15:9-17

Jesus loves each one of us.
What does he want us to do?

Use the code to find what Jesus says in John 15:9, 12

__ __ __ __ __ __ __   __ __
i v n z r m   r m

__ __   __ __ __   __ •
n b   o l e   v

__ __ __   __   __ __ __ __
o l e   v   v z x s

__ __ __ __ __ •
l g s v i

z	**A**	m	**N**
y	**B**	l	**O**
x	**C**	k	**P**
w	**D**	j	**Q**
v	**E**	i	**R**
u	**F**	h	**S**
t	**G**	g	**T**
s	**H**	f	**U**
r	**I**	e	**V**
q	**J**	d	**W**
p	**K**	c	**X**
o	**L**	b	**Y**
n	**M**	a	**Z**

THINK and LOOK ahead

Which feast day
do we celebrate
on Thursday?

Use the code to fill in the blanks

A = •
E = ◁
H = ◇
O = ◯
R = ▷
S = ↑

T __◇__ __◁__   __•__ S C __◁__ N __↑__ I __◯__ N

OF   T __▷__ __◁__   L __◯__ __◇__ D

How can we remain in Christ's love?

Unscramble the words of Jesus!

FI OYU
EPKE YM
MMOCNAEDMTNS

JOHN 15:10

If we do all these things, what will Jesus call us?

Use the picture clues to complete the puzzle.
The answer will appear in the bold squares

JOHN 15:14

Jesus prays for us

JOHN 17:11-19

Jesus said a prayer to his Father for his followers.

Add or subtract letters to find his words

A B C D E F G H I J K L M N O P Q R S T U V W X Y Z

E+1 F−5 J+10 E+3 I−4 P+2 G+4 C+2 J−5 O+1

Q+3 D+4 K−6 N−1 Z−6 L+6 V−1 A+4

W−3 G+8 Z−1 V−7 T+1 S−1

L+2 I−8 L+1 J−5

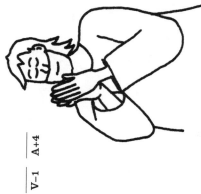

JOHN 17:11

THINK and LOOK ahead

Which "helper" does Jesus promise to send from his Father?

JOHN 15:26

Answer

— — — — — —

— — —

— —

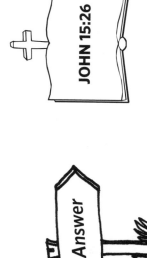

Write the first letter of each object in order on the lines above

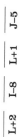

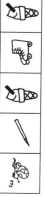

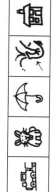

What did Jesus want to share?

Follow the arrows to find Jesus' words in John 17:13

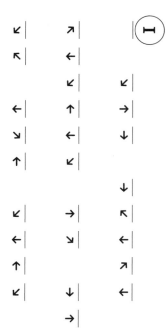

Ⓘ					
I	A	Y	T	E	S
T	S	H	R	A	M
H	E	E	H	Y	O
N	I	O	S	J	W
G	T	P	E	T	I
L	S	M	H	W	H

Ⓘ

What did Jesus pass on to ALL of us?

Follow the instructions to find out

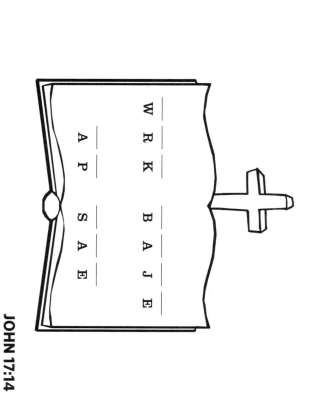

W R K   B A J E
_ _ _ _ _ _ _ _

A P   S A E
_ _   _ _ _

JOHN 17:14

1. Change **A** to **O**
2. Change **E** to **D**
3. Change **K** to **E**
4. Change **R** to **H**
5. Change **S** to **G**
6. Change **P** to **F**
7. Change **B** to **W**
8. Change **J** to **R**
9. Change **W** to **T**

The Holy Spirit comes!

ACTS 2:1-11; JOHN 15:26-27; 16:12-15

The Holy Spirit rested on the disciples and gave them the gift of expression! *What happened next?*

Use the code cracker to find out!

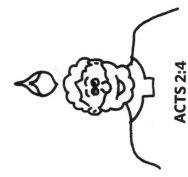

B G E S A N L T O H U Y P R K F I

ACTS 2:4

THINK and LOOK ahead

What do we celebrate next Sunday?

Write the letter missing from the sequence to find out!

PQRSU

NOPQS

HJKLM

MOPQR

EFGHJ

SUVWX

VWXZA

QRTUV

TVWXY

LMOPQ

ABCEF

XYZBC

WXZAB

Many people from different countries could hear the disciples preaching in their own languages!

Jesus sent the Spirit to help the disciples to be his witnesses.

Find these places hidden in the word search puzzle!

Circle them

JUDAEA   MESOPOTAMIA   CAPPADOCIA   ASIA

PONTUS   EGYPT   LIBYA   PHRYGIA   ROME

```
B C A P P A D O C I A
J A M C O P R S E B I
U L A I G Y R H P F I
D P M K C A P S O E P
A I M A T O P O S E M
E B N S P R O S E M A
A E P I Y M B M I Y A
L S J A G C O S B B Y
K P R L E R R I E S E
P O N T U S L L Y M G
```

Find the words of Jesus taken from John 16:13–14 by writing the next letter of the alphabet above the letters given.

For example, D will be written above C

"

G D __ V H K K __ K D Z C __ X N T __

S N __ B N L O K D S D __

S Q T S G __ Z K K __ G D __

S D K K R __ X N T __ B N L D R __

E Q N L L D __ . "

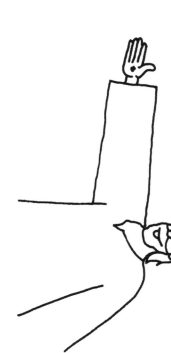

A B C D E F G H I J K L M N O P Q R S T U V W X Y Z

Father, Son, and Holy Spirit

MATTHEW 28:16–20

The disciples set off for Galilee to meet Jesus as arranged.

Use the grid references to help the disciples find the mountain where they are to meet

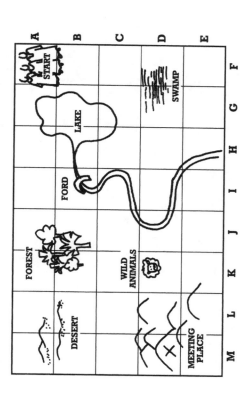

MAP REF

BF, CG, CH, BH, BI, AI, AJ, AK, BL, CL, DL, DM

Write the missing letter to find when Jesus is with us!

In **BALL** , but not in **BILL** _____

In **LETTER** 🖼 but not in **BETTER** _____

In **WELL** 🔔 but not in **BELL** " _____ ,

In **HAT** 👝 but not in **HOT** _____

In **SILLY** but not in **SILL** _____

In **STOP** 🛑 But not in **TOP** 👕 _____

MATTHEW 28:20

Jesus told them...

Go make disciples of all nations

MATTHEW 28:19

Find Jesus' words in the word search below

B	H	A	Z	G	A	D	O	C	I	A
J	A	M	C	O	P	R	S	S	B	I
N	A	T	I	O	N	S	E	P	E	I
D	P	M	K	C	A	L	S	O	K	P
A	T	M	A	T	P	P	Z	S	A	M
E	B	N	S	I	R	O	S	E	M	A
A	E	P	C	Y	M	B	M	P	Y	A
L	S	S	A	G	A	O	F	B	B	Y
K	I	R	L	E	R	L	I	E	S	E
D	O	N	T	U	S	B	L	Y	M	G

In whose names
did the disciples have to
baptize people?

Add or subtract words and letters to find the answer!

— LOWER +  — B + — PA ___ ___ ___ ___ ___

— UN + ⊕ — BUTT ___ ___ — H ___

— RSE + ✶ — HOL ___ ___ ___

— OON + — FE + — KE ___ ___ ___ ___ ___

MATTHEW 28:19

Lamb of God

JOHN 1:35–42

What did John the Baptist say when he saw Jesus?

His words have been written backward!
Write the letters in the correct order to read what he said

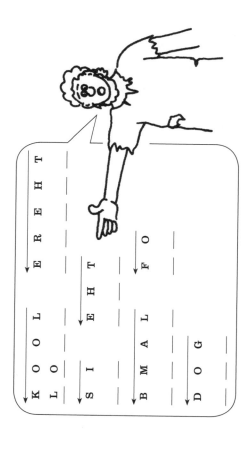

```
K  O  O  L    E  R  E  H  T
L  O
___ ___ ___   ___ ___ ___ ___ ___

S  I    E  H  T
___ ___   ___ ___ ___

B  M  A  L    F  O
___ ___ ___ ___   ___ ___

D  O  G
___ ___ ___
```

JOHN 1:36

THINK and LOOK ahead

What did Andrew and Simon Peter do for a living?

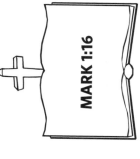

Find out

MARK 1:16

THEY WERE

___ ___ ___ ___ ___ ___ ___

Two of John's disciples followed Jesus. The one called Andrew had a brother.

What was his name?

Use the clues to find out!

1	2	3	4	5

6	7	8	9	10

CLUES

1. Third letter of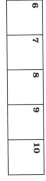

2. First letter of

3. Second letter of

4. Third letter of

5. Third letter of

6. First letter of

7. Fifth letter of

8. First letter of

9. Fifth letter of

10. Second letter of

Andrew took his brother to meet Jesus.

What did Jesus say to him?

Use the code to find his words

___ ___ ___ ___ ___
1,2   2,3   5

___ ___ ___ ___ ___
3   5,6   2   4   2,3

___ ___ ___ ___ ___
4,5   3   1   7   3,4

___ ___ ___ ___ ___
1   2   6,7   3   2

___ ___
4,5   2

L	Y	E	O	A	H	T	C	U	R	B	D	P	G	S
1	2	3	4	5	6	7	8

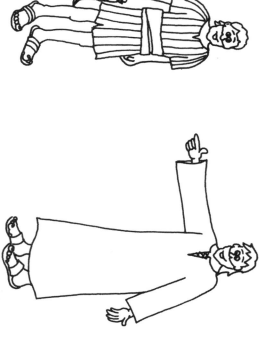

Follow me!

MARK 1:14–20

After John's arrest, Jesus went to Galilee.

What did he do there?

Use the code breaker to find the answer

$\overline{8}\ \overline{5}$

$\overline{16}\ \overline{18}\ \overline{15}\ \overline{3}\ \overline{12}\ \overline{1}\ \overline{9}\ \overline{13}\ \overline{5}\ \overline{4}$

$\overline{20}\ \overline{8}\ \overline{5}$ $\overline{7}\ \overline{15}\ \overline{15}\ \overline{4}$

$\overline{14}\ \overline{5}\ \overline{23}\ \overline{19}$ $\overline{6}\ \overline{18}\ \overline{15}\ \overline{13}$

$\overline{7}\ \overline{15}\ \overline{4}$

1 A	14 N
2 B	15 O
3 C	16 P
4 D	17 Q
5 E	18 R
6 F	19 S
7 G	20 T
8 H	21 U
9 I	22 V
10 J	23 W
11 K	24 X
12 L	25 Y
13 M	26 Z

MARK 1:14

Then he called James and his brother John to follow him too!

Draw straight lines between dots with the same number to see what James and John are mending

Where was Jesus walking when he saw Simon and his brother Andrew?

Use the picture clues to complete the puzzle.
The letters in the bold boxes will spell out the answer

What did Jesus say to them?

Find the numbered words in their net and write them in order on the lines

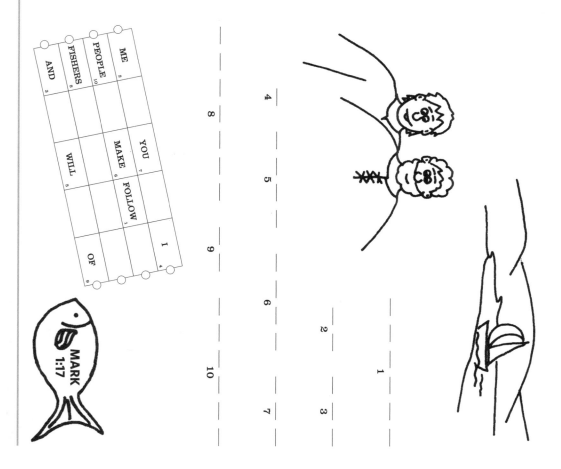

MARK 1:17

The power of Jesus!

MARK 1:21-28

Which town did Jesus go to visit?

Cross out the following letters and
fill in the blanks with those that are left

S S Z S C S A Z S Z P S E S Z Z S R S N S Z A Z U S S M S

1. Cross out the letters that sound like a snake

2. Cross out the "sleepy" letters

MARK 1:21

The people were amazed by what they heard and saw!

Fit the words in the boxes to see what they are thinking!

E V E N   H I M   T E A C H I N G   T H E   T H I S

I S   S P I R I T S   N E W

O B E Y

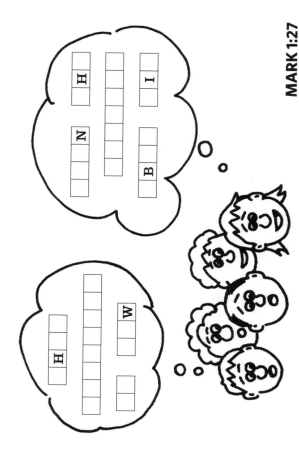

MARK 1:27

Where did Jesus go
to teach the people?

Hold this picture in front a mirror
to see if your answer was right!

THE SYNAGOGUE

Jesus was interrupted
by a man with an unclean spirit
who shouted at him!

What did Jesus say to the unclean spirit?

Use the code to find his words

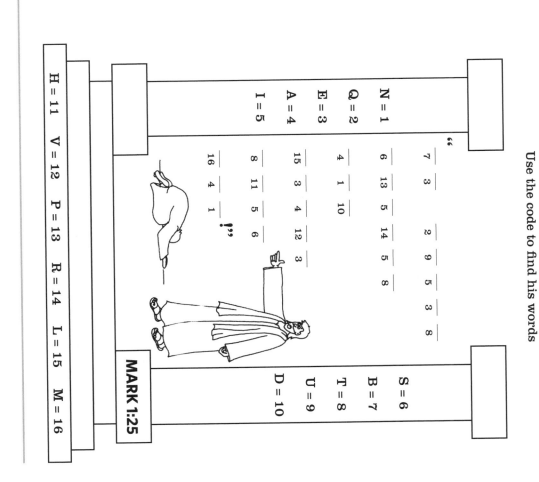

"___ ___ ___   ___ ___ ___ ___ ___ ___ ___ ___
7 3   6 13 5 14 5 3 8

___ ___   ___ ___
2 9 5 8

___ ___ ___   ___ ___ ___ ___
4 1 10

___ ___ ___ ___   ___ ___ ___
15 3 4 12 3

___ ___ ___ ___   ___ ___ ___ !"
8 11 5 6   16 4 1

N = 1   S = 6

Q = 2   B = 7

E = 3   T = 8

A = 4   U = 9

I = 5   D = 10

H = 11   V = 12   P = 13   R = 14   L = 15   M = 16

MARK 1:25

Jesus cures the sick

MARK 1:29–39

I was sick, but Jesus made me well again!

Who am I?

Unscramble the letters

IMOSSN   THOMRE – NI – ALW

_____

MARK 1:30–31

THINK and LOOK ahead

Who asks Jesus
for help next Sunday?

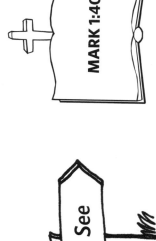

See

A

MARK 1:40

_ _ _

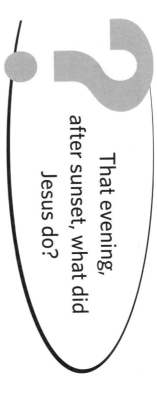

That evening, after sunset, what did Jesus do?

What did Jesus do long before dawn?

Solve the problems to complete the code and then find the missing letters!

Use the code cracker to see!

	O	G	S	F
☀	O	G	S	F
☽	E	U	W	H
✿	R	C	A	D
☾	N	M	I	Y
	□	△	○	◇

CODE

E = (9 x 2) – 4 _____

A = (16 ÷ 2) + 2 _____

O = 4 + 7 + 4 _____

P = (5 x 2) + 3 _____

T = (22 – 11) + 1 _____

H __ 14

W __ 14   N __ 12

__ __ L __ Y
12 15

L __ 15   N __ 14   __ N 14   __ L 14   __ Y

R __ 10   C __ 14   __ N 10   __ N D

__ __ R __ 10   Y __ 14   __ D
13

__ R 13   __ H 14   __ R 14

Jesus cures a leper!

MARK 1:40-45

A leper came to Jesus to ask for his help.

What did the leper say?

Use the symbols to find what the leper said

O = ⌐	A = |O|	M = ◇	N = Ξ	T = ≫	F = Ō	W = ∿
C = ≪	U = →	Y = |||	I = ⌐	E = ◇	R = ↑	

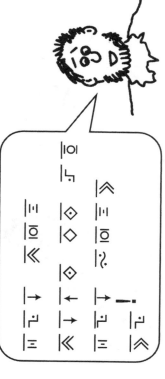

MARK 1:40

What did the
cured man do next?

Follow the arrows to find out!

S	H	T	E	L	D	U
J	M	H	O	S	E	R
E	T	O	B	V	O	Y
J	S	U	P	A	N	R
B	J	E	S	E	B	H

MARK 1:45

What did Jesus say to him?

Use the code to find the letters in the squares and write them in the spaces

O	F	W	R	S	I	C	L	A
U	E	C	K	E	P	W	Y	B

1 2 3 4 5 6 7 8

"
___ ___   ___ ___ ___ ___ ___ ___
1A 2A   3B 1A 1B 4A 5A 2B

___   ___ ___ ___ ___
6A   7B 6A 8A 8A

___ ___ ___ ___ ___ ___
7A 1B 4A 5B 8B 1A 1B !"

MARK 1:41

What two things did the cured man have to do?

Choose the odd word from each set and write it on the numbered line

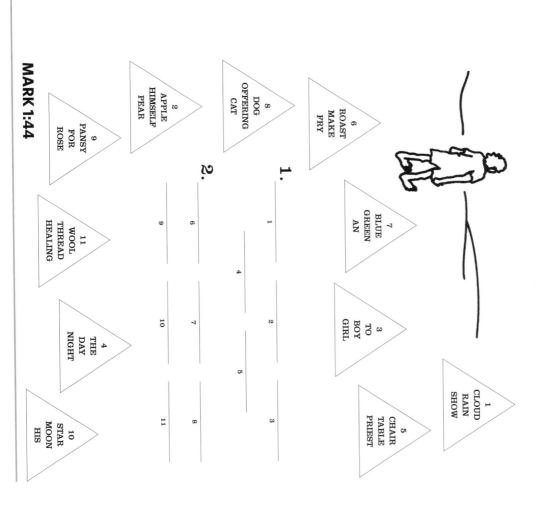

MARK 1:44

Don't give up!

MARK 2:1-12

Crowds of people who wanted to be cured were following Jesus.

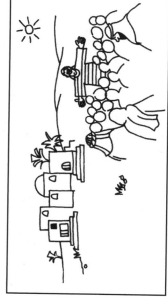

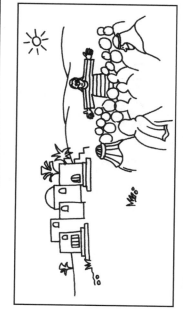

Can you find ten differences in the bottom picture?

The man got up and walked away! *What did the crowd say?*

Use the code to find what the crowd said

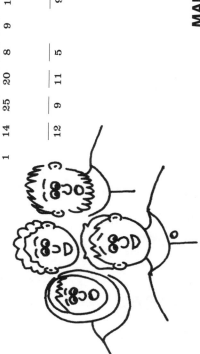

A 1	N 14
B 2	O 15
C 3	P 16
D 4	Q 17
E 5	R 18
F 6	S 19
G 7	T 20
H 8	U 21
I 9	V 22
J 10	W 23
K 11	X 24
L 12	Y 25
M 13	Z 26

‾23 ‾5   ‾8 ‾1 ‾22 ‾5

‾14 ‾5 ‾22 ‾5 ‾18   ‾19 ‾5 ‾5 ‾14

‾1 ‾14 ‾25 ‾20 ‾8 ‾9 ‾14 ‾7

‾12 ‾9 ‾11 ‾5   ‾20 ‾8 ‾9 ‾19

‾9 ‾14   ‾9 ‾20 ‾19

‾20 ‾8 ‾5   ‾23 ‾8 ‾15 ‾12 ‾5   ‾12 ‾9 ‾6 ‾5 !

MARK 2:12

Four men found an unusual way to get their friend to Jesus!

Connect the dots to complete the scene

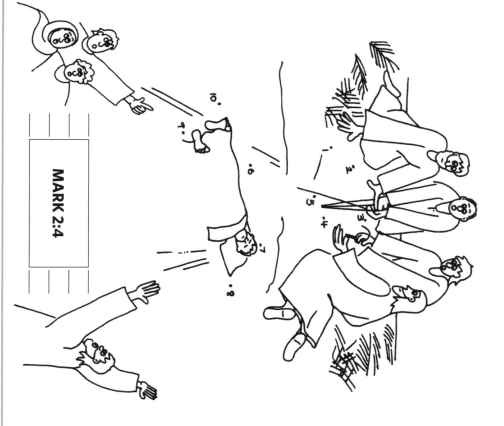

MARK 2:4

What did Jesus say to the man who could not walk?

Write the next letter of the alphabet on the line above. For example, **E** will be written above **D**

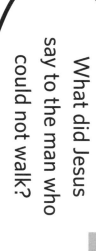

"
___ ___ ___ ___ !
F D S T O

___ ___ ___ ___ ___ ___ ___
S Z J D X N T Q

___ ___ ___ ___ ___ ___ ___
R S Q D S B G D Q

___ ___ ___ ___
Z M C F N

___ ___ ___
G N L D
"

MARK 2:11

A B C D E F G H I J K L M N O P Q R S T U V W X Y Z

Jesus pours love into our lives

MARK 2:18-22

One day some of the people put a question to Jesus.

Moving clockwise around the circle, write down every other letter. Do this twice to find out what they said

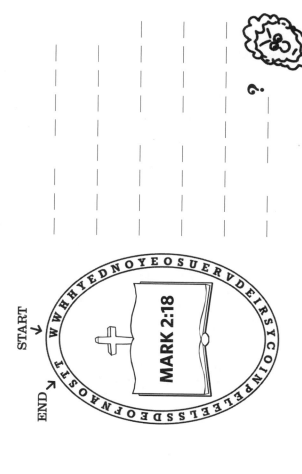

START

END

MARK 2:18

Which people were set in their ways and unable to accept the Good News that Jesus came to pour into their lives?

Use the picture clues to spell out the answer

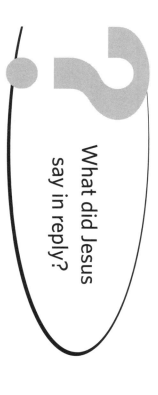

What did Jesus say in reply?

Fit the jigsaw pieces together to find his answer in Mark 2:19

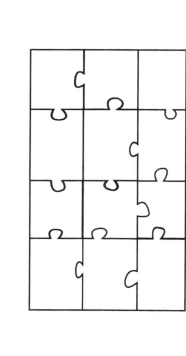

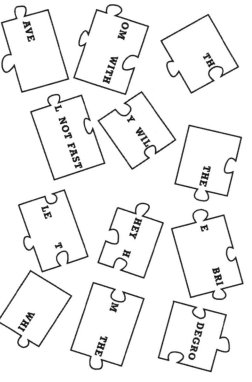

Jigsaw pieces: AVE, OM WITH, TH, Y WILL, L NOT FAST, THE, E BRI, LE T, HEY H, M THE, WHI, DEGRO

Wine was often stored in animal skins.
Can you remember what Jesus said about them?

Use the code to find Jesus' words in Mark 2:22

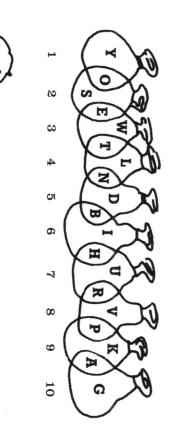

Code vessels:
1 Y
2 O S
3 E W
4 T L
5 N D
6 B I
7 H U
8 R V
9 P K
10 A G

"

___ ___ ___   ___ ___   ___ ___ ___   ___ ___ ___ ___
4,5 2,3 3   6   1,2 4,5 2,3   6   4,5 2,3   8,9 1,2 7 7,8

___ ___   ___ ___ ___   ___ ___ ___   ___ ___ ___
1,2 4   5   3   6   4,5 2,3 2   9   6   4,5 3,4 1,2

___ ___ ___   ___ ___ ___   ___ ___ ___
3,4 6,7 2,3   2   9   6   4,5 2

___ ___ ___ ___   ___ ___ ___ ___ ___
3   1,2 7   4   5   5,6 7   7,8 2   3,4

___ ___ ___ ___ ___ ___   ___ ___ ___ ___
2,3 8   2,3 7,8 1   3,4 6,7 6   4,5 10   3   1,2 7   4   5

___ ___
5,6 2,3   4   1,2 2   3,4

99

Choose God's way

MARK 2:27—3:6

This man was in the synagogue.
What was wrong with him?

Copy the letters in order on to the lines above the symbols

H S A D A W T E E // I H N W S I H R D

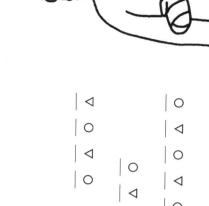

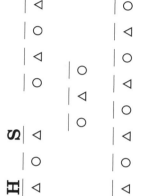

Jesus chose
to act with kindness
and love!

Complete the picture below by giving the man a healthy hand

Stretch out
your hand!

MARK 2:5

Which day of the week was it?

CLUES

Write the word that fits the clue.
The first letter of each word will spell out the answer

1. A clock tells you this
2. The opposite of COLD
3. Birds lay these
4. A legless hissing reptile
5. The forbidden fruit
6. A nocturnal flying mammal
7. Something you sleep on
8. The opposite of **BEFORE**
9. Clothing for legs
10. Protective headgear

1.	2.	3.	4.	5.	6.	7.	8.	9.	10.

— — — — — — — — — —

The Pharisees watched Jesus
to see if he would cure the man.
What did Jesus ask them?

Use the code to find his words in Mark 2:4

	iⱼ	KĿ	MṄ
AḂ	OṖ	QR	ST
GḢ			
EḞ	UV̇	wx	yż

☐ = R ㄱ = V ∨ = A

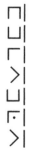

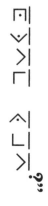

The family of God

MARK 3:20-35

Such a crowd gathered that it was impossible
for Jesus to have a meal!

Fill the page with faces surrounding Jesus

MARK 3:20

We all belong
to one family of God!

Draw pictures of people you know who belong to God's family

His friends and relatives came to take care of him. They sent Jesus a message.

Use the secret code to read what it said!

1 = O	3 = S	5 = T	7 = A	9 = N	11 = M	13 = Y
2 = U	4 = E	6 = R	8 = D	10 = I	12 = B	14 = H

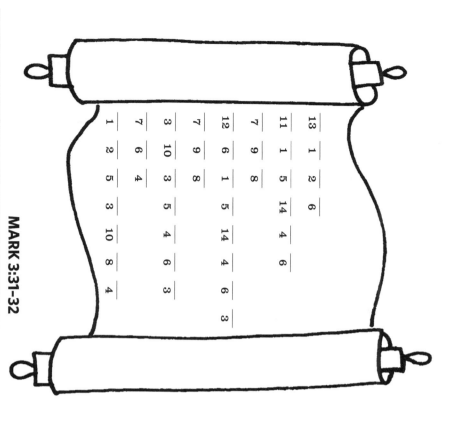

13 1 2 6

11 1 5 14 4 6

7 9 8

12 6 1 5 14 4 6 3

7 9 8

3 10 3 5 4 6 3

7 6 4

1 2 5 3 10 8 4

MARK 3:31-32

What did Jesus say when he received the message?

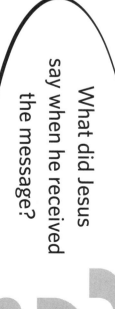

Use the code to find out

z y x w v u t s r q p o n m l k j i h g f e d c b a
A B C D E F G H I J K L M N O P Q R S T U V W X Y Z

"

d s l r h n b u z n r o b ?

z m b l m v d s l w i v h

t l w h d r o o z n w

y i l g s v i z m w

h r h g v i z m w

n l g s v i !"

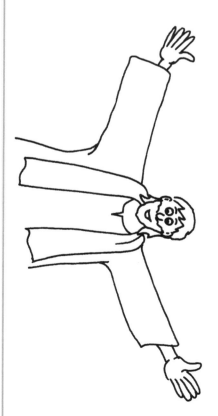

God's kingdom

MARK 4:26-34

Jesus used simple stories to teach the people and help them to understand his message.

What do we call these stories?

In the box write the letter that is missing from the second word

In	TAP	but not in	TAN
In	PAN	but not in	PIN
In	BREAD	but not in	BEAD
In	SAW	but not in	SOW
In	BREAK	but not in	RAKE
In	BALL	but not in	BAT
In	MEAT	but not in	MAT
In	SUN	but not in	FUN

What was Jesus trying to explain in these parables?

Write the first letter of each picture to see!

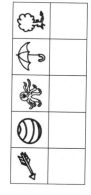
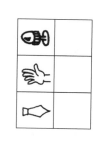
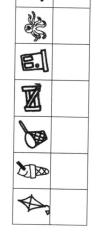
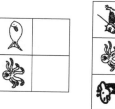
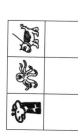

Jesus told a parable
about a seed growing by itself to
produce a great harvest!

Can you number these pictures 1 to 4
to put them in the right order?

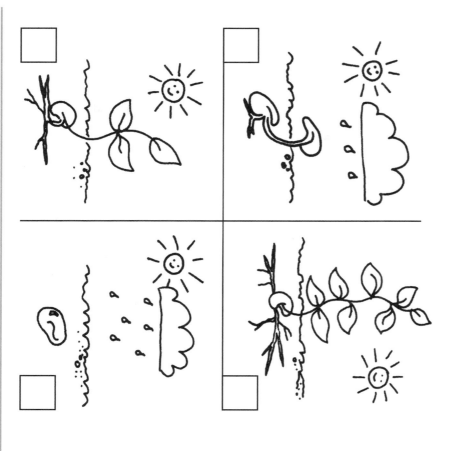

Jesus told another parable
about the tiny mustard seed.

Can you fit these words into the boxes to complete this poem?

ME   WIDE   SEE   SMALL   HIDE

TALL

A mustard seed is very

and yet it grows so very T

It puts out branches strong and

in which so many birds can W

God plants his words of love in

and so his kingdom grows, you

Lord of wind and sea

MARK 4:35-41

Jesus and his disciples decided to cross the Sea of Galilee.

Plot a safe course for them to get to the other side

COURSE

2E,

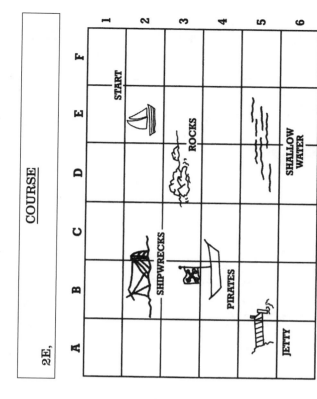

MARK 4:35-36

What do we need to have at "stormy" times of our lives?

Use the clues to find the answer

1.	2.	3.	4.	5.

CLUES

2. Fourth letter of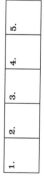

3. Second letter of

4. Third letter of

5. Second letter of

1. First letter of

A terrible storm blew up and the disciples were afraid as huge waves washed the boat!

Jesus awoke and scolded the sea and the wind.

Use the clues to find the code and then use the code to find out what the disciples said to Jesus

A young dog

Season following autumn

A tune that is sung

Something to wipe your feet on

Someone you visit when ill

Use the secret code to find out what he said

SECRET CODE

1 = Q 2 = C 3 = U 4 = P 5 = A 6 = I

7 = E 8 = B 9 = T 10 = W 11 = N 12 = O

"
___ ___ ___ ___ ___ ___ ___ ___
1   3   6   7   9   11 12 10

___ ___ ___ ___ ___ ___ !
8   7   9   4   7   5   2

___
7

"

Jesus gives us new life!

MARK 5:21–43

A synagogue leader asked Jesus
to save his daughter who was dying.

Come and
lay your hands
on her.

Write the first letter of
each object to find out the
man's name

MARK 5:23

Jesus went to the little girl...

Little girl, get up!

Draw a picture of what happened next!

A woman in the crowd believed that touching Jesus would cure her illness!

Use the numbered letters to see what Jesus said to her

"__ __ __ __ __ __ __ __ __
 6 1 8 12 3 9 7 2 13

__ __ __
13 9 10

__ __ __ __ __ __
13 4 9 11 4 5

__ __ __ !"
 6 1 8

1=O
2=T
3=F
4=E
5=D
6=Y
7=I
8=U
9=A
10=S
11=L
12=R
13=H

MARK 5:34

News came that the little girl was dead!
What did Jesus say to her father?

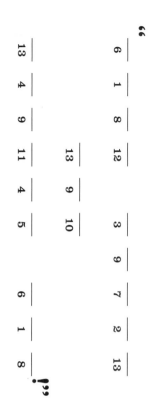

MARK 5:36

Add or subtract letters to find out

A B C D E F G H I J K L M N O P Q R S T U V W X Y Z

"D __ __ __ T __ E __ R __ ID!
   J+5 U-7 T-5 A+1 G-6 C+3 M-12

__ __ IE __ E __ __ __
I-7 A+4 F+6 Z-4 K-2 H+6 Q-4

Jesus is rejected

MARK 6:1-6

Jesus went with his disciples to his hometown.

Follow the road to see where they were going

NAZARETH

BETHLEHEM

JERUSALEM

THINK and LOOK ahead

Which one thing are the disciples instructed to take on their journey?

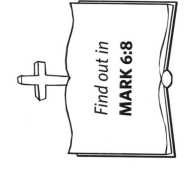

Find out in **MARK 6:8**

A _ _ _ _ _

On the Sabbath
Jesus began teaching
in the synagogue.

The people
would not accept him
in his own town.

Use the code to see what the people in the crowd were thinking

CODE

			1	2	3	4
△	S	U	E	O		
□	L	A	Y	N		
◇	C	R	M	I		
○	H	P	T	J		

1△ 2◇ 3△ 1□ 3○

3◇ 2□ 2◇ 3△ 1△

4○ 3△ 1△ 2△ 1△   1△ 4△ 4○

3◇ 2□ 2◇ 3□ 1△   3○ 1○ 4◇ 1△   4◇ 1△

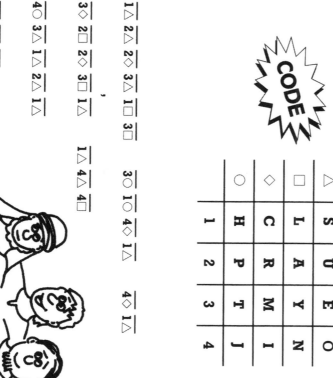

1○ 2□ 2◇ 2○ 3△ 4○ 3○ 3△ 2◇

Write the first letter of each picture
on the line above to find out Jesus' reaction

J __ __ US W __ __ __ Y

AM __ ZE __ __ A __ EIR

O __

FA __ __ __

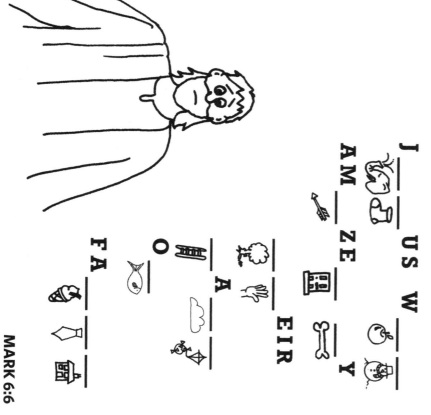

Messengers for Jesus

MARK 6:7-13

Jesus sent the twelve apostles out in pairs
(Mark 6:7).

How many pairs did he send?
Solve the problem below to check your answer!

Add up the number of staffs, multiply the answer by the
number of tunics, then subtract the number of sandals!

_____ = [   ]

THINK and LOOK ahead

Next Sunday what does
Jesus decide that the apostles need?

MARK 6:31

Answer

ANSWER CHECK

Write every SECOND letter in order on the lines above

STMOBRCEDSPTRFBOJRCAPWKHJIMLRE

Jesus told them what they did and did not need for the journey.

The apostles set off to share the Good News of God's love!

Use the symbols to complete the lists below

✈ = A
★ = E
◆ = I
❀ = O
↔ = U

YOU WILL NEED

S T ✈ F F

❀ N ★ T ↔ N ◆ C

S ✈ N D ✈ L S

YOU WILL NOT NEED

B R ★ ✈ D

H ✈ V ★ R S ✈ C K

M ❀ N ★ Y

Find and circle these words in the word search below

PREACH   REPENTANCE   ANOINT
LOVE   CURE   HEAL   MESSENGERS

G	E	P	R	E	A	C	H	V	O
S	E	M	L	A	E	V	O	L	S
S	R	E	G	N	E	S	S	E	M
K	U	H	L	O	R	E	S	A	C
M	C	A	B	I	J	P	R	O	V
R	E	P	E	N	T	A	N	C	E
H	T	E	J	T	M	P	U	S	P
S	R	P	L	R	T	O	V	P	E

MARK 6:8-9

Jesus cares for the people

MARK 6:30–34

The apostles returned to Jesus and told him about everything they had done!

Help each pair to find their way back to Jesus

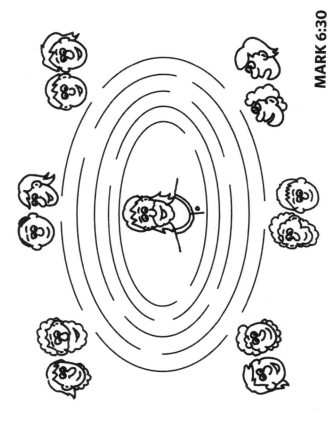

MARK 6:30

THINK and LOOK ahead

What other name was given to the Sea of Galilee?

JOHN 6:1

Find out in

The sea of

_ _ _ _ _ _ _ _ _

Crowds of people followed them, and the apostles had no time even to eat!

Follow the arrows to see what Jesus said to them

J	P	B	C	Y	T	B	O	C
L	R	A	O	A	E	L	B	
M	M	W	E	M	L	M	E	Y
P	E	A	P	(C)	O	N	P	L
S	A	W	O	E	S	A	L	E
W	O	R	F	T	R	N	C	E
H	I	W	E	M	S	D	A	B
P	S	L	I	R	P	M	C	F

"C → | → ↖ | ↗ | ↑ | ↖ | ↙ | → | ↑
→ | ↙ | → | ↗ | ↘ | ↖ | ↗ | → | ↘
↓ | ↗ | ↖ | ↙ | ↖ | ↗ | ↓ | ↙
↖ | ↘ | ↙ | ↖ | ↙ | ↗ | → | ↖
↑ | ↘ | ↖ | ↗ | ↖ | ↓ | ↖
↙ | ↖ | ↘ | ↓ | ↘ | ↗ "

MARK 6:31

They set off by boat but a large crowd waited to greet them!

Why did Jesus have pity on them?

Use the code to find out!

| B | E | A | H | S | U | C | R | Y | W | K | O | L | I | P | T | D |
| 1 | | 2 | | 3 | | 4 | | 5 | | 6 | | 7 | | 8 | | 9 |

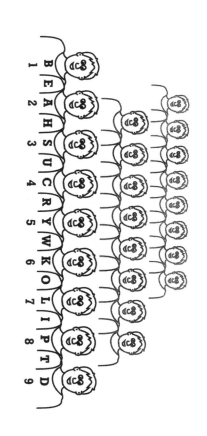

1 ___ ___ ___ ___ ___ ___ ___ ___ ___
1,2 4 2 3,4 3 1,2 8,9 2,3 1,2

5,6 ___ ___ ___ 7 ___ ___
1,2 4,5 1,2 7,8 6 1,2

3 ___ ___ ___
2,3 1,2 1,2 8

5,6 ___ ___ ___ ___ ___ ___
7,8 8,9 2,3 2,3 6,7 3,4 8,9

2 ___ ___ ___ ___ ___ ___ ___
3 2,3 1,2 8 2,3 1,2 4,5 9

MARK 6:34

Jesus feeds the people

JOHN 6:1-15

A huge crowd had followed Jesus and, as time passed, they grew hungry.

Follow the arrows to find how much food they had to share!

F-I-V-E-B
Y-E-L-R-A
L-O-A-V-E
T-D-N-A-S
W-O-F-I-S-H.

JOHN 6:9

Jesus fed 5,000 people with five loaves and two fish!

What do we call such an extraordinary event?

Write the first letter of each object

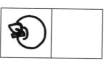

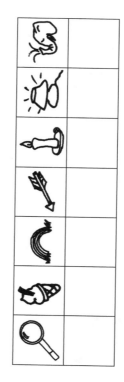

Jesus told
the people to sit down.
What did he do next?

Use the code to find his instructions

1 A	14 N
2 B	15 O
3 C	16 P
4 D	17 Q
5 E	18 R
6 F	19 S
7 G	20 T
8 H	21 U
9 I	22 V
10 J	23 W
11 K	24 X
12 L	25 Y
13 M	26 Z

8 __ 5 __

12 __ 15 __ 1 __ 22 __ 5 __ 19 ' __

7 __ 1 __ 22 __ 5 __

20 __ 8 __ 1 __ 14 __ 11 __ 19 __

8 __ 5 __ 20 __ 8 __ 5 __ 13 __

9 __ 1 __ 18 __ 4 __

1 __ 14 __ 4 __

20 __ 8 __ 5 __

6 __ 19 __ 8 __ 1 __ 14 __ 4 __

20 __ 8 __ 5 __ 23 __ 9 __ 20 __ 8 __

20 __ 8 __ 5 __ 16 __ 5 __ 15 __ 16 __ 12 __ 5 __ . __

13 __ 26 __ 14 __

20 __ 8 __ 5 __ 19 __ 1 __ 13 __ 5 __

23 __ 9 __ 8 __ 5 __ 4 __ 9 __ 4 __

23 __

6 __ 9 __ 19 __ 8 __ . __

Jesus told them to pick up the scraps
so nothing was wasted.
How many baskets did they fill?

Solve the problems and use the code to spell out the answer

$$\begin{array}{r} 18 \\ -4 \\ \hline \end{array} \quad \begin{array}{r} 4 \\ \times 4 \\ \hline \end{array} \quad \begin{array}{r} 16 \\ -7 \\ \hline \end{array} \quad \begin{array}{r} 15 \\ \div 3 \\ \hline \end{array} \quad \begin{array}{r} 7 \\ +5 \\ \hline \end{array} \quad \begin{array}{r} 3 \\ \times 3 \\ \hline \end{array}$$

__ __ __ __ __ __

CODE

12	5	9	16	14
V	L	E	W	T

JOHN 6:13

Use the code cracker to find out what else Jesus told the people

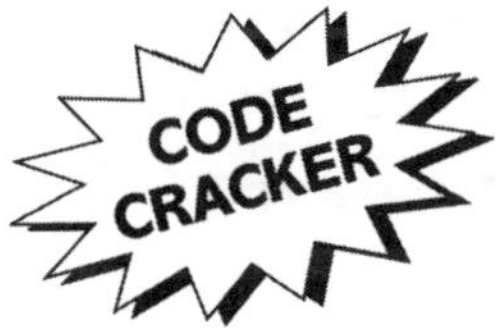
CODE
CRACKER

z y x w v u t s r q p o n m l k j i h g f e d c b a
A B C D E F G H I J K L M N O P Q R S T U V W X Y Z

r z n g s v y i v z w

l u o r u v

z m b l m v d s l

x l n v h

g l n v

d r o o

m v e v i

y v s f m t i b

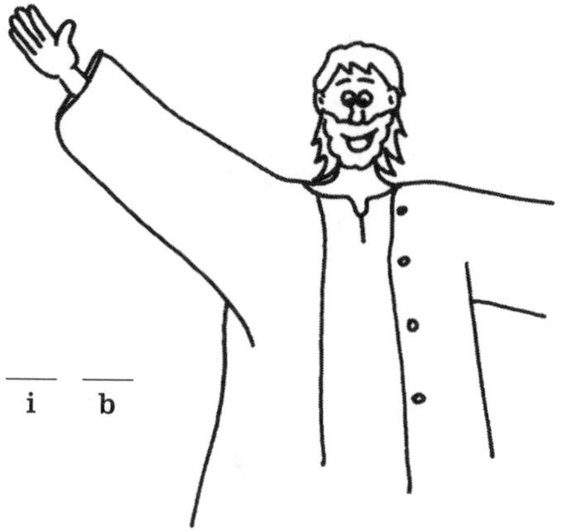

JOHN 6:35

Bread from heaven

EXODUS 16:2–4; JOHN 6:24–35

As Moses and the Israelites crossed the wilderness, the people grew hungry and afraid.

Use the code to find God's words to Moses in Exodus 16:4

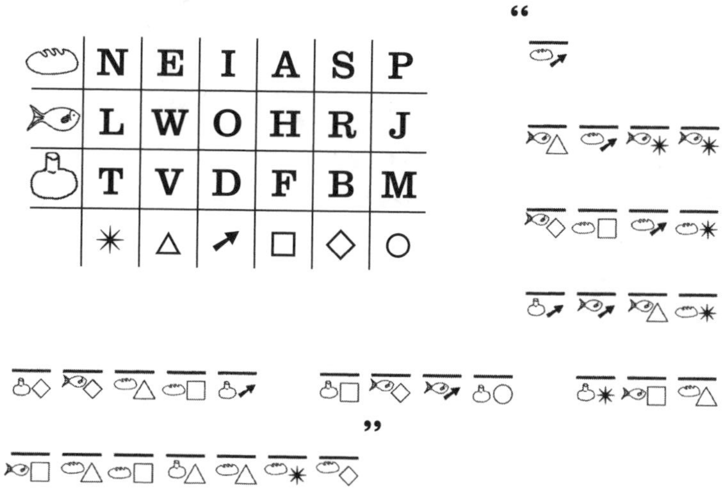
N E I A S P
L W O H R J
T V D F B M
“
”

What do we call the food
God provided for his people in
the wilderness?

The people asked Jesus a question...

How can
we carry out
God's work?

Use the symbols to
find Jesus' answer

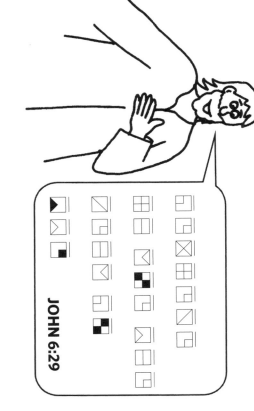

JOHN 6:29

▨ = V   ▨ = H   ◨ = E   ◪ = O   ⊠ = L
◱ = B   ◩ = T   ▩ = Y   ◫ = N   ◰ = D
◿ = S   ⊞ = I   ◣ = G

Write the letter that is missing
from the second word in the box

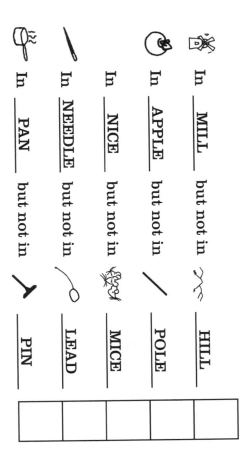

In **MILL** but not in **HILL**

In **APPLE** but not in **POLE**

In **NICE** but not in **MICE**

In **NEEDLE** but not in **LEAD**

In **PAN** but not in **PIN**

God cares for his people

1 KINGS 19:4-8; JOHN 6:41-51

Elijah was tired and hungry,
so God sent a messenger with food and
water to give him strength.

Who was that messenger?

Starting at the arrow,
write down every other letter

T _ _ _ _ _ _ _ _

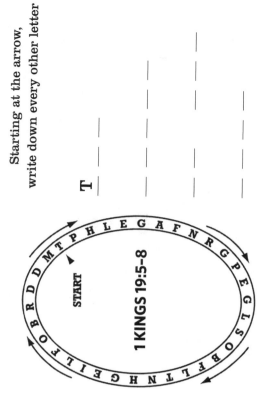

START

1 KINGS 19:5-8

Jesus came to
share his life with
the world!

Fit the shapes in the puzzle to find his words to the people

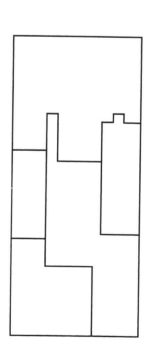

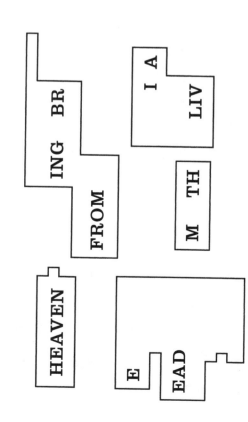

ING   BR

FROM

I A

LIV

M   TH

HEAVEN

E

EAD

Many people thought that Jesus was just an ordinary person.

How can he say he is from heaven?

When...

Unscramble these letters to find their words from John 6:42

"

U R L E S Y   H T I S   S I

___ ___ ___ ___ ___   ___ ___ ___ ___   ___ ___

S O J P E H S   O N S ,

___ ___ ___ ___ ___ ___   ___ ___ ___

E S J S U

___ ___ ___ ___ ___ !"

Use the code to find the missing letters to complete their words

" W ___ ___   K ___ ___ W

H ___ ___   F ___ ___ H ___ R

N D   M ___ ___ H ___ R !"

△ = E	◁ = A	
□ = O	▽ = N	
⊃ = T	◇ = I	

JOHN 6:42

The Bread of Life

JOHN 6:51-58

What does Jesus, the Bread of Life, give to us?

Write the name of each object in the numbered boxes.
The first letters will spell out the answer

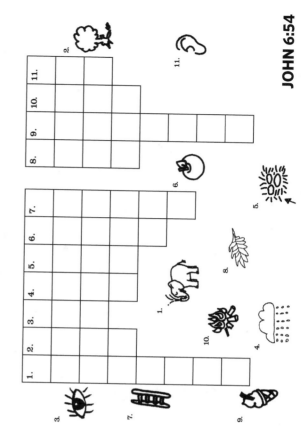

JOHN 6:54

THINK and LOOK ahead

Jesus had described himself as the "Bread of Life" who had "come down from heaven."

How did these words make the people feel about him?

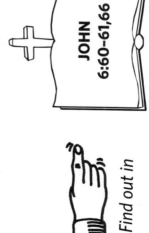

Find out in

JOHN 6:60–61,66

Draw their expressions

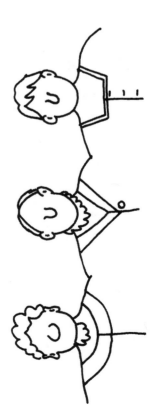

Jesus wants to live
in our hearts!

How many hearts can you find in this puzzle?
Write the answer below

ANSWER

Jesus will help us
to become more and more
like him. He will give us strength
and courage.

Find these words in the puzzle below and circle them

UNDERSTANDING   COURAGE

LOVE   PATIENCE   FORGIVENESS   FAITH

WISDOM   KNOWLEDGE   TRUTH

```
F B C S M N M O D S I W P E O
A A S M I F E T R I L J F D T
E F I D B K C G S R M E C F R
G P S T L K N O W L E D G E U
A R M L H J E O B L J K P S T
R Z A R M P I Q M R X S B Z H
U N D E R S T A N D I N G M O
O L P M F H A V G R N J Z S E
C M R J P E P A K T Y C G V L
B N B S S E N E V I G R O F I
E S C E F Q W D U I L L H X B
```

We believe in you

JOHN 6:60-69

Many of the people were angered by what Jesus told them.

Use the code to find their words

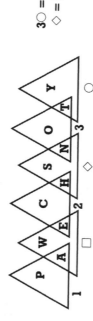
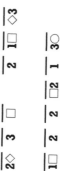

$3\bigcirc = T$

$\diamond = S$

JOHN 6:60

THINK and **LOOK** ahead

Find out why Jesus and his disciples are in trouble with the Pharisees next Sunday!

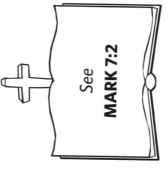

See **MARK 7:2**

CLUES

Many would not believe in Jesus and they went away.

Simon Peter answered Jesus!

Use this code to find what Jesus said to his disciples

A·	B·	C·
D·	E·	F·
G·	H·	I·

J	K	L
M	N	O
P	Q	R

·S·	
V·	S·
U·	T·

W	
Y	Z
	X

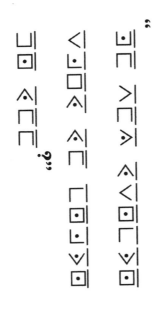

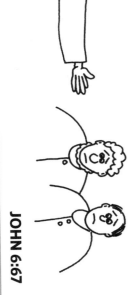

JOHN 6:67

His words have been written back to front.
Rearrange the letters to read what he said in John 6:69

"L O R D,

D R O L E W   E V E I L E B

N I   U O Y   E W   W O N K

U O Y   E R A   S D O G

Y L O H   E N O !"

A clean heart

MARK 7:1-8, 14-15, 21-23

The Pharisees had many rules and laws that they obeyed.

Use the secret code to find which rule is written on the scroll

SECRET CODE	A	E	G	F	S	I	W	R	N	H	T	B	O

THINK and LOOK ahead

MARK 7:31

From which district does Jesus return next Sunday?

ANSWER CHECK

Write the missing letter	Q R S U V
	W X Z A B
	P Q S T U
	C D F G H

Sometimes the Pharisees placed too much importance on such rules.

Add or subtract letters to find their words to Jesus

A B C D E F G H I J K L M N O P Q R S T U V W X Y Z

"

$\overline{\text{Z-3}}$ $\overline{\text{I-1}}$ $\overline{\text{T+5}}$ $\overline{\text{C+1}}$ $\overline{\text{I+6}}$ $\overline{\text{Z-1}}$ $\overline{\text{V-7}}$ $\overline{\text{S+2}}$ $\overline{\text{Q-3}}$ $\overline{\text{H+7}}$ $\overline{\text{U-1}}$

$\overline{\text{G+11}}$ $\overline{\text{A+4}}$ $\overline{\text{X-5}}$ $\overline{\text{J+6}}$ $\overline{\text{H-3}}$ $\overline{\text{B+1}}$ $\overline{\text{Q+3}}$ $\overline{\text{U-6}}$ $\overline{\text{L+9}}$ $\overline{\text{P+2}}$

$\overline{\text{I-6}}$ $\overline{\text{P+5}}$ $\overline{\text{T-1}}$ $\overline{\text{W-3}}$ $\overline{\text{F+9}}$ $\overline{\text{C+10}}$ $\overline{\text{Y-6}}$, $\overline{\text{E-4}}$ $\overline{\text{K+3}}$ $\overline{\text{C+1}}$

$\overline{\text{L-7}}$ $\overline{\text{B-1}}$ $\overline{\text{Q+3}}$ $\overline{\text{X-1}}$ $\overline{\text{D+5}}$ $\overline{\text{R+2}}$ $\overline{\text{V-14}}$ $\overline{\text{N+7}}$ $\overline{\text{L+2}}$ $\overline{\text{H-5}}$ $\overline{\text{J+2}}$ $\overline{\text{F-1}}$ $\overline{\text{B-1}}$ $\overline{\text{K+3}}$

$\overline{\text{P-8}}$ $\overline{\text{F-5}}$ $\overline{\text{K+3}}$ $\overline{\text{F-2}}$ $\overline{\text{H+11}}$?"

MARK 7:5

Look at these sets of words.
Find the odd one out and write it on the numbered line

4
PEN
MAKES
PENCIL

2
WICKED
RAIN
SNOW

1
MOTH
A
BUTTERFLY

7
UNCLEAN
SAUSAGE
BACON

5
A
DOOR
WINDOW

6
CAT
DOG
PERSON

3
SHOE
BOOT
HEART

"

1 _ _ _ _ _

2 _ _ _ _ _

3 _ _ _ _ _

4 _ _ _ _ _

5 _ _ _ _ _

6 _ _ _ _ _

7 _ _ _ _ _

"

MARK 7:20-23

Jesus cures a deaf man

MARK 7:31-37

The people brought a deaf man who could not speak properly to meet Jesus.

Did they take road A, B, or C? Circle the letter

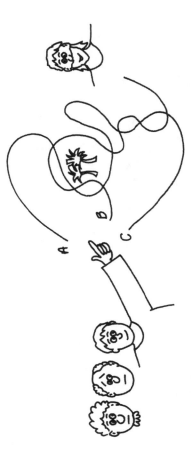

Jesus opens OUR ears and mouths too!

What does Jesus want us to do?

Cross out every word with a *

When Jesus was alone with the man, what did he do?

Use these clues to find the missing letters and decode the answer

The opposite of low

The Son of God

Describes a person who cannot hear

The opposite of quickly

A birthday celebration

A theater for watching films

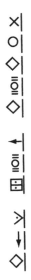

Then looking up to heaven, Jesus prayed to God and the man was healed!

Ephphatha!

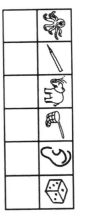

Write the first letter of each object to find what this word means

Jesus is the Son of God

MARK 8:27–35

Jesus asked his disciples a question.

Use the code cracker to find his words

	L	A	M	O	E
△	□	I	W	H	P
◇	◇	S	✳	D	Y
	✂	✂	✳	✿	↑

MARK 8:27

What are these disciples arguing about next Sunday?

Find out in

MARK 9:33–34

Simon Peter spoke up
and answered him.

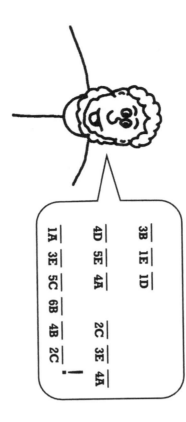

Find the letters and complete Peter's words

$\overline{3B}$ $\overline{1E}$ $\overline{1D}$

$\overline{4D}$ $\overline{5E}$ $\overline{4A}$ $\overline{2C}$ $\overline{3E}$ $\overline{4A}$

$\overline{1A}$ $\overline{3E}$ $\overline{5C}$ $\overline{6B}$ $\overline{4B}$ $\overline{2C}$!

MARK 8:29

	1	2	3	4	5	6	
C	H	B	E	O	P		A
R	L	Y	S	M	I		B
J	T	Z	N	R	K		C
U	M	Q	A	P	X		D
O	S	H	L	R	E		E

Jesus calls us to
follow him, even though it is
not always easy to do!

Color the squares with a * or a •
to see what each of us must carry!

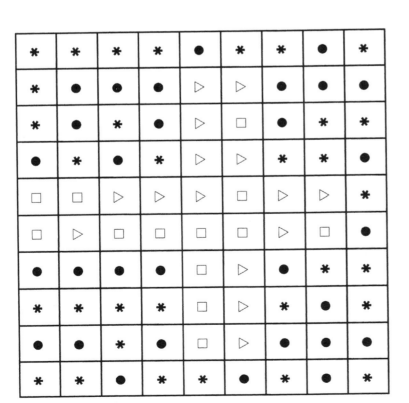

The last shall be first

MARK 9:30-37

The disciples had been arguing about which of them was the greatest!

Use the letter code
to find what Jesus said
to them

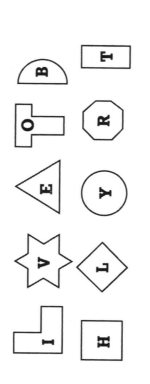

Z 1	M 14	
Y 2	L 15	
X 3	K 16	
W 4	J 17	
V 5	I 18	
U 6	H 19	
T 7	G 20	
S 8	F 21	
R 9	E 22	
Q 10	D 23	
P 11	C 24	
O 12	B 25	
N 13	A 26	

MARK 9:35

THINK and LOOK ahead

How do we recognize
other followers of Christ?

Use the shapes to decode the answer

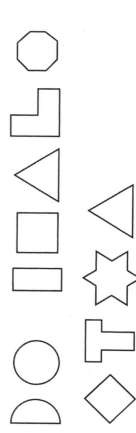

Everyone is good at something!

Draw a picture of yourself doing something you are good at!

God measures our greatness
by our goodness!

A good person welcomes others and
puts their needs above their own.

Write the names of some good people you know
at home, at school, and at church

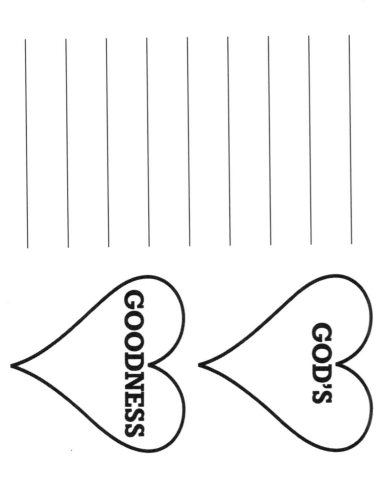

GOD'S

GOODNESS

All goodness comes from God

MARK 9:38–50

Jesus told his disciples...

Use the code pad to find his words

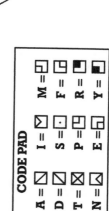

MARK 9:39

CODE PAD

U =	A =	I =	M =
H =	D =	S =	F =
G =	T =	P =	R =
O =	N =	E =	Y =

THINK and **LOOK** ahead

Next Sunday
the people bring their children
to meet Jesus.

Draw a picture of yourself and some of your friends with Jesus

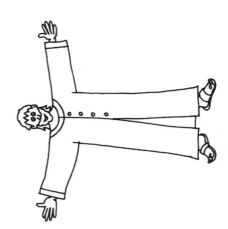

What must
we try to do?

The answer has been torn into pieces.
Put the pieces together to read what it says

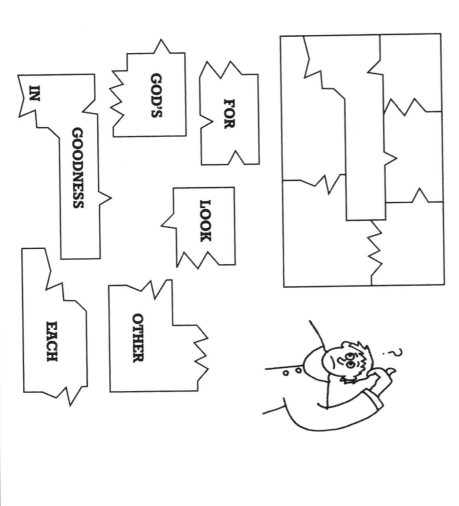

IN

GOD'S

GOODNESS

FOR

LOOK

EACH

OTHER

Who sees and
rewards every act
of goodness?

Write every letter with an even number
in order on the lines below

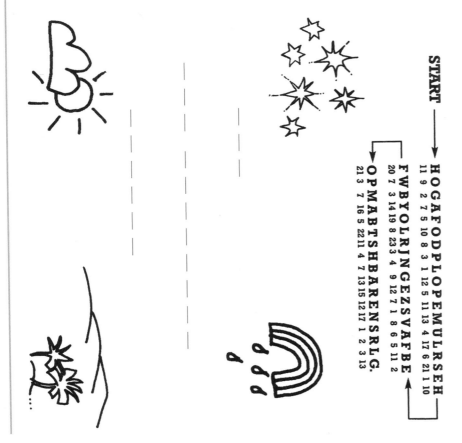

START ——▶

H O G A F O D P L O P E M U L R S E H
11 9 2 7 5 10 8 3 1 12 5 11 13 4 17 6 21 1 10

F W B Y O L R J N G E Z S V A F B E
20 7 3 14 19 8 23 3 4 9 12 7 18 6 5 11 2

O P M A B T S H B A R E N S R L G .
21 3 7 16 5 22 11 4 7 13 15 12 17 1 2 3 13

The children's friend

MARK 10:2-16

Why did Jesus scold his disciples?

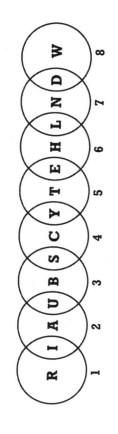

Use the code to find out!

| R | I | A | U | B | S | C | Y | T | E | H | L | N | D | W |
| 1 | 2 | 3 | 4 | 5 | 6 | 7 | 8 |

$\overline{3}\ \overline{5,6}\ \overline{4}\ \overline{2}\ \overline{2,3}\ \overline{3,4}\ \overline{5,6}$

$\overline{5}\ \overline{6}\ \overline{5,6}\ \overline{4,5}\ \quad\ \overline{3,4}\ \overline{5,6}\ \overline{7}\ \overline{5}$

$\overline{5}\ \overline{6}\ \overline{5,6}\ \quad\ \overline{4}\ \overline{6}\ \overline{1,2}\ \overline{6,7}\ \overline{7,8}\ \overline{1}\ \overline{5,6}\ \overline{7}$

$\overline{2}\ \overline{8}\ \overline{2}\ \overline{4,5}\ !$

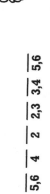

MARK 10:14

THINK and LOOK ahead

Next week's gospel talks about an animal passing through the eye of a needle.

What is that animal?

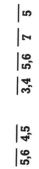

MARK 10:25

Answer

A ___ ___ ___

___ ___ ___ ___

Jesus is a special friend who is ALWAYS ready to listen to children!

Follow the arrows to spell out the words of Jesus in Mark 10:14

A	T	K	G	D	O	J	V	K	F
M	E	N	I	A	M	E	A	C	I
(T)	H	D	E	O	H	N	B	T	H
M	F	T	S	F	N	L	E	E	K
J	O	P	H	G	O	G	I	K	S
T	U	C	I	D	R	L	Q	L	E
O	R	L	S	E	N	H	L	E	N

"

"

Jesus welcomed the children and blessed them.

Write the first letter of each object to find the words of Jesus

"

"

MARK 10:14

The camel and the needle!

MARK 10:17-30

A rich man came to Jesus and asked a question.

Moving clockwise around the circle, write down every other letter. Do this twice to find what he asked

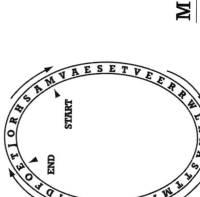

M _ _ _ _ _ _

_ _ _ _ _ _ _ ?

MARK 10:17

THINK and LOOK ahead

James and John appear in next Sunday's gospel.

Find out the name of their father.

Look in **MARK 10:35**

ANSWER CHECK

1. First letter of

2. Third letter of

3. First letter of

4. Fifth letter of

5. Fourth letter of

6. Third letter of

7. Fifth letter of

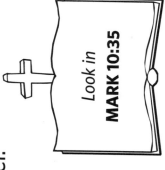

1.	2.	3.	4.	5.	6.	7.

The man was sad to hear Jesus' answer because he was very wealthy.

Find the missing words to read what Jesus told him

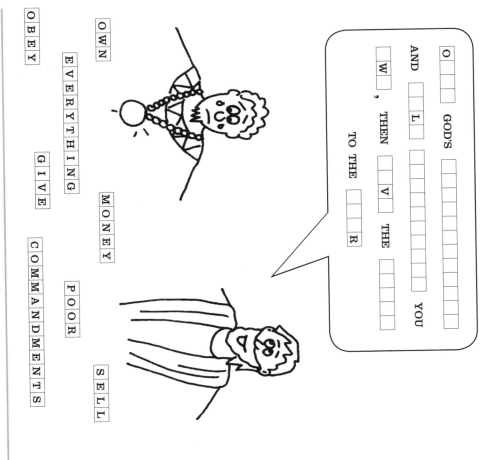

O ☐☐☐ GOD'S ☐☐☐☐☐☐

AND ☐☐L☐ ☐☐☐☐☐☐☐☐☐☐

W☐☐☐ , THEN ☐V☐ THE ☐☐☐☐

TO THE ☐☐☐R

YOU

OWN   MONEY   SELL

EVERYTHING   POOR   GIVE

OBEY   COMMANDMENTS

It is more important to have riches in heaven than riches on earth!

Add or subtract letters to see what Jesus said in Mark 10:25

A B C D E F G H I J K L M N O P Q R S T U V W X Y Z

<u>I</u>   <u>E</u>   <u>I</u>   <u>R</u>
L+8   D-3   B+3   N+1

<u>C</u>   <u>E</u>   <u>P</u>   <u>A</u>
F+3 M-6   Q+2   B+17 W-4

J-9 I+4   O+5 S-4   K-5

<u>R</u>   <u>E</u>   <u>H</u>   <u>A</u>
G-6   V-10

<u>Z</u>   <u>U</u>   <u>T</u>   <u>H</u>
G+1   D+3   I-8 M+1

Z-6   L-7 X+1 A+4   C<u>H</u>   <u>M</u><u>A</u>
K+3 J-5   A+7 K-6 O-14 U+1   Q-3

<u>L</u><u>E</u>'   <u>C</u>   <u>T</u>
P-15   H+10 H+1

<u>R</u>   <u>T</u>   <u>R</u>   <u>E</u>
O-9 L+3   P-1   F-1   X-10 !

U-1 J+5   R-13 G+7

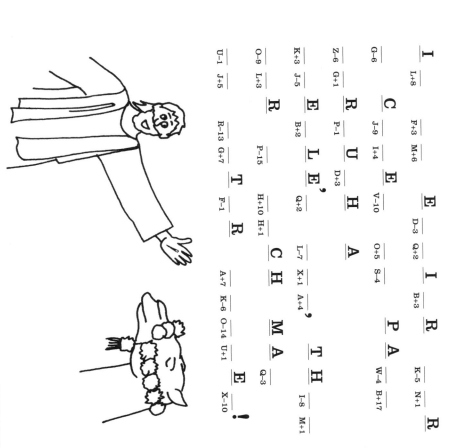

A place in heaven

MARK 10:35-45

The sons of Zebedee wanted Jesus
to promise them a special place in heaven.

Unscramble their names

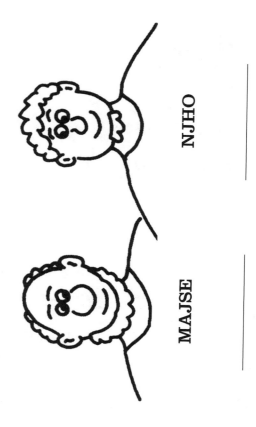

MAJSE

NJHO

What did Jesus come to do?

Write the next letter of the alphabet above the given letters.
For example, E will be written above D

A B C D E F G H I J K L M N O P Q R S T U V W X Y Z

___ ___ ___ ___ ___   ___ ___ ___
S G D   R N M   N E L Z M

___ ___ ___   ___ ___   ___ ___ ___ ___
B Z L   D S N   R D Q U D

___ ___ ___   ___ ___   ___ ___ ___ ___
Z M C   S N   F H U D

___ ___ ___   ___ ___ ___   ___ ___ ___
G H R   K H E D   E N Q

___ ___ ___ ___
L Z M X

MARK 10:45

Find what Jesus told them
by using the code to fill in the blanks

3☆ 2☀ 3☀ 4☀ 2☀ 1☀   1) 3) 4☀   1) 3☆ 2☀ 2) 4)

2) 4☀   1◌ 1☀   2◌ 2☀ 1☀ 3☆ 2)   3◌ 1☆ 4) 2)

1◌ 1☀   2◌ 1☀ 3☆ 4◌ 3☀   2) 4☀

4) 1☀ 2☀ 4☆ 1☀   1☀ 4☆ 1☀ 2☆ 3☀ 4☀ 2☀ 1☀

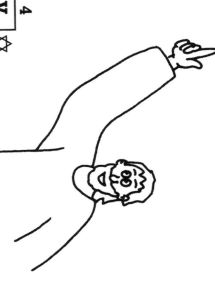

	1	2	3	4
1	U	R	A	V
2	E	N	Y	O
3	W	T	H	S
4	B	G	M	D

☆   ☀   )   ◌

God will measure
our greatness by how much
we serve others and put their
needs before our own.

Write some ways you can serve other people.
Use the pictures to give you some ideas

Master, let me see!

MARK 10:46-52

Jesus and his disciples set off
with a large crowd.

Which town were they passing through?

Use the clues to spell out the answer

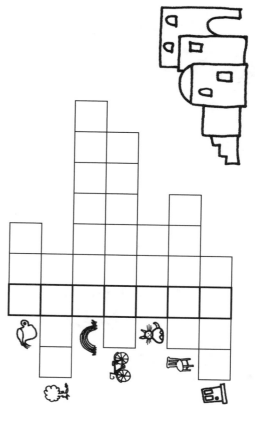

MARK 10:46

Like Bartimaeus,
what do we need
to have?

Find the missing numbers to spell out the answer

3 = I   4 = F   7 = H   8 = M   9 = R   12 = A

14 = P   15 = J   16 = T   21 = S

17	4	11	9	(3 x 3)
-13	x 3	- 8	+ 7	- 2

___   ___   ___   ___   ___

I CAN SEE!

A blind man called Bartimaeus began shouting loudly at Jesus!

Use the code cracker to find his words

CODE CRACKER

	♥	✎	★	▲	✎
1	U	Y	A	E	S
2	M	L	J	H	D
3	T	P	N	V	I

"

2★ ___ 1▲ ___ 1✎ ___ 1♥ ___ 1✎ ___

3▲ ___ 3✎ ___ 3♥ ___

2▲ ___ 1★ ___ 3▲ ___ 1▲ ___

1★ ___ 3★ ___ 1✎ ___

3▲ ___ 3✎ ___ 3♥ ___

2▲ ___ 1▲ ___ 2✎ ___ 3✎ ___

2♥ ___ 1▲ ___ ___ !"

MARK 10:47

Bartimaeus kept on shouting until Jesus heard his cry for help.

These pictures show what happened but they have been jumbled up! Decide what order they should be in and write the numbers below

1.

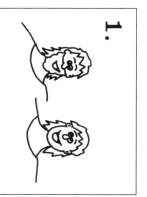

Jesus said: "Because you believed in me you can see!"

2.

Bartimaeus calling for pity

3.

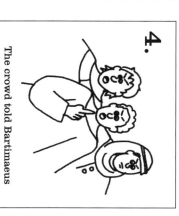

Jesus said: "Bring that man to me"

4.

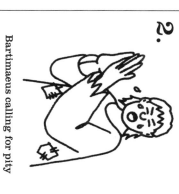

The crowd told Bartimaeus to be quiet

The two greatest commandments

MARK 12:28-34

One of the scribes asked Jesus an important question.

Use the alphabet code to find out what they asked

A B C D E F G H I J K L M N O P Q R S T U V W X Y Z
z y x w v u t s r q p o n m l k j i h g f e d c b a

" __d__ __s__ __r__ __x__ __s__ __r__ __h__ __g__ __s__ __v__

__n__ __l__ __h__ __g__ __r__ __n__ __k__ __l__ __i__ __g__ __z__ __m__ __g__

__x__ __l__ __n__ __n__ __z__ __m__ __w__ __n__ __v__ __m__ __g__

__l__ __u__ __z__ __o__ __o__ __o__ ?"

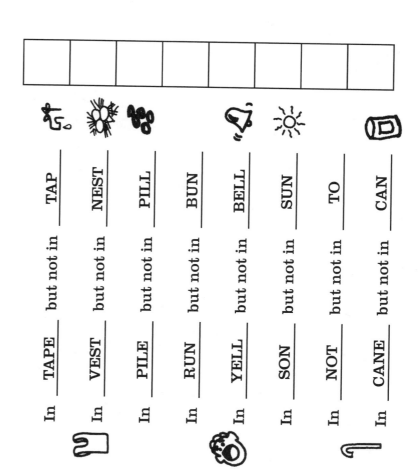

MARK 12:28

Who is YOUR neighbor?

Write in the box the letter that is missing from the second word to spell out the answer

In __TAPE__ but not in __TAP__

In __VEST__ but not in __NEST__

In __PILE__ but not in __PILL__

In __RUN__ but not in __BUN__

In __YELL__ but not in __BELL__

In __SON__ but not in __SUN__

In __NOT__ but not in __TO__

In __CANE__ but not in __CAN__

Hold this page in front of a mirror to read Jesus' answer!

To love God with all your heart, soul, mind, and strength!

MARK 12:30

Then Jesus told him the second most important commandment.

Love your neighbor as yourself.

MARK 12:33

Using the code below, turn the words of Jesus into a coded message

1	2	3	4	5	6	7	8	9	10	11	12	13	14	15
H	N	Y	E	L	R	S	O	G	A	V	B	U	I	F

L O V E   Y O U R   N E I G H B O R
5 8

A S   Y O U R S E L F

The generous widow

MARK 12:38-44

Jesus sat in the Temple and watched the people making their offerings.

There are ten coins hidden in this picture! Find them and mark them with a cross

THINK and LOOK ahead

Jesus mentions a sign that tells us that summer is near!

Find what it is in Mark 13:28

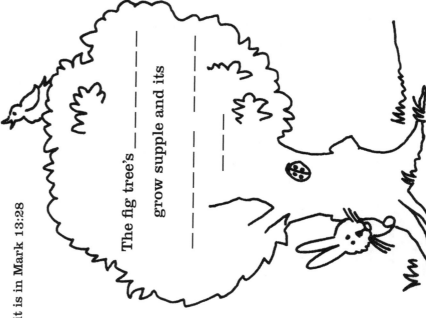

The fig tree's ___ ___ grow supple and its ___ ___

Find the words missing from the poem

As Jesus sat in the Temple one _____

a widow woman came to pay

a Temple offering which was so _____

it hardly seemed worth giving at all.

Rich folk brought large bags of _____ ;

their offerings plain to behold.

Just _____ small coins the widow brought,

no admiration or thanks she sought.

The _____ gave all she had;

her generous act made _____ glad.

"She had no extra to give away,

such generous love will be repaid."

GOLD   WIDOW   DAY   JESUS

TWO   SMALL

It is not how MUCH you give that is important to Jesus, but HOW you give it!

Use the coin code below to find what Jesus said in Mark 12:43

COIN CODE

W-1 L/A-2 S/D-3 T/E-4 R/I-5 O/H-6 N/P-7 G/V-8 Q/M-9

(Coin code circles top letters: W L A D S E T I R O H P N G V Q M; numbers: 1 2 3 4 5 6 7 8 9)

" __ __ __ __ __ __
  4 5,6 4,5 3 6,7 6 5

__ __ __ __ __ __ __
1 6 9 2 7 5,6 2 3

__ __ __ __ __ __ __
7,8 4,5 8 3,4 7 2 1,2 1,2

__ __ __ __ __ __
4 5,6 2 4 3 5,6 3,4

__ __ __
5,6 2 2,3 "

Jesus will return

MARK 13:24–32

One day Jesus will return in glory.

Use the numbered pictures to see what prophecy
Jesus made about the end of time

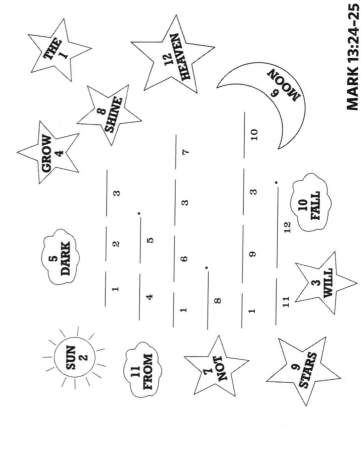

MARK 13:24-25

THINK and LOOK ahead

What do we celebrate next Sunday?

Use the calculator buttons to find the answer!

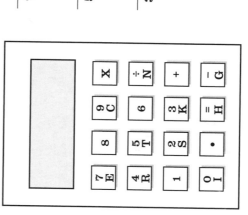

Jesus will welcome us to his kingdom.

Use the picture clues to find out who will be sent to gather God's chosen ones

We must try to be ready to greet Jesus whenever he returns.

Use the code cracker to find what Jesus says in Mark 13:32

	1	2	3	4	5	6
(	M	S	D	O	E	U
☀	A	C	N	T	I	W
☆	B	F	H	K	Y	R

"

3☀ __ 4(__

2☀ __ 1☀ __

4☀ __ 3☆ __

4☀ __ 5☀ __

4(__ 4(__

3☀ __ 4(__

1☀ __ 4☀ __ 3☆ __

5(__ 5(__

6(__ 4☀ __

6☀ __ 5☀ __ 4☆ __

3☀ __ 6☆ __

1☀ __ 5☆ __

3(__ 1(__

4(__ 6☆ __

1☀ __ 6(__

4☀ __ 3☀ __

4(__ 6☀ __

4☀ __ 3☆ __

2(__

5(__

"

Jesus is King!

JOHN 18:33-37

Pilate, the Roman governor, asked Jesus a question.

Follow the arrows to find his words

A – R – E – Y
H – T – U – O
E – K – I – N
T – F – O – G
H – E – J – E
S – W

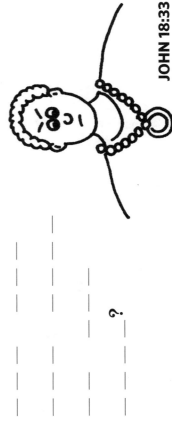

_ _ _ _

_ _ _ _ ?

JOHN 18:33

THINK and LOOK ahead

As our Christmas preparations begin, what will we light next Sunday?

Write the first letter of each object to find out

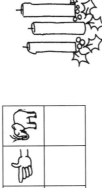

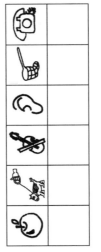

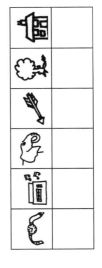

Pilate was
confused when Jesus
answered him.

Use the code to read Jesus' reply

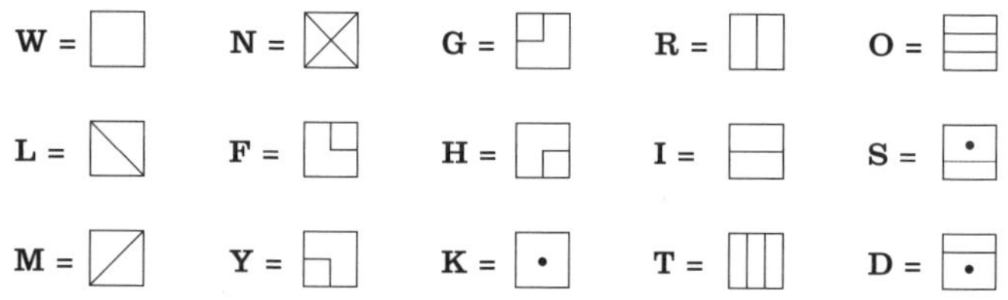

W = 　　N = 　　G = 　　R = 　　O =

L = 　　F = 　　H = 　　I = 　　S =

M = 　　Y = 　　K = 　　T = 　　D =

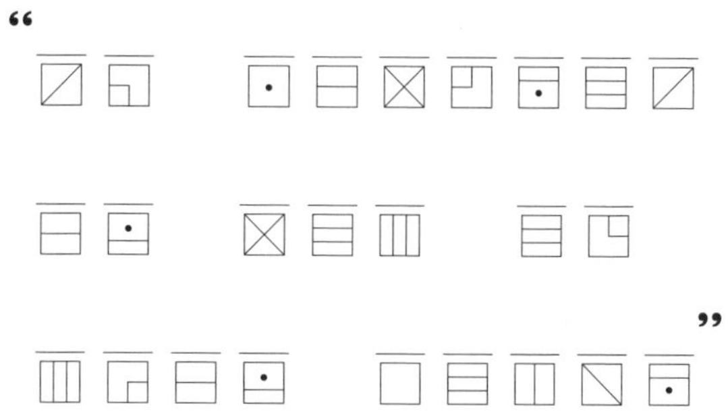

"

"

JOHN 18:36

Then Jesus told Pilate...

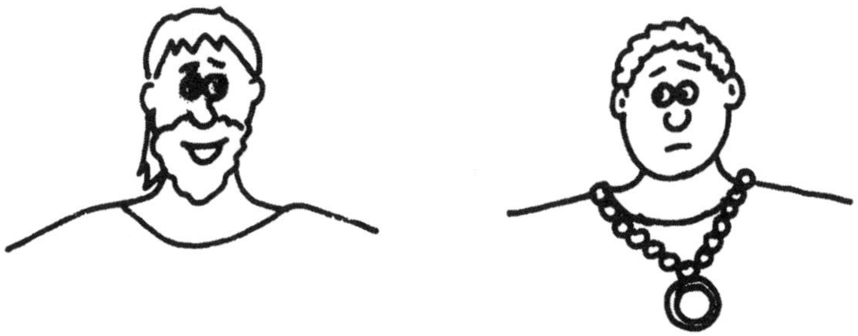

Follow the arrows to spell out his words

L	K	I	S	P	R	L	E
J	N	G	A	M	D	T	N	F
A	A	I	K	E	A	I	E	B
M	C	N	B	T	W	R	S	E
E	I	O	D	S	H	T	H	T
S	H	T	R	L	O	T	E	U
C	W	O	F	I	Z	G	R	D

I

!

JOHN 18:37

Year C

Be ready to welcome Jesus!

LUKE 21:25-28, 34-36

Jesus will come again—but only God knows when

Write the letter that is missing from the second word in the box

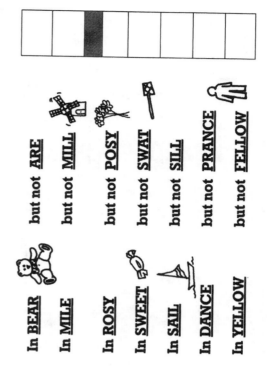

In **BEAR**   but not **ARE**

In **MILE**   but not **MILL**

In **ROSY**   but not **POSY**

In **SWEET**   but not **SWAT**

In **SAIL**   but not **SILL**

In **DANCE**   but not **PRANCE**

In **YELLOW**   but not **FELLOW**

What must we remember to do? _____

THINK and LOOK ahead

Find out in **LUKE 3:2**

Who does the word of God come to next week?

Follow the arrows to check your answer

P	M	N	T	L	P
S	O	J	R	C	N
S	Z	E	O	H	W
A	H	Q	C	S	A
I	O	H	R	O	E
K	R	A	B	F	D

Z _____ ,

Jesus told us
how we will know that the end
of time has come.

Use the code to fill in the blanks
and find out what we must watch for!

ABCDEFGHIJKLMNOPQRSTUVWXYZ
1 2 3 4 5 6 7 8 9 10 11 12 13 14 15 16 17 18 19 20 21 22 23 24 25 26

"
__ __ __   __ __ __ __   __ __
20 8 5   23 9 12 12   2 5

__ __ __ __ __   __ __   __ __ __
19 9 7 14 19   9 14   20 8 5

__ __ __   __ __ __   __ __ __ __   __ __ __
19 21 14   1 14 4   13 15 15 14   1 14 4

__ __ __   __ __ __ __ __
1 14 4   19 20 1 18 19
"

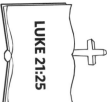

The word "Advent" means "coming."
Today is the First Sunday of Advent
when we light the first candle
on our wreath.

Find the words missing from the poem below

Jesus' _____ is not far away,
and we must be ready for _____ Day.

As we light the _____ candle on our Advent ring,
we begin to prepare for the _____ of our King.

Like the ring of _____ holly and _____
that we see,
God's love is _____, and will always be.

As the light from the _____ grows brighter and
strong,
we watch and we _____ as time draws on.

WAIT	CHRISTMAS	BIRTHDAY CANDLES
PINE	FIRST	GREEN UNENDING BIRTH

Be prepared

LUKE 3:1-6

God sent John the Baptist
to prepare the way for Jesus.

LUKE 3:4

Use the code to find out what Isaiah said John would do

CODE

△	A	F	O	T
○	D	H	P	W
□	E	L	R	Y
	1	2	3	4

"

3○ 3□ 1□ 3○ 1△ 3□ 1□

1△ 4○ 1△ 4□ 2△ 3△ 3□

4△ 2○ 1□ 2□ 3△ 3□ 1○

"

THINK and LOOK ahead

LUKE
3:10-14

?

JOHN THE
BAPTIST

THE
PEOPLE

What three things did John tell the people they must do?

1. _____

2. _____

3. _____

? !

What came to John the Baptist in the wilderness?

Use the clues to find the missing letters and decode the answer

A place where trees grow

△ ⊡ ◇ ○ ≪ ╄

What a kangaroo does

⌐ ⊡ ❋ ≪

Baseball bats are made from this

∼ ⊡ ⊡ ∧

A very thick mist

△ ⊡ =○=

Opposite of enemy

△ ◇ ❋ ○ ⊓ ∧

Season following autumn

∼ ❋ ⊓ ╄ ○ ◇

↑ ⌐ ○ ∼ ⊡ ◇ ∧
⊡ △ =○= ⊡ ∧

LUKE 3:2

Today is the Second Sunday of Advent and we light two candles on our wreath.

Write the first letter of each picture to find the missing words in the poem!

On this ___ ___ ___ Sunday,

The ___ ___ ___ candles we light,

Is now twice as ___ ___ ___ from our wreath,

___ sent John the Baptist,

To help change our ___ ___ ___ ___ ___,

And show us the ___ ___ ___ to make a fresh start

In the words of ___ ___ ___ ___, "prepare a way,"

So that we will be ready for ___ ___ ___ ___ ___ ___ day!

Turn back to God

LUKE 3:10-18

God sent John the Baptist to tell the people about Jesus his Son.

Find the letters hidden in the picture!

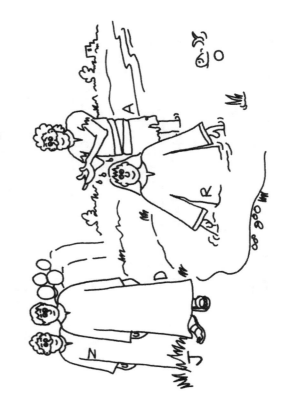

John baptized people in the River

THINK and LOOK ahead

Next week Mary goes to visit John the Baptist's mother.

Find out the names of John's parents in Luke 1:57–66

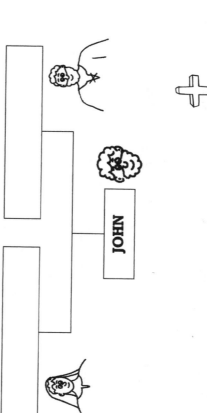

JOHN

LUKE 1:11–16

Who brought some very good news for them?

The people asked John
what God wanted them to do.

Last week did you find out what he told them?

Add or subtract letters to find out whether you were right!

A B C D E F G H I J K L M N O P Q R S T U V W X Y Z

1.

— — — — — — — — — — —
M+6 D+4 G–6 P+2 Q–12   Z–3 G+1 F–5 X–4 D+1 S+3 G–2 V–4

— — — — — — — —
Z–1 D+11 P+5   G+1 L–11 T+2 D+1

2.

— — — — — — — — — —
C–1 A+4   N–6 L+3 P–2 J–5 Q+2 Y–5

3.

— — — — — — — — — — — — —
F–4 F–1   A+2 K+4 A+13 V–2 F–1 M+1 X–4

Some people thought
that John was the Savior
promised by God.

Use the code to find out what he told them

P	U	S	M	K
◇	☾	I	T	O	L	R

○	I	T	O	L	R
◇	E	N	W	Z
□	Y	B	A	C	G
❋	♡	☺	△	☆

"

LUKE 3:16

A special visitor

LUKE 1:39–44

Mary went to visit her cousin Elizabeth.

Help Mary to find the right way to Elizabeth's house

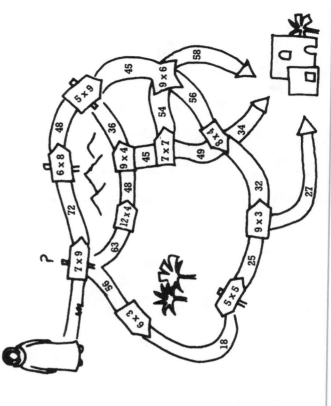

THINK and LOOK ahead

Now four candles
are lit on the
Advent wreath;
Christmas
is almost here!

MERRY CHRISTMAS
EVERYONE

Find these words hidden in the word search puzzle.
They go down, across, backward, and diagonally!

STAR   SHEPHERDS   STABLE   ANGELS
BETHLEHEM   MARY   JESUS   JOSEPH   REJOICE

Y	B	A	R	P	S	A	J	M
N	R	M	N	T	D	O	E	L
J	S	A	G	R	H	S	H	E
O	A	B	M	O	E	P	U	C
S	L	D	J	L	H	L	S	I
E	W	A	H	O	P	E	S	O
P	D	T	B	R	E	S	E	J
H	E	L	O	M	H	A	C	E
B	A	K	P	E	S	T	A	R

Use the picture clues to discover Elizabeth's greeting to Mary.

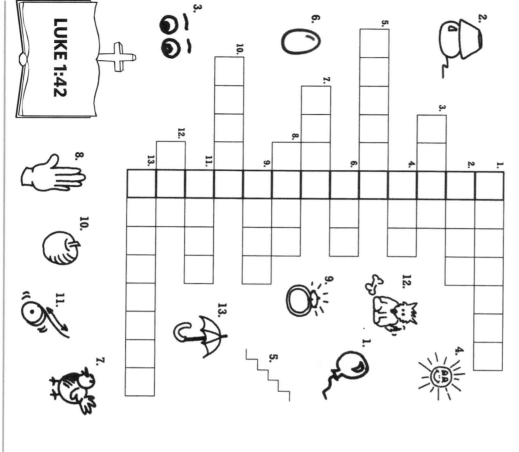

LUKE 1:42

Today is the Fourth Sunday of Advent. Four candles are lit today!

Connect the dots and then add four flames to the picture

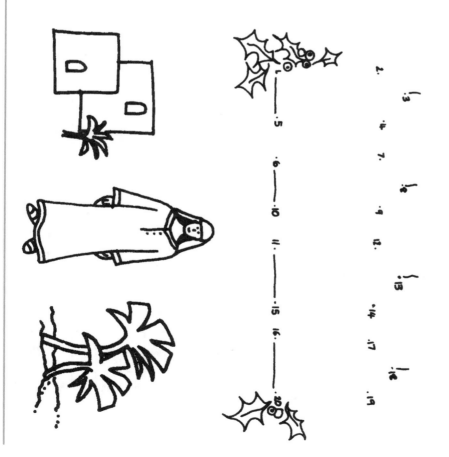

Jesus is born!

LUKE 2:15-20

Mary's child was almost ready to be born when she and Joseph had to make a long journey to Bethlehem.

Add the numbers together to find how many kilometers they had to travel

25 + 15 + 10 + 27 + 15 + 17 + 13

_____ kilometers

THINK and LOOK ahead

What do we celebrate on the Sunday after Christmas?

Look in your Sunday missal or use this code to find the answer

(1) = **M** (2) = **T** (3) = **F** (4) = **A** (5) = **L** (6) = **H**

(7) = **E** (8) = **S** (9) = **O** (10) = **Y** (11) = **I**

$\overline{(2)}\ \overline{(6)}\ \overline{(7)}$ $\overline{(3)}\ \overline{(7)}\ \overline{(4)}\ \overline{(8)}\ \overline{(2)}$

$\overline{(9)}\ \overline{(3)}$ $\overline{(2)}\ \overline{(6)}\ \overline{(7)}$

$\overline{(6)}\ \overline{(9)}\ \overline{(5)}\ \overline{(10)}$ $\overline{(3)}\ \overline{(4)}\ \overline{(1)}\ \overline{(11)}\ \overline{(5)}\ \overline{(10)}$

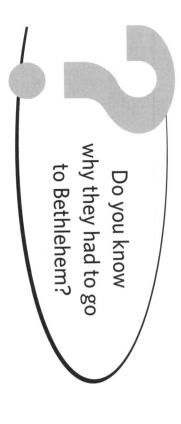

Do you know why they had to go to Bethlehem?

Moving clockwise around the circle, write down every other letter. Do this twice to find the answer

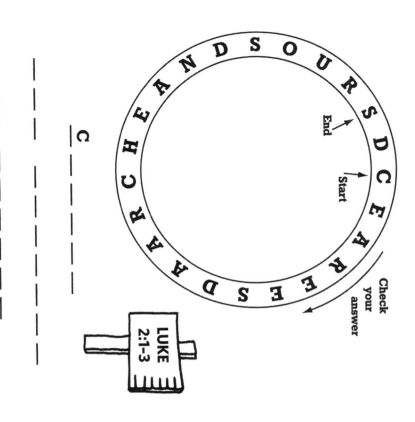

Start

End

Check your answer

LUKE 2:1-3

C _ _ _ _ _

_ _ _ _ _ _ _

While in Bethlehem the time came for Mary to have her baby. They named him Jesus, just as the angel had told them.

The name Jesus means "God is with us."

Find the letter missing from each group to spell out another name given to Jesus

CDFGHI			
JKLNOP			
LNOPQR			
XYZBCD			
IJKLMO			
RSTVWX			
BCDFGH			
HIJKMN			

MATTHEW 1:23

Jesus goes missing!

LUKE 2:41-52

Jesus went missing in Jerusalem!

LUKE 2:46

Solve the puzzles to find the
answers to the questions below

Where did Mary and Joseph eventually find him?

T	M	N	H
✋	E	P	I
🔔	L	T	E
		✳	○

How long did they search for him?

(4 x 3) - 10 = _____ x 8 = _____ ÷ 4 = _____ - 1 = _____ **days**

Help Mary and
Joseph to find their way through
the streets of Jerusalem
to the Temple.

Jesus sat listening and asking questions in the Temple.

Circle eight things that are different in the bottom picture

What did Jesus say to Mary and Joseph when they found him?

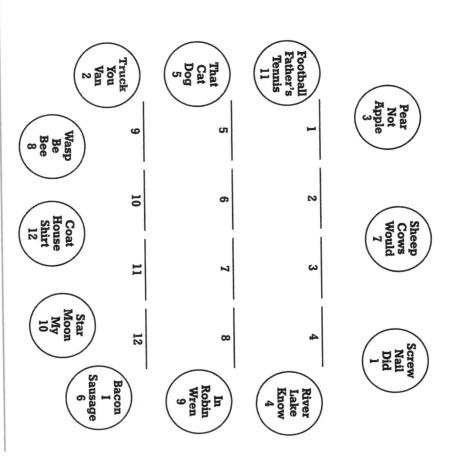

Underline the word in each group that doesn't belong.
Write these words on the lines

Pear
Not
Apple
3

Sheep
Cows
Would
7

Screw
Nail
Did
1

Football
Father's
Tennis
11

River
Lake
Know
4

In
Robin
Wren
9

That
Cat
Dog
5

Truck
You
Van
2

Wasp
Be
Bee
8

Coat
House
Shirt
12

Star
Moon
My
10

Bacon
I
Sausage
6

1 ___ 2 ___ 3 ___ 4 ___

5 ___ 6 ___ 7 ___ 8 ___

9 ___ 10 ___ 11 ___ 12 ___

Jesus is baptized

LUKE 3:15-16, 21-22

The people thought that John the Baptist was the Savior promised by God.

Use the code to find out what John told them

Check your answer in

LUKE 3:16

THINK and LOOK ahead

Next week Jesus goes to a wedding where something very special happens!

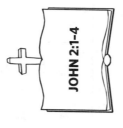

Find out in

JOHN 2:1-4

Find the missing numbers to spell out the answer!

7	12	8	17	11	19	7	27
+8	+9	×2	-6	+4	+3	+3	-24
—	—	—	—	—	—	—	—

3 = E   10 = L   11 = R   15 = A

16 = I   21 = M   22 = C

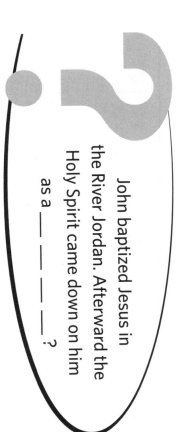

John baptized Jesus in the River Jordan. Afterward the Holy Spirit came down on him as a __ __ __ ?

Write the letter that is missing from the second word in the box to find the answer

In DOG but not BOG

In OTHER but not EITHER

In VAN but not PAN

In END but not AND

Use the code to find out other ways the Holy Spirit has appeared

A B C D E F G H I J K L M N O P Q R S T U V W X Y Z
1 2 3 4 5 6 7 8 9 10 11 12 13 14 15 16 17 18 19 20 21 22 23 24 25 26

__ __ __ __ __ __ __   __ __   __ __ __ __
20 15 14 7   21 5   19   15 6   6   9   18 5

__ __ __ __ __ __ __   __ __   __ __ __ __
18 15 1   18 9   14 7   15 6   23 9   14 4

Find out in **ACTS 2:1-3**

Then a voice from heaven spoke!

Follow the arrows to spell out what it said

J	E	D	A	O	D
V	T →	H	S	N	R
O	W	I	L	I	S
A	L	E	S	M	O
E	F	B	Y	G	K
S	J	R	I	P	O

T ↘ ↓ ↗ ↗ ↗ ↘
↓ ↘ ↗ ↗ ↗ ↗
↖ ↗ ↗ ↓ ↗ ↓

Jesus is put to the test

LUKE 4:1-13

Today is the First Sunday of Lent. The word "Lent" comes from the old English word *lencten*.

Use the clues to find out what the word "Lent" means

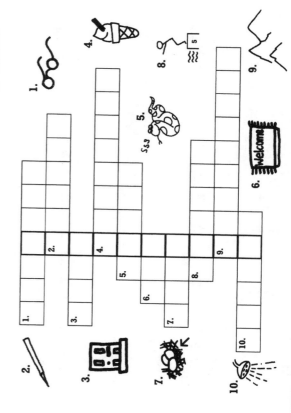

THINK and LOOK ahead

Next week Jesus takes three of his disciples up a mountain to show them something very special.

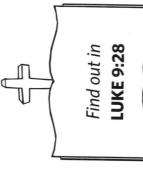

Find out in **LUKE 9:28**

Which three friends went with him?

1. — — — — — —

2. — — — — — —

3. — — — — — —

Where did Jesus go for forty days and what did he do there?

Add or subtract letters to crack the code

A B C D E F G H I J K L M N O P Q R S T U V W X Y Z

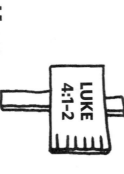

LUKE 4:1-2

" __The__
Z-7 M+3 H+1 U-3 J-1 K+9

led Jesus

__through the__
R+5 C+6 O-3 R-14 A+4 O+3 M+1 C+2 Y-6 P+3

__for__
D+2 J+5 C+15 V-2 X+1

days, he

__had__
L+2 V-7 S+1 B+6 G+2 K+3 N-7

to

A+4 E-4 L+8

there

__because he was__
C+3 B-1 R+1 W-3 Q-8 L+2 J-3

"

Jesus was tempted to use his powers in the wrong way.

What were the three tests he had to face?

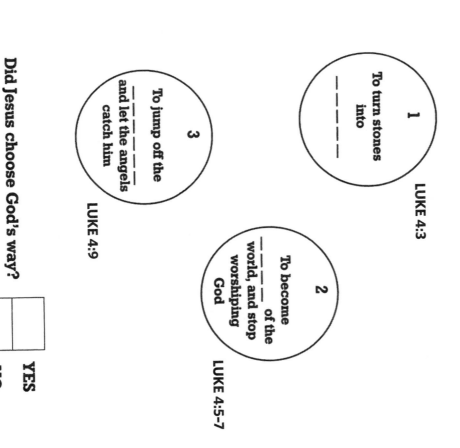

1

To turn stones into

_ _ _ _

LUKE 4:3

2

To become

_ _ _ of the world, and stop worshiping God

LUKE 4:5-7

3

To jump off the

_ _ _ _ and let the angels catch him

LUKE 4:9

Did Jesus choose God's way?

YES   NO

Jesus shines like the sun

LUKE 9:28–36

Something marvelous happened on the mountain!

What did Peter, James, and John see?

Write the first letter of each object

Another word for "changed" is

THINK and LOOK ahead

Next week Jesus tells a parable about a fig tree.

Look up Luke 13:6–9 and find out what the angry vineyard owner and his gardener are saying

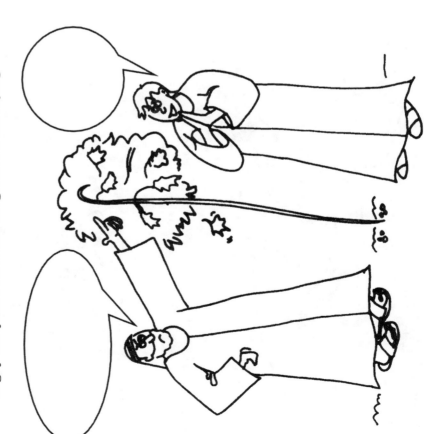

Two other people appeared next to Jesus and spoke to him.
Who were they?

Follow the arrows to spell out their names

M →	R	K	A	E	B
Q	O	P	S	O	L
B	S	E	D	C	I
D	F	G	A	J	A
O	M	N	L	H	L
P	R	J	H	E	I

M → ↙ ↑ ↗ → ↘ ↙ ↘ and ↗ → ↙ ↘ ↙ ↘ ↙ ↗ ↙

The disciples were even more amazed when they heard a voice coming from a cloud.

Unscramble the jumbled letters to read what it said

"This is my **EBVOLDE SNO. NESIIT** to him!"

God gives us another chance

LUKE 13:1-9

These pictures telling the story of the fruitless fig tree are in the wrong order. Put the letters of the pictures in the correct order on the lines below

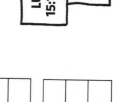

See LUKE 13:6-9

A

It produced no fruit for three years

B
The owner came to cut it down

The Fig tree parable

C
A fig tree grew in a vineyard

D
The gardener gave it special care. If fruit still would not grow then he would cut it down

E
The gardener asked him to give it a chance

THINK and LOOK ahead

Next week Jesus tells

another parable about someone who

was given a second chance.

Write the letter that is not in the second word to find out who it is

 LUKE 15:11-32

In **HEART** but not **HEAR**
In **BATH** but not **BAT**
In **CARE** but not **CAR**

In **REAP** but not **ARE**
In **PEAR** but not **PEACH**
In **LOST** but not **LAST**
In **DOOR** but not **POOR**
In **BIBLE** but not **BABBLE**
In **GOOD** but not **HOOD**
In **HAM** but not **HIM**
In **LETTER** but not **BETTER**

In **SAND** but not **HAND**
In **JOLLY** but not **JELLY**
in **DINNER** but not **RIDE**

God is always ready
to give us another chance
to try again.

Color the pictures below

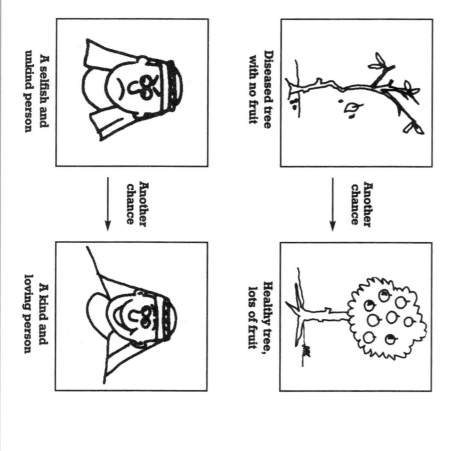

Diseased tree
with no fruit

Another
chance

Healthy tree,
lots of fruit

A selfish and
unkind person

Another
chance

A kind and
loving person

Jesus will help us to
bear the fruits of God's love
in our lives.

Cross out each "FRUIT" and copy the hidden
words on to the tree below

KIFRUITNDNESS LFRUITOVE FORFRUITGIVENESS
GENEFRUITROSITY HONEFRUITSTY SHFRUITARING

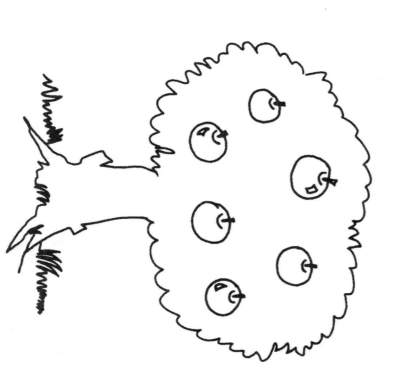

The son who came back

LUKE 15:1-3, 11-32

The story of the prodigal son
is a very well-known parable.

Choose words from the list below to complete the story

FATHER   SAD   PENNILESS   FORTUNE

MONEY   HOME   SONS

A man had two _____ . The younger son

asked his _____ for his share of the

father's _____ . The son left _____ ,

and his father was very _____ . The son

spent all his _____ enjoying himself

and soon he was _____ and hungry.

"What should I do?" he asked himself.

THINK and LOOK ahead

Next week Jesus shows us that
often we see the faults in others before
we notice our own!

**Who brought a woman
to Jesus to be judged?**

The ____ ____ ____ ____

and ____ ____ ____ ____

**How did they want
to punish her?**

By ____ ____ ____

her ____ ____ ____

Find out
JOHN 8:3

Find out
JOHN 8:5

WHO?

**Find out
next week**

HOW?

What did
the prodigal son
do next?

Cross out the wrong words to see what he decided

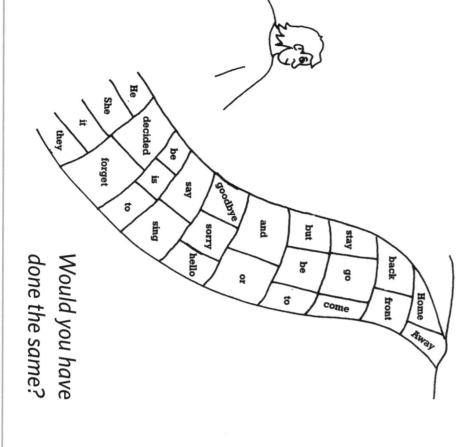

He / She / it / they decided / be / is / forget / to / say / sing / goodbye / sorry / hello / and / or / but / be / stay / go / back / front / come / to / Home / Away

Would you have
done the same?

When the father
saw his son coming he ran
to greet him.

Use the code to find out what the father said to his son

A B D E F H I L N O S T U V W
1 2 3 4 5 6 7 8 9 10 11 12 13 14 15

"

___ ___ ___ ___   ___ ___ ___ ___   ___ ___ ___ ___ ___
6   4   15 1 11   3   4   1   3   1   8   7   14 4 !

___ ___ ___   ___ ___   ___ ___ ___
9   10 15   6   4   7   11

___ ___ ___   ___ ___ ___   ___ ___ ___
8   10 11   15 1   11   2   13 12

___ ___ ___   ___ ___   ___ ___ ___
6   4   2   13   7   11

___ ___ ___   ___ ___
9   10 15   6   4

___ ___ ___ ___ ___
5   10 13 9   3

"

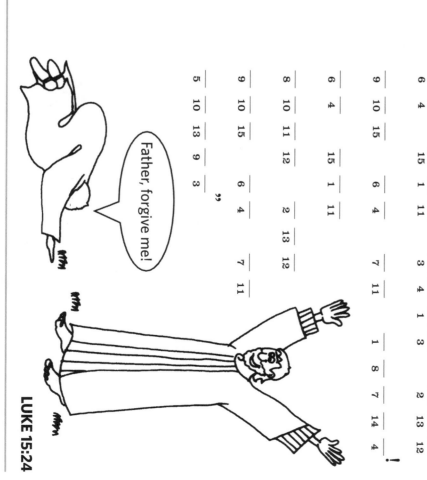

Father, forgive me!

Jesus forgives a woman

JOHN 8:1-11

The Scribes and Pharisees brought a woman to Jesus. She had been caught doing wrong, and they wanted to punish her.

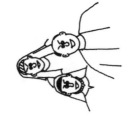

Use the code to find out what they said to Jesus

T	A	W	L	H
♥	♣	—	◇	☞
O	Y	S	R	D
☆	⬆	✳	☞	△
M	E	U	I	N
◇	✳	☞	☆	▷

Example: ☞⬆ = R

JOHN 8:5

THINK and LOOK ahead

Next Sunday is the beginning of Holy Week.

Which two names are given to next Sunday?

Write the first letter of each object

OR

SUNDAY!

After pausing
for a moment, Jesus
answered them.

Color the numbered spaces listed below to read his answer

1 3 4 12 27 10 29 5 6 8 22 16 20 24 11 14 18 26

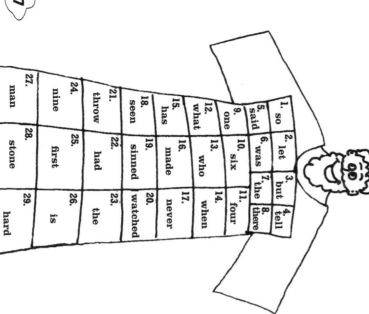

1. so	2. let	3. but	4. tell
5. said	6. was	7. the	8. there
9. one	10. six	11. four	
12. what	13. who	14. when	
15. has	16. made	17. never	
18. seen	19. sinned	20. watched	
21. throw	22. had	23. the	
24. nine	25. first	26. is	
27. man	28. stone	29. hard	

JOHN 8:7

One by one the
crowd dropped their stones
and walked away.

Use the code to find the missing words

Jesus said to the woman:

"You are

Go
___ ___ ___
1   14 4

no ___ ___ ___ ___ ___
   13 15 18 5

___ ___ ___ ___ ___ ___ ___ ___ ___ ___ ___ ___.
6   15 18 7   9   14   19 9   14

6 15 18 7 9 14   22 5   14 ."

JOHN 8:11

1	A	14	N
2	B	15	O
3	C	16	P
4	D	17	Q
5	E	18	R
6	F	19	S
7	G	20	T
8	H	21	U
9	I	22	V
10	J	23	W
11	K	24	X
12	L	25	Y
13	M	26	Z

We all make mistakes!

Jesus enters Jerusalem

LUKE 19:28-40

Jesus sent his disciples off to find a colt for him to ride.

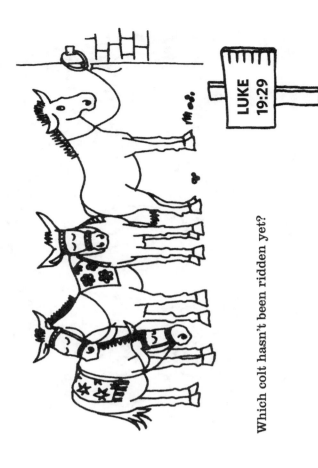

LUKE 19:29

Which colt hasn't been ridden yet?

THINK and LOOK ahead

Next week is Easter Sunday.
What do we celebrate then?

Write the word that fits the clue.
The first letter of the words will spell out the answer

CLUES

1. Water that falls from clouds
2. You hear with these
3. Frozen flakes of water
4. You use one when it rains
5. You drive on it
6. A red-breasted bird
7. Our planet
8. Christmas songs
9. They travel on rails not roads
10. Used to remove creases
11. Vegetable that makes eyes water
12. Opposite of yes

THE

1	2	3	4	5	6	7	8	9	10	11	12
☐	☐	☐	☐	☐	☐	☐	☐	☐	☐	☐	☐

— — — — — — —

OF JESUS!

The people waved palm branches and spread their coats on the road for Jesus to walk on.

The people welcomed Jesus with shouts of adoration.

Find the way to Jerusalem. Choose A, B, or C

LUKE 19:38

Solve the math problems and use the code to find the missing letters

A B C D E F G H I J K L M N O P Q R S T U V W X Y Z
1 2 3 4 5 6 7 8 9 10 11 12 13 14 15 16 17 18 19 20 21 22 23 24 25 26

"____ ____ ____

2   6   3   20   17   10   2
−0   x2   +2   −1   +2   −5   x2
____   ____   ____   ____   ____ ____   ____

IS

19   5   10   3   20   7   8   11   4   7
+4   +3   +5   x1   −5   +6   −3   +8   x2   −2
____   ____   ____   ____   ____   ____   ____   ____   ____ ____

IN

6   22   12   2   12   2   10   11   15
+6   −7   +6   x2   +7   x7   −9   +2   −10
____   ____   ____   ____   ____   ____   ____   ____   ____

THE ____ ____ ____ ____ ____ , ____ ____ ____ ____ ____ ____ ."

EASTER SUNDAY, YEAR C

Jesus is risen!

JOHN 20:1-9

What did Mary of Magdala see when she went to the tomb?

Use the symbols written under the lines to find the missing letters

For example: ♥ = D

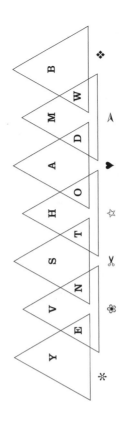

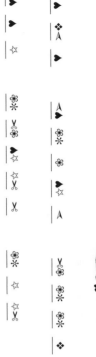

JOHN 20:1

THINK and LOOK ahead

What did Jesus say to his disciples when he saw them for the first time after the Resurrection?

Use the clues below to spell out the answer

" ___ ___ ___ ___ ___ ___ ___
  1   2   3   4   5   6   7

___ ___ ___ ___ ___ ___ ___ "
8   9 10 11 12 13 14

JOHN 20:19

1. Second letter of
2. First letter of
3. Second letter of
4. First letter of
5. Fifth letter of
6. First letter of
7. Fourth letter of
8. First letter of
9. Third letter of
10. Sixth letter of
11. First letter of
12. Second letter of
13. Second letter of
14. First letter of

Mary ran to tell
two of the disciples that
Jesus had gone.

Follow the arrows to spell out their names

S→	A	C	N	F	E
I	J	P	H	N	O
E	M	O	T	S	L
P	N	L	J	A	D
N	E	A	R	H	M
B	T	E	C	D	T

S ↓ ↘ ↓ ↓ ↖ ↖ ↖ ← ← ← ↓ ↓ ↓ ↗

AND

↑ ↖ ↗ →

They found the tomb empty!
The linen cloths lay rolled up on the ground.
Now they understood the Scriptures!

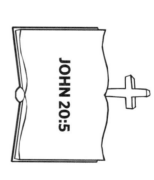

JOHN 20:5

Using the code,
see if YOU can understand
what was written!

A	D	E	F	H	I	M	O	R	S	T	U
·	◁	≥	◇	⊹	△	)	· ⌐	∨	⊙	⊹	∥

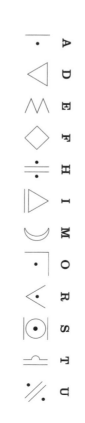

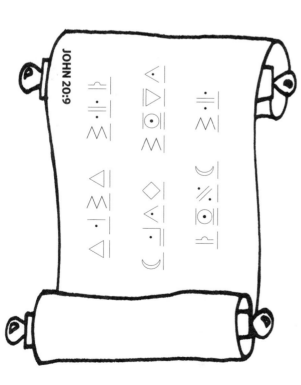

JOHN 20:9

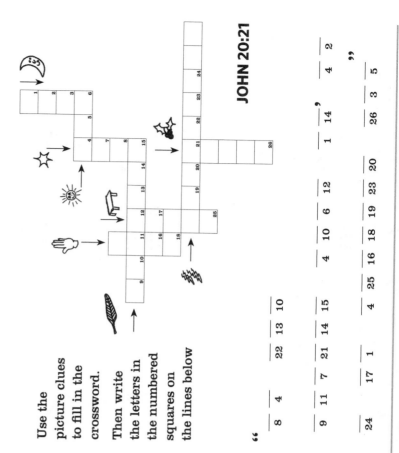

Peace be with you!

JOHN 20:19-31

The disciples were filled with joy to see Jesus.
He sent them to share his words with others.

Use the
picture clues
to fill in the
crossword.

Then write
the letters in
the numbered
squares on
the lines below

JOHN 20:21

" __ __   __ __ __   __ __ __ __
  8 4   22 13 10   9 11 7 21 14 15

__ __ __ __ __ __   __ __ __ __ __ __ __
4 10 6 12 4 25 16   18 19 23 20 24 17 1

__ __ __ __ "
1 14 4 2 26 3 5

THINK and LOOK ahead

Next week Jesus appears to his disciples
again while they are out fishing.

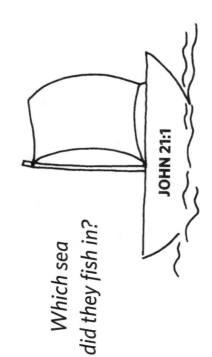

JOHN 21:1

*Which sea
did they fish in?*

The sea of

_____

CLUE

*It begins with
the twentieth letter
of the alphabet*

Then Jesus gave them a very special gift to help them with their work.

Write the letter that is missing from the second word to spell out what it was!

In **HEART** but not **HEAR**

In **HAND** but not **BAND**

In **LIME** but not **LIMB**

In **HOUSE** but not **MOUSE**

In **OTHER** but not **EITHER**

In **LIGHT** but not **MIGHT**

In **YELLOW** but not **MELLOW**

In **WEST** but not **WET**

In **PAN** but not **CAN**

In **MAIN** but not **MAN**

In **WRITE** but not **WHITE**

In **VAIN** but not **VAN**

In **TABLE** but not **ABLE**

One of the disciples was missing when Jesus appeared. He did not believe that Jesus was alive.

Unscramble the letters to find his name

MHSAOT _____

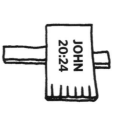

JOHN 20:24

Jesus showed him his wounds and then he believed!

Use the code to find what Jesus said to him

A 1	N 14	
B 2	O 15	
C 3	P 16	
D 4	Q 17	
E 5	R 18	
F 6	S 19	
G 7	T 20	
H 8	U 21	
I 9	V 22	
J 10	W 23	
K 11	X 24	
L 12	Y 25	
M 13	Z 26	

" __ __ __ __ __ __ __ __ __ __ __
  8 1 16 16 25   1 18 5

  __ __ __ __ __ __ __ __ __ __
  20 8 15 19 5   23 8 15

  __ __ __ __ __ __ __ __ __ __
  8 1 22 5   14 15 20

  __ __ __ __ __ __ __ __ __ __ __
  19 5 5 14   1 14 4

  __ __ __ __ __ __ __ __ __ __ __ __
  25 5 20   2 5 12 9 5 22 5 "

See **JOHN 20:29**

Jesus on the shore

JOHN 21:1-19

Peter and his friends had been fishing all night but had caught nothing. Then someone they did not recognize told them to try again.

Solve each math problem to find out how many fish they caught

1. $(5 \times 5) + 2$ = _____

2. $14 + 22 - 3$ = _____

3. $(9 \div 3) \times 7$ = _____

4. $(17 - 2) \times 2$ = _____

5. $(3 + 3) \times 7$ = _____

   TOTAL = _____ fish!

THINK and LOOK ahead

How did Jesus describe himself?

JOHN 10:14

Find out

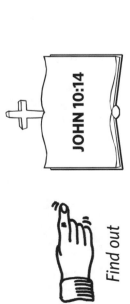

Write the answer below

" _____ _____ _____

_____ _____ "

The disciples recognized Jesus and
they came ashore to have breakfast with him.
Jesus asked Peter the same question
three times, and Peter gave the
same answer each time.

Use the code to find out what they said to each other

z y x w v u t s r q p o n m l k j i h g f e d c b a
A B C D E F G H I J K L M N O P Q R S T U V W X Y Z

Then Jesus told
Peter what he wanted
him to do.

Add or subtract words and letters to find the missing words

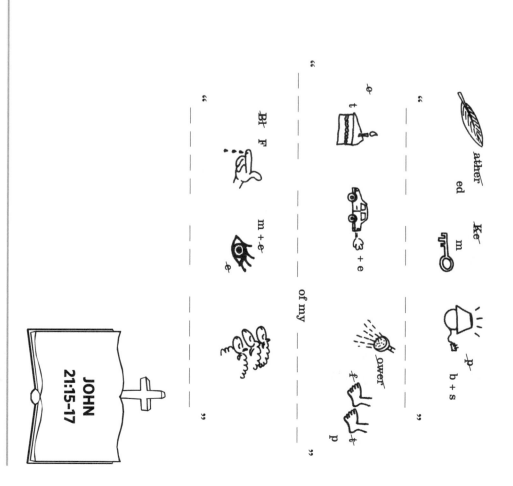

JOHN
21:15-17

The Good Shepherd

JOHN 10:27-30

Help the sheep to find their way to the shepherd

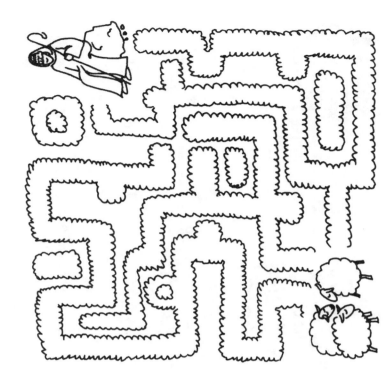

THINK and LOOK ahead

How do people recognize us as disciples of Jesus?

JOHN 13:35

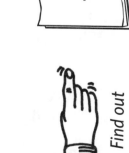

Find out

Add or subtract letters to spell out the answer

‾G–5 ‾X+1   ‾S–4 ‾W–2 ‾K+7   ‾I+3 ‾Z–11 ‾F+16 ‾H–3

‾C+3 ‾D+11 ‾T–2   ‾I–4 ‾J–9 ‾A+2 ‾Q–9

‾M+2 ‾X–4 ‾F+2 ‾P–11 ‾L+6

A B C D E F G H I J K L M N O P Q R S T U V W X Y Z

Who are the "sheep" that belong to Jesus?

Write the next letter of the alphabet above the letters given.

For example, E will be written above D

O D N O K D V G N

K H R S D M S N G H R

U N H B D Z M C

E N K K N V G H L

JOHN
10:27

Find three pairs of sheep

A

B

C

D

E

F

What will Jesus give to his sheep?

_____

Write the first letter of each object on the line above

A new commandment

JOHN 13:31-35

Jesus gave us a new commandment that would mark us out as his disciples. *What was it?*

Begin at the heart.
Moving clockwise, write down every other word

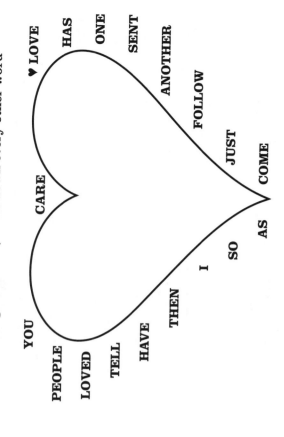

♥ LOVE
HAS
ONE
SENT
ANOTHER
FOLLOW
JUST
COME
AS
SO
I
THEN
HAVE
TELL
LOVED
PEOPLE
YOU
CARE

THINK and LOOK ahead

What special gift did Jesus give to his friends?

Use the clues to find the answer!

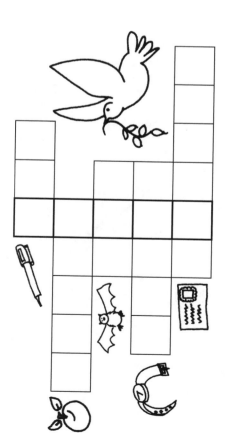

JOHN 14:27

Jesus showed us all how to love each other by his words and actions.

Ask someone to help you look up these stories

MARK 1:40–45

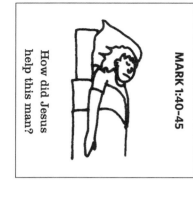

How did Jesus help this man?

JOHN 8:1–11

What did Jesus do for this woman?

LUKE 19:1–10

Why was this man so pleased to have Jesus as a friend?

MARK 5:35–43

What did Jesus do for this little girl?

Find ten hearts hidden in this picture

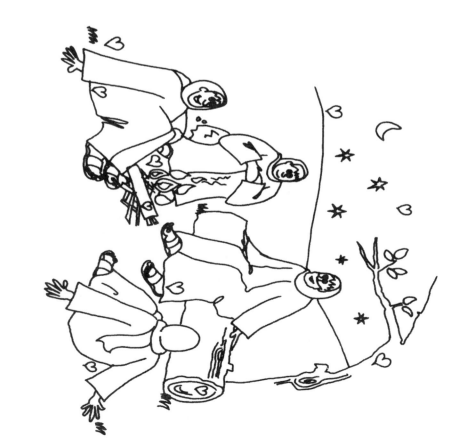

Do not be afraid

JOHN 14:23-29

Use the code to find out what Jesus said

	L	F	U	R
✎	S	E	N	W
☞	T	I	Y	A
✂	H	D	O	B
➤	1	2	3	4

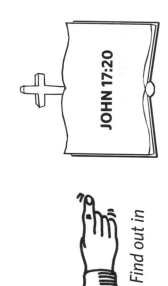

THINK and LOOK ahead

Jesus did something that
each one of us should do every day.

What was it?

JOHN 17:20

Find out in

Arrange the letters in the correct numerical order

P₃	H₁	E₇	R₄	D₈	A₅	E₂	Y₆

___ ___ ___ ___ ___ ___ ___ ___
1   2   3   4   5   6   7   8

Jesus said that God would send the Holy Spirit to be with the disciples.

What other name did Jesus use for the Holy Spirit?

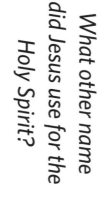

*Check your answer in **JOHN 14:26***

Find the missing numbers to solve the mystery!

5 = A 8 = C 9 = D 11 = E 12 = H

17 = O 20 = T 32 = V

16	6	9
+4	x 2	+2
—	—	—

17	5	8	9	25	30	4	46
-12	+4	x 4	+8	-17	-25	x 5	-35
—	—	—	—	—	—	—	—

This word means "someone who comes to help"!

What did Jesus say that the Holy Spirit would do?

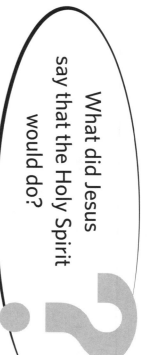

Use the clues to find the missing letters

The opposite of hot is

You put flowers in a

The opposite of sad is

You have five on each hand

You dry yourself with a

You put one up in the rain

AND

May they all be one

JOHN 17:20-26

Jesus prayed not only for his disciples
but that everyone might believe in him.

Use the code breakers to find his words

	IJ	KL	MN
	OP	QR	ST
	UV	WX	YZ

AB		CD
GH		EF
		EF

Examples:

$\llcorner$ = N $\vee$ = A

$\sqcap$ = W $\diamond$ = H

JOHN 17:20

THINK and LOOK ahead

Next week Jesus sends
the Holy Spirit as he promised to help
the disciples.

*What special name is given
to next Sunday?*

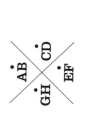

ACTS 2:1

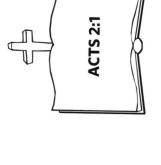

Find out

Fill in the missing letters

__ __ __ E   __ E   O __ __ __ __ T

The disciples shared the words and teachings of Jesus, and through them many did come to believe in him.

What name is sometimes given to a person who does such work?

Write the missing letter to find out

In <u>MOUSE</u> but not <u>HOUSE</u>

In <u>BIN</u> but not <u>BUN</u>

In <u>SEAT</u> but not <u>NEAT</u>

In <u>STAR</u> but not <u>CART</u>

In <u>EITHER</u> but not <u>OTHER</u>

In <u>DOVE</u> but not <u>DIVE</u>

In <u>NOSE</u> but not <u>HOSE</u>

In <u>HAT</u> but not <u>HIT</u>

In <u>RABBIT</u> but not <u>HABIT</u>

In <u>BOY</u> but not <u>BOOK</u>

These two pictures might look the same but can you find ten differences?

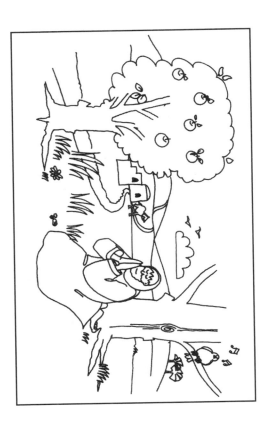

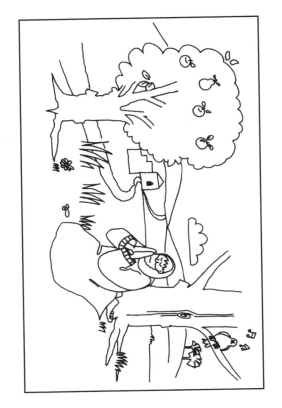

The Holy Spirit comes!

JOHN 14:15-16, 23-26; ACTS 2:1-11

Jesus asks us to do something for him if we love him.

What is it?

Hold this message up to a mirror read what it says

Commandments

"Keep my

JOHN 14:15

The Spirit gave the disciples the courage and power to preach to the people, just as Jesus had told them to do.

These pictures are in the wrong order. Put the letter for each picture in the right order on the lines below

A

B

C

D

_____ _____ _____ _____

Jesus promised to send the Holy Spirit to everyone who keeps his word.

How did the Spirit appear to the disciples at Pentecost?

Write the next letter of the alphabet above the letters given.

For example, G will be written above F

A B C D E F G H I J K L M N O P Q R S T U V W X Y Z

___ ___
R Z

___ ___ ___ ___ ___ ___ ___ ___ ___ ___
N V D Q E T K V H M C

___ ___ ___
M C

___ ___ ___ ___ ___
N M F T D R

___ ___ ___ ___ ___
E E H Q D

ACTS
2:2-3

When do WE receive the Holy Spirit in a special way?

Write the first letter of each object

AT

AND

How many gifts does the Spirit bring?

Solve the math problem to find out!

$(4 \times 3) + 24 - 3 + (2 \times 8) \div 7 = $ ___

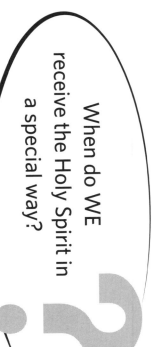

One God, three persons

JOHN 16:12-15

How and when does Jesus speak to us?

Copy the letters in order on the lines above the symbols as shown

TRUHHSII / HOGTEPRT

ALHTM / LTEIE

Find these words in the word search below and circle them

SAVIOR   HOLY SPIRIT   ADVOCATE

REDEEMER   LORD   FATHER   SON OF GOD

PARACLETE   EMMANUEL   MESSIAH

S A O E D R O I V A S B
L E T R T M E S S I A H
E M I A P A V I A U R O
I M R H M C C L D M S E
L A I R A A E O T K O T
A N P S S I G H V H D E
S U S A I F L E R D E L
E E Y S O L O A F O A C
O L L N P N R T R S N A
N P O S R E D E E M E R
M S H E H R I T R S P A
L T G R E H T A F T O P

The Spirit comes to show us God's way.

Use the code below to find out what Jesus says

Jesus said...

"

1,6 1,8   1,7 3,8 2,5 2,5

2,8 2,7 1,5   2,4 2,7   2,5 1,8 3,5 3,7

1,4 2,7 3,4 2,6 2,5 1,8 2,4 1,8

2,4 1,6 1,8

2,4 3,6 1,5 2,4 1,6

"

	4	5	6	7	8
1	C	U	H	W	E
2	T	L	P	O	Y
3	M	A	R	D	I

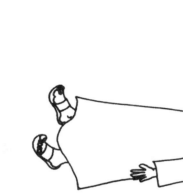

JOHN 16:13

On Trinity Sunday we give glory and praise to....?

Fit the pieces in the puzzle

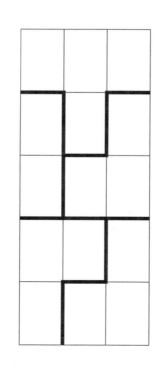

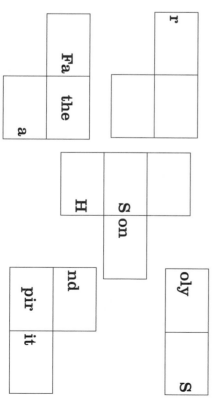

r

Fa | the | a

Son | H

oly | S

nd | pir | it

A wedding party

JOHN 2:1-11

Jesus and his mother were invited to a wedding at Cana in Galilee.

Help them to find their way using the directions below

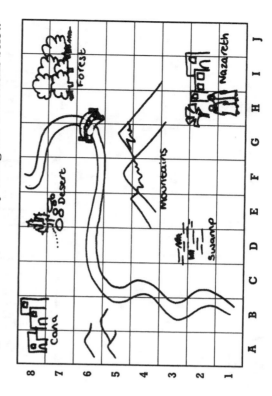

Directions to Cana

I1, I2, J3, I4, I5, H6, G6, F6, E7, D7, C8, B8

THINK and LOOK ahead

Where did Jesus go to read Scriptures and teach the people?

A B C D E F G H I J K L M N O P Q R S T U V W X Y Z

Add or subtract letters to find out

X – 4	
E + 3	
J – 5	

Q + 2	
Z – 1	
L + 2	
I – 8	
C + 4	
P – 1	
P – 9	
Q + 4	
F – 1	

See
LUKE 4:15-17

When they ran out
of wine Mary knew that
Jesus could help.

Use the numbers written under the lines to
find the missing letters and spell out what Mary said

For example: 4,5 = L

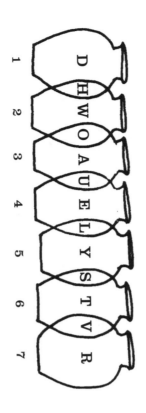

D	H W O	A U	E L Y	S	T V	R
1	2	3	4	5	6	7

"

___ ___ ___ ___ ___ ___ ___ ___
1 2,3   2 1,2 3   6   4 6,7 4   7   1,2 4

___ ___ ___ ___   ___ ___ ___
6   4 4,5 4,5 5,6   5 2,3 3,4

"

JOHN
2:5

They filled six stone jars with water,
and Jesus changed them into wine.

? Who else believed in Jesus when they saw
what he had done?

Write down every other letter on the line below

T O H A E R / D P I A S E C S I E P B L O E A S

T _____ / _____

? How many gallons of water could each
stone jar hold?

Do the math to find the answer

(60 – 15) – 20 – (3 + 2) = _____ or _____ gallons

120
–90
——

JOHN
2:6

Check your answer

Jesus begins his work

LUKE 1:1–4; 4:14–21

Jesus began preaching to the people and sharing the good news of God's love

Crack the code below to find out what helped him with this work

CODE CRACKER

1 A	14 N
2 B	15 O
3 C	16 P
4 D	17 Q
5 E	18 R
6 F	19 S
7 G	20 T
8 H	21 U
9 I	22 V
10 J	23 W
11 K	24 X
12 L	25 Y
13 M	26 Z

__ __ __
20 8 5

__ __ __ __ __
16 15 23 5 18

__ __
15 6

__ __ __
20 8 5

__ __ __ __ __
19 16 9 18 20

LUKE 4:14

Write the words of Jesus in order on the lines below

1 ___ 2 ___ 3 ___ 4 ___

5 ___ 6 ___ 7 ___ 8 ___

9 ___ 10 ___

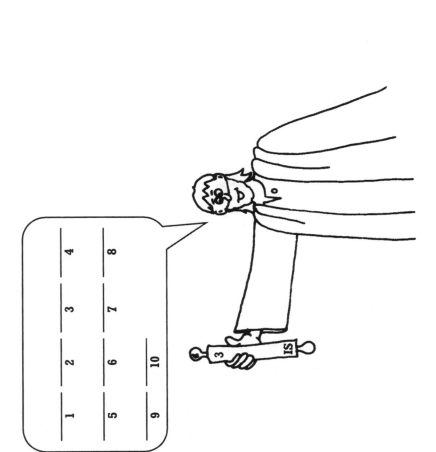

3 IS

10 LISTEN
5 FULFILLED
1 THIS
6 TODAY

4 BEING
2 TEXT
9 YOU
8 AS
7 EVEN
10 LISTEN

LUKE 4:21

Jesus went to read the Scriptures in a synagogue in which town?

Use the clues below to spell out the name of the town

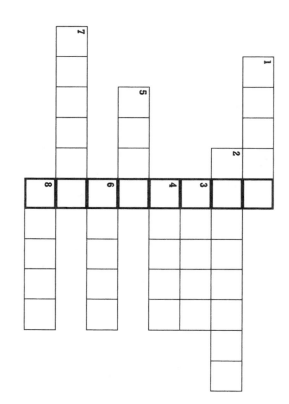

1. The color of grass
2. Decorations worn on the ears
3. A "stripy" horse
4. The opposite of below
5. It grows on your head
6. Our planet
7. An orange vegetable
8. They are attached to your wrists

Jesus read the words of the prophet Isaiah

Use the key to find out what was written

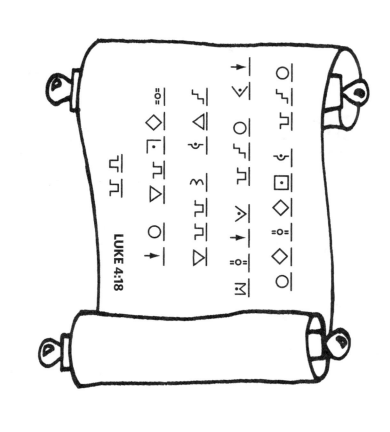

LUKE 4:18

| A | B | D | E | F | G | H | I | L | M | N | O | P | R | S | T | V |

Good news for everyone!

LUKE 4:21-30

The people of Nazareth heard Jesus preaching in the synagogue and were amazed.

Find out what they were thinking! Match the words with the spaces

SON   JOSEPH'S   THIS   IS   SURELY

Jesus managed to slip away unharmed.

Use the code cracker to find his words below

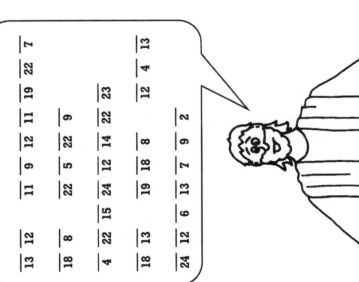

LUKE 4:24

1 Z	14 M
2 Y	15 L
3 X	16 K
4 W	17 J
5 V	18 I
6 U	19 H
7 T	20 G
8 S	21 F
9 R	22 E
10 Q	23 D
11 P	24 C
12 O	25 B
13 N	26 A

Jesus spoke about the prophets Elijah and Elisha. They were sent to tell EVERYONE about God, not just their own people.

Write the first letter of each object

Who was Elijah sent to?

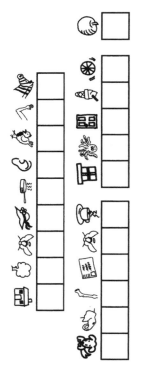

Who was Elisha sent to?

The people grew angry with Jesus! *What did they want to do to him?*

Use the code breaker to find out

C = ☀   L = ᙎ   E = ◠   M = ⊞   F = ∂g   O = ◯

H = ☆   R = ◠   I = ꓭ   T = ⚡   W = ◯

The marvelous catch

LUKE 5:1-11

Jesus sat in a boat by the shore and preached to the crowd. The boat belonged to Simon Peter the fisherman.

Find the letters
S-I-M-O-N P-E-T-E-R
hidden in the picture

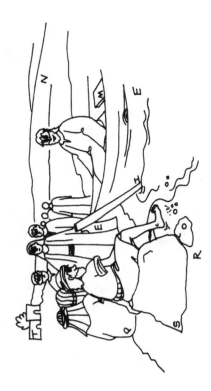

Jesus asked them to come and share his work telling people about God.

What did they do?

Cross out every other letter.
Write the remaining letters in order below

Start →	T	H	O	E	A
Y	B	L	A	E	T	F	R
T	O	E	B	V	D	E	T	R	O
Y	A	T	L	H	E	I	S	N	B
G	D	A	C	N	A	D	L
F	T	O	S	L	F
L	R	O	W
W	A	E	O
D	E

_ _ _ _ _

_ _ _ _ _ _

_ _ _ _

LUKE 5:11

Simon Peter and his friends had been fishing all night and had caught nothing, but Jesus told them to try again.

These pictures show what happened next but they are in the wrong order. Put the number of each picture in the correct order below

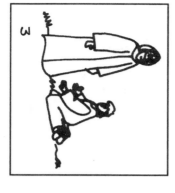

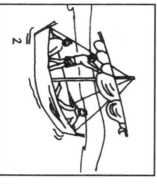

___ ___ ___ ___

The sons of Zebedee, who fished with Simon Peter, were also amazed by this marvelous catch!

Color the following boxes to find their names

2A 4C 1D 5B 7E 1B 6C 2C 3E
5D 7B 4E 6B 3B 2E 4B 2D 1C
7D 1E 3D 6E 5C 7C 3A 6D

	1	2	3	4	5	6	7	
	J	C	O	J	O	H	N	A
	J	A	E	M	S	A	E	B
	O	E	M	S	J	S	N	C
	H	O	J	E	N	E	O	D
	S	H	A	N	S	J	A	E

Happiness is...

LUKE 6:17, 20–26

People came from far and wide to hear Jesus and to be healed.

Fit the shapes into the puzzle below and find out where some of the crowds came from

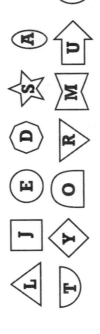
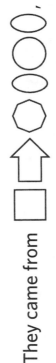
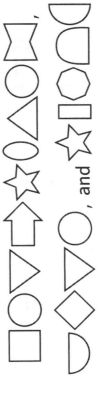

They came from ⬜ ⬜ ⭐ ⬤ ◗ , ◺ ◁ ◇ ◗ , and ⬜ ⬡ ⭐ ⬡ ◗ .

LUKE 6:17

God's love makes us happy and we share that happiness with others!

Draw a picture of yourself doing something that makes you or someone else feel happy

The people sat on a hillside by the Sea of Galilee and listened to Jesus preaching.

Jesus wanted to tell the people how to be truly happy.

Unscramble the letters below to find a name often used for the sermon Jesus gave that day

ETH _____

MNORSE _____

NO _____

HET _____

TMUNO _____

Find Luke 6:20–21 using the code cracker!

1	2	3	4	5	6	7	8	9	10	11	12	13
Z	Y	X	W	V	U	T	S	R	Q	P	O	N

14	15	16	17	18	19	20	21	22	23	24	25	26
M	L	K	J	I	H	G	F	E	D	C	B	A

"

19 26 11 11 2   26 9 22   7 19 22

16 18 13 20 23 12 14   12 21   7 12

25 22 15 12 13 20 8   7 19 22

11 12 12 9 '   7 19 22

19 26 11 11 2   11 2   26 9 22   7   19 22

19 26 11 11 2   11 2   26 9 22   7 19 22

"

19 6 13 20 9 2   21 12 9   7 19 22 2

8 19 26 15 15   25 22

8 26 7 18 8 21 18 22 23

"

Love your enemies

LUKE 6:27-38; SAMUEL 26:2-23

How did Jesus tell us to treat our enemies?

Cross out the words that are wrong

"HATE/LOVE your ENEMIES/FRIENDS;

do GOOD/BAD to those who LOVE/HATE you;

BLESS/CURSE those who curse you;

pray for those who treat you BADLY/WELL."

LUKE 6:27-28

God will
reward us for our love
and goodness.

Copy every other letter on to the lines below

A T E H I E O A U M B O C U O N E T F Y G O H U
I G J I K V A E I W O I U L A L C B D E F G Z I X V
Y E W N L B M A N C O K P T Q O R Y S O T U

" _ _ _ _ _ _ _ _ _ _

_ _ _ _ _

_ _ _ _ _ _ _ !"

LUKE 6:38

Jesus wants us to love others without expecting something in return!

Add or subtract letters to find out what Jesus said

A B C D E F G H I J K L M N O P Q R S T U V W X Y Z

B+2 J+5   ___ ___ ___ ___ ___
             K-4 L+3 V-7 A+3

___ ___ ___ ,
X+3 P-2 F-2

C+4 J-1 R+4 C+2   ___ ___ ___ ___ ___
                       Z-3 E+4 X-4 M-5 N+1 W-2 W-3

Q-9 J+5 L+4 H-3   ___ ___ ___
                      K+4 H-2

___ ___ ___ ___ ___ ___ ___
N+4 C+2 M+7 Y-4 J+8 O-1

Do you think this is easy to do?

YES ☐   NO ☐

In today's Old Testament story who was ready to forgive his enemy?

Use the clues to spell out the answer

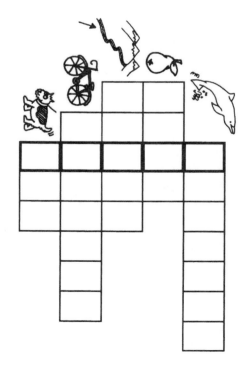

SAMUEL 26:2-23

The fruits of goodness

LUKE 6:39-45

One day Jesus told a parable...

Find the right words and write them in the spaces

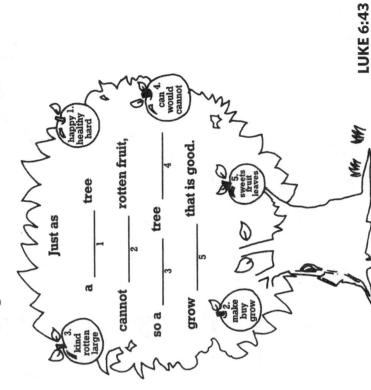

Just as a ___ tree
              1

cannot ___ rotten fruit,
        2

so a ___ tree
      3

grow ___ that is good.
      5

1. happy
   healthy
   hard

2. make
   buy
   grow

3. kind
   rotten
   large

4. can
   would
   cannot

5. sweets
   fruit
   leaves

LUKE 6:43

How do people
know when our hearts are
full of goodness?

Follow the arrows to find out!

I	O	U	S	A	N
Y	D	E	A	D	A
E	Y	W	C	Y	W
B	W	T	T	H	F
D	E	H	A	W	E

B ___

Find four differences between the two trees
and write them below

Tree A

Tree B

Tree B is different from Tree A because

1. _____

2. _____

3. _____

4. _____

LUKE 6:45

What is the
source of someone's
goodness?

Use the code to find the words of Jesus

"_____ _____ _____

_____ _____ _____

_____ _____ _____

_____ _____ _____

_____ _____ _____ ,,

The faithful centurion

LUKE 7:1-10

The centurion's faith was rewarded!

What happened to his favorite servant?

Find the missing numbers and fill in the letters below

KEY

4 = H 6 = A 8 = S 9 = D

10 = W 11 = E 15 = L

16	6	7	19	4
−12	+5	+3	−13	x2
___	___	___	___	___

12	7	3	30	9	4
−8	+4	x2	−15	+2	+5
___	___	___	___	___	___

A Roman centurion sent a message to Jesus to ask for his help. *Why?*

	1	2	3	4	5	6	
	K	U	N	A	S	E	A
	C	O	H	V	W	T	B
	D	B	R	I	L	F	C

Using the clues, find the letters and write them on the lines

___ ___ ___   ___ ___ ___ ___ ___ ___ ___ ___
3B 4C 5A   6C 4A 4B 2B 3C 4C 6B 6A

___ ___ ___ ___ ___ ___ ___   ___ ___ ___
5A 6A 3C 4B 4A 3A 6B   5B 4A 5A

___ ___ ___ ___   ___ ___ ___   ___ ___ ___ ___ ___
5A 4C 1B 1A   4A 3A 1C   1B 5C 2B 5A 6A

___ ___   ___ ___ ___ ___ ___
6B 2B   1C 6A 4A 6B 3B

LUKE 7:2

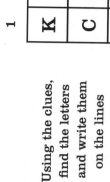

LUKE 7:10

As Jesus was on his way, the soldier sent him a message.

The words are written backward. Write them the correct way on the lines to read what the message says

suseJ, I ma ton yhtrow ot eviecer

_____

uoy, tub tsuj evig eht drow dna ym

_____

tnavres lliw eb deruc.

_____

dengis,

_____

eht noirutnec

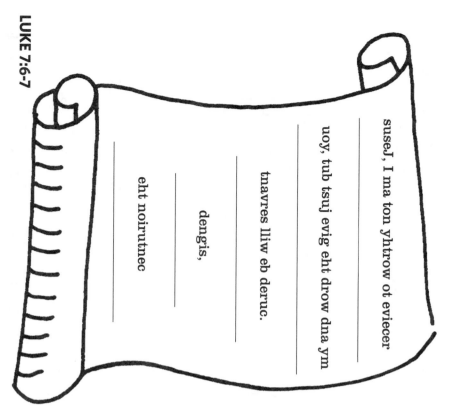

Jesus was amazed by the centurion's great _____ *?*

Write the word that fits the clue.
The first letter of the words will spell out the answer

CLUES

1. Birds can do this
2. Place where planes land and take off
3. Liquid that flows from pens
4. A slow-moving reptile with a shell on its back
5. The opposite of sad

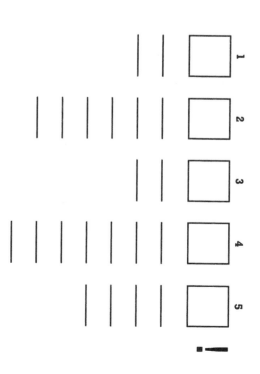

Jesus takes pity

LUKE 7:11-17

A large crowd followed Jesus and his disciples to a town called Nain.

Help them to find their way safely using the directions below

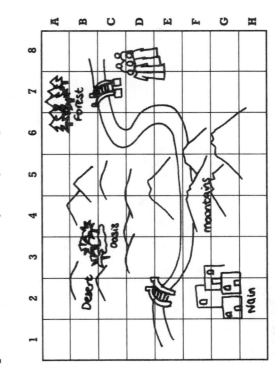

Directions to Nain
8C, 7C, 7B, 6B, 5C, 4B, 3B, 2C, 2D, 2E, 1E, 1F, 1G, 2G

The crowd was filled with wonder and amazement.

Use the symbols to find out what they said

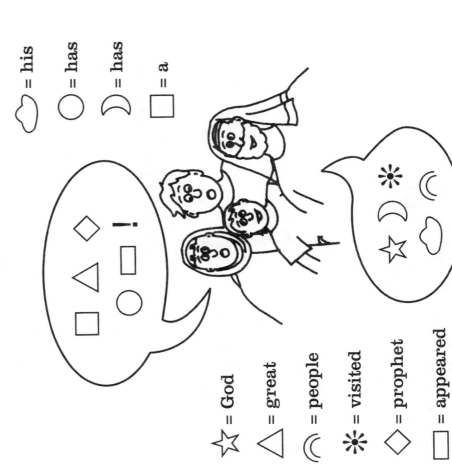

⌢ = his

◯ = has

☾ = has

▢ = a

☆ = God

△ = great

☾ = people

✳ = visited

◇ = prophet

▢ = appeared

?

What did they
see as they arrived
at the town?

Write the next letter of the alphabet above the given letters.
For example, D will be written above C

Z | C D Z C | L Z M

A D H M F | B Z Q Q H D C

N T S | E N Q | A T Q H Z K

LUKE 7:12

Jesus was filled with pity to see so much
sadness and he stopped to help.

Young man, get up!
(Luke 7:14)

Find out what happened
next by using the symbols to
find the missing letters

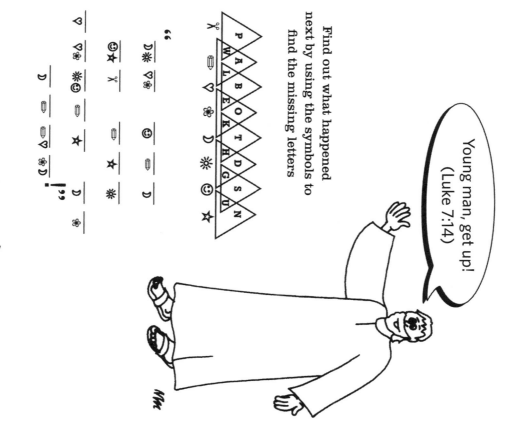

P A B O T D S N
W L E K H G U

Check your
answer in

3
+4
x5
:

Jesus forgives a sinner

LUKE 7:36—8:3

While Jesus was having dinner with Simon the Pharisee, who came to find him?

Use the code breaker to find out!

For example:

□ = Q
⌐ˑ = Z
∨ = A
◇ˑ = H

	IJ̇	KL̇	MṄ
AḂ			
CḊ	OṖ	Q̇R	ṠT
EḞ	UV̇	WẊ	YŻ
GH			

7:37

THINK and LOOK ahead

Next week Jesus asks the disciples a question.

Find out in **LUKE 9:20**

Who gives the correct answer?

Add or subtract letters to check your answer

A B C D E F G H I J K L M N O P Q R S T U V W X Y Z

G + 9

M – 8

P + 4

J – 5

C + 15

The woman was sorry for everything she had done wrong.

Simon was annoyed because Jesus did not send the woman away.

Fill in the words that are missing from the poem below

WASH   FORGIVENESS   WOMAN   SORRY
TEARS   LOVE   JESUS   OINTMENT

The _____ was _____ for

the wrong she had done.

To ask for _____ to

she'd come.

She used her own _____ to

_____ the Lord's feet.

With kisses and _____ her

_____ was complete.

Use the code to find out what Jesus said to Simon and the woman

Jesus said to Simon:

$\overline{8}$ $\overline{5}$ $\overline{18}$ $\overline{19}$ $\overline{9}$ $\overline{14}$ $\overline{19}$ $\overline{1}$ $\overline{18}$ $\overline{5}$

$\overline{6}$ $\overline{15}$ $\overline{18}$ $\overline{7}$ $\overline{9}$ $\overline{22}$ $\overline{5}$ $\overline{14}$ '

$\overline{6}$ $\overline{15}$ $\overline{18}$ $\overline{19}$ $\overline{8}$ $\overline{5}$ $\overline{8}$ $\overline{1}$ $\overline{19}$

$\overline{19}$ $\overline{8}$ $\overline{15}$ $\overline{23}$ $\overline{14}$ $\overline{7}$ $\overline{18}$ $\overline{5}$ $\overline{1}$ $\overline{20}$

$\overline{12}$ $\overline{15}$ $\overline{22}$ $\overline{5}$

Then Jesus said to the woman:

$\overline{25}$ $\overline{15}$ $\overline{21}$ $\overline{18}$ $\overline{6}$ $\overline{1}$ $\overline{9}$ $\overline{20}$ $\overline{8}$

$\overline{8}$ $\overline{1}$ $\overline{19}$ $\overline{19}$ $\overline{1}$ $\overline{22}$ $\overline{5}$ $\overline{4}$ $\overline{25}$ $\overline{15}$ $\overline{21}$

$\overline{7}$ $\overline{15}$ $\overline{9}$ $\overline{14}$ $\overline{16}$ $\overline{5}$ $\overline{1}$ $\overline{3}$ $\overline{5}$.

1 A	14 N	
2 B	15 O	
3 C	16 P	
4 D	17 Q	
5 E	18 R	
6 F	19 S	
7 G	20 T	
8 H	21 U	
9 I	22 V	
10 J	23 W	
11 K	24 X	
12 L	25 Y	
13 M	26 Z	

LUKE 7:47-48

The Son of God

LUKE 9:18–24

One day Jesus and his disciples were praying together when he asked them a question.

Cross out the letters with odd numbers and copy the remaining letters in order on the lines below

Start → A O W E H S O R D L F O S P L M E R O
1 5 2 3 6 9 8 5 4 7 13 14 11 2 7 9 8 15 4

M P K L J E E S P A N Y A I R A T E M
17 12 13 14 11 13 6 25 12 21 8 3 22 5 14 17 23 6

" _ _ _ _ _ _ _ _ _ _

_ _ _ _ _ _ _ _

_ _ _ _ ? "

Use the code below to find the words of Jesus in Luke 9:24

A	D	E	F	H	I	K	L	M	N	O	R	S	T	V	W	Y
1	2	3	4	5	6	7	8	9	10	11	12	13	14	15	16	17	18

1 11 18 12 11 4   17 6 12

9 12 16 4 14   15 6 4 7 13

9 7 5 4   5 12 13   10 18

14 1 8 4   17 7 9 9

2 4   14 1 16 4 3

Only Simon Peter knew the answer to Jesus' question.

Unscramble the letters to read what Simon Peter said

OYU RAE ETH
NOS FO DGO

Simon Peter had seen Jesus do many things that only the Son of God could do!

Match each picture with the correct caption

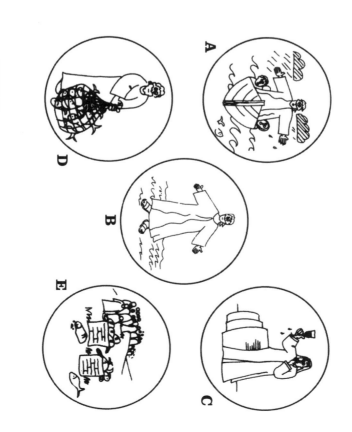

TITLE

1. **The miracle at Cana** (JOHN 2:1–11)
2. **Calming the storm** (MARK 4:35–41)
3. **Feeding five thousand** (MATTHEW 14:13–21)
4. **Walking on water** (MATTHEW 14:25–33)
5. **The marvelous catch** (JOHN 21:1–17)

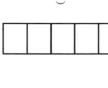

Make Jesus welcome

LUKE 9:51–62

Jesus and his disciples set off for Jerusalem, intending to stop and rest at a village on the way.

Who lived in this village?

Find the missing letters to spell the answer

In <u>S</u>UN but not BUN
In <u>HAVE</u> but not <u>HIVE</u>
In <u>MOUNTAIN</u> but not <u>FOUNTAIN</u>
In <u>BATH</u> but not <u>BOTH</u>
In <u>RABBIT</u> but not <u>HABIT</u>
In <u>INK</u> but not <u>ANKLE</u>
In <u>TOW</u> but not <u>ROW</u>
In <u>NAP</u> but not <u>NIP</u>
In <u>NOSE</u> but not <u>HOSE</u>
In <u>SAD</u> but not <u>GLAD</u>

LUKE 9:52

THINK and LOOK ahead

Jesus sent his disciples ahead of him to the village he planned to visit.

1. How many disciples did he send?

CLUE $(7 \times 2) + (8 \times 8) - (3 \times 2) = $ ____

2. Jesus sent them off in pairs, so how many pairs of disciples set out?

CLUE Answer 1 ÷ 2 = ____

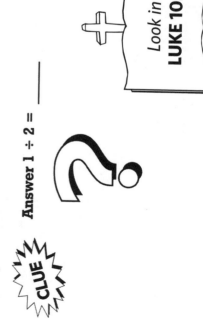

Look in
LUKE 10:1

The Samaritans and the Jews had a strong dislike for each other!

Use the code to find out what happened next

CODE BREAKER

1	V	O	T	A	W
2	M	E	H	S	D
3	T	I	N	R	Y

| 1 | ☀ | ➘ | ☁ | ☽ | ♌ |

Jesus was not angry, and instead went to another village where he would be welcomed.

Fit the pieces in the puzzle to find out what we should remember!

LUKE 9:53

Share the Good News

LUKE 10:1-12

Jesus sent seventy-two disciples out in pairs to the surrounding towns and villages.

Add or subtract letters to find out what Jesus told them to say. For example, S+2=U

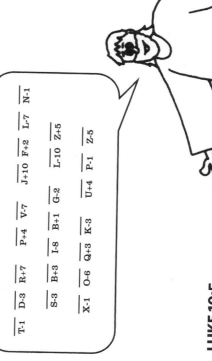

T-1 D-3 R+7 P+4 V-7 J+10 F+2 L-7 N-1

S-3 B+3 I-8 B+1 G-2 L-10 Z+5

X-1 O-6 Q+3 K-3 U+4 P-1 Z-5

LUKE 10:5

THINK and LOOK ahead

Next week Jesus is asked the question, "Who is my neighbor?" He tells a well-known story in reply.

Look up the reference to find the story and write the title below

LUKE 10:30-35

FIND OUT

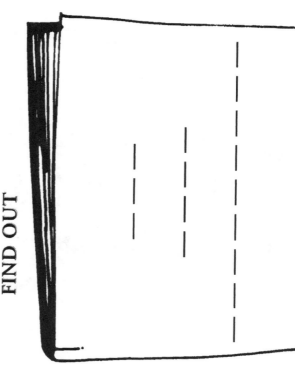

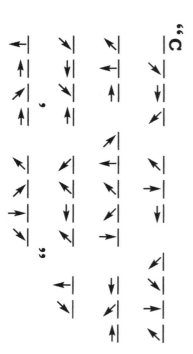

What did Jesus tell them to do whenever they were made welcome?

Soon the disciples returned and told Jesus about the marvelous things they had seen and done.

Follow the arrows to reveal the answer

L	U	R	O	S	C
C	H	H	E	K	I
A	A	S	T	S	R
E	E	H	D	A	S
A	T	E	G	N	D
V	R	E	H	E	W
O	I	S	D	S	F
P	L	G	L	O	G

"C → ↘ ↗ ↗ ↘

↗ → ↙ ↗ ↗ ↑ ↗

↗ ↑ ↘ ↗ ↑ →

↗ → ↗ ↘ ↙ ↘ ↗

↑ ↗ → ↑ ↗ ↙ ↗ ↗

↑ ↘ ↗ , ↗ ↗ ↗ ↑ ↑

↑ → ↘ ↗ ↗ ↑ →

↑ → ↗ ↗ ↗ ↗ ↗ ↗ "

Cross out every third word to reveal what Jesus said to them

BE HAPPY FOR BECAUSE YOUR LIVES NAMES ARE WILL WRITTEN IN BOOKS HEAVEN

The good Samaritan

LUKE 10:25–37

Where was the merchant traveling from and going to when the robbers attacked him?

Write the first letter of each object

From

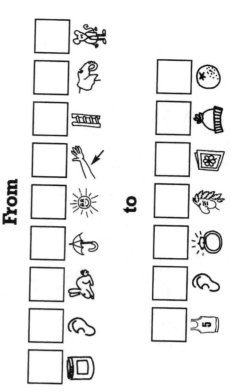

to

THINK and LOOK ahead

Next week Jesus goes to visit two sisters.

Write the missing letter in the series to find their names

IJKLN
WXYZB
OPQST
SUVWX
EFGIJ
YZBCD

and

LNOPQ
ZBCDE
OPQST
WXZAB

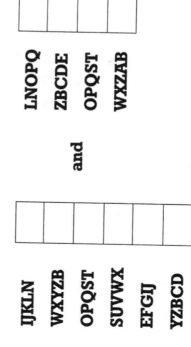

LUKE 10:38, 39

CHECK YOUR ANSWERS

Two men passed by and did not stop to help.
Then a Samaritan took pity on the
traveler and cared for him.

Read Luke 10:34–35 and find four things that the
good Samaritan used to take care of the traveler

1. _____
2. _____
3. _____
4. _____

Circle the clues in the picture!

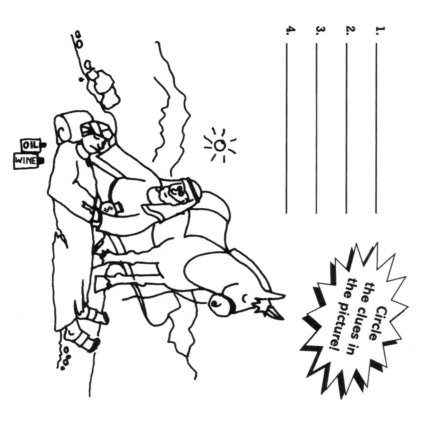

Jesus told this story
to explain what it means to love
your neighbor as yourself.

Using the code below, find the words of Jesus
that are written in Luke 10:37

z y x w v u t s r q p o n m l k j i h g f e d c b a
A B C D E F G H I J K L M N O P Q R S T U V W X Y Z

For example: j = Q

"

___ ___ ___ ___ ___ ___ ___
t l   z m w   w l   g s v

___ ___ ___ ___ ___
h z n v   u l i

___ ___ ___ ___ ___ ___ ___ ___
z m b l m v   d s l

___ ___ ___ ___ ___ ___ ___
m v v w h   b l f
"

Making time for Jesus

LUKE 10:38-42

Two sisters called Martha and Mary invited Jesus to their house.

Find ten differences between these two pictures

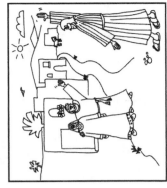

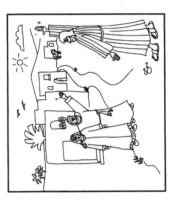

Draw a picture of yourself making time for Jesus

Listening to God's word

Talking to God at prayer time

Martha busied herself
serving her guests, while Mary
sat next to Jesus and listened
to him speaking.

Martha felt angry with her sister!

What did she say?

Use the code to
read her words

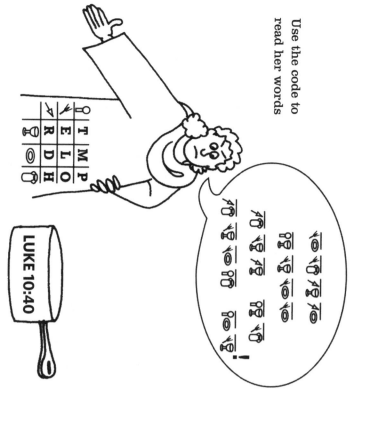

LUKE 10:40

Unscramble the words below to find Jesus' reply

has ₂

Mary ₁

anything ₁₄

important ₁₂

to ₆

is ₁₀

than ₁₃

to ₄

chosen ₃

listen ₅

and ₈

that ₉

more ₁₁

me ₇

Teach us to pray

LUKE 11:1-13

One day the disciples asked
Jesus to teach them how to pray.

Fill in the missing words

FORGIVE   BREAD   TRESPASS   US   EVIL
KINGDOM   NAME   EARTH   FATHER   HEAVEN

Our _____ who art in heaven,

hallowed be thy _____ ;

thy _____ come;

thy will be done,

on _____ as it is in _____ .

Give us this day our daily _____ ,

and _____ us our trespasses,

as we forgive those

who _____ against us.

And lead _____ not into temptation,

but deliver us from _____ . Amen.

THINK and LOOK ahead

I am in a parable
that Jesus tells next
week. I am someone
with a good harvest.

Who am I?

LUKE 12:16

Use the code to see if you are right

A = 1¢   M = $1
C = 5¢   N = $5
E = 10¢   R = $10
H = 25¢   T = $20
I = 50¢

Jesus taught us to think of God as a Father who loves each one of us.

Use the clues to find the missing letters and read his words

Color the picture using the number key given below

A young goat is called a...

Whoever comes first in a race

The number of fingers on each hand

A young dog is called a...

A cat meows and a dog...

The opposite of cold

Rain falls from these

"

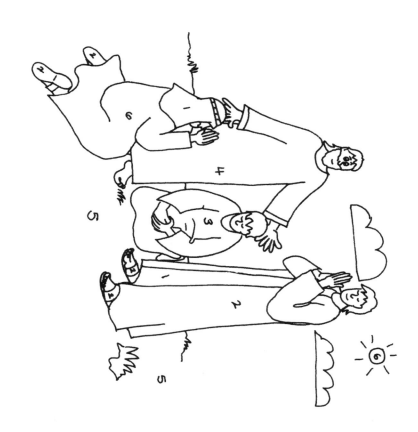

1	Blue
2	Brown
3	Pink
4	Yellow
5	Green
6	Orange

The foolish man

LUKE 12:13–21

Jesus told a parable about a rich man whose crops would not fit in his many barns.

Write the next letter of the alphabet above the given letters to find out what the rich man said.

For example, E will be written above D

"
‾‾ H

‾‾ ‾‾ ‾‾ ‾‾   ‾‾ ‾‾ ‾‾
V H K K   O T K K

‾‾ ‾‾ ‾‾ ‾‾   ‾‾ ‾‾   ‾‾ ‾‾ ‾‾ ‾‾ ‾‾
C N V M   L X   A Z Q M R

‾‾ ‾‾ ‾‾   ‾‾ ‾‾ ‾‾ ‾‾ ‾‾
Z M C   A T H K C

‾‾ ‾‾ ‾‾ ‾‾ ‾‾ ‾‾
A H F F D Q
                    "
‾‾ ‾‾ ‾‾ ‾‾
N M D R

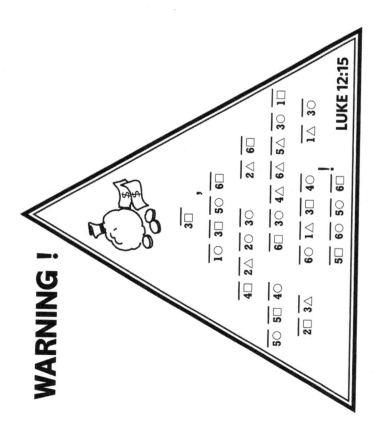

LUKE 12:18

Use the code cracker to find a warning!

□	D	B	A	L	O	S
○	M	F	E	T	N	W
△	H	I	Y	C	R	U
	1	2	3	4	5	6

WARNING!

‾‾
3□

,

‾‾ ‾‾ ‾‾ ‾‾
1○ 3□ 5○ 6□

‾‾ ‾‾ ‾‾   ‾‾ ‾‾
4□ 2△ 2○ 3○   2△ 6□

‾‾ ‾‾   ‾‾ ‾‾ ‾‾ ‾‾ ‾‾ ‾‾
5○ 5□ 4○   6□ 3○ 4△ 6△ 5△ 3○   1△ 3○

‾‾ ‾‾   ‾‾ ‾‾ ‾‾   ‾‾ ‾‾ ‾‾   ‾‾ ‾‾ ‾‾ ‾‾ ‾‾ 1□
2□ 3△   6○ 1△ 3□ 4○ !   5□ 6○ 5○ 6□

LUKE 12:15

The rich man was foolish and greedy. He chose to store up his earthly riches instead of treasure in heaven.

Circle these words in the puzzle below

SELFISH GREEDY FOOLISH RICH
TREASURE BARNS CROPS

H	A	R	N	S	G	E
E	S	M	H	C	I	R	H
O	L	I	R	B	U	E	S
F	R	O	F	S	A	E	I
B	P	K	A	L	M	D	L
S	N	E	L	A	E	Y	O
P	R	L	A	E	M	S	O
T	A	R	E	S	A	M	F

Lead the rich man to the real treasure Jesus told us about.

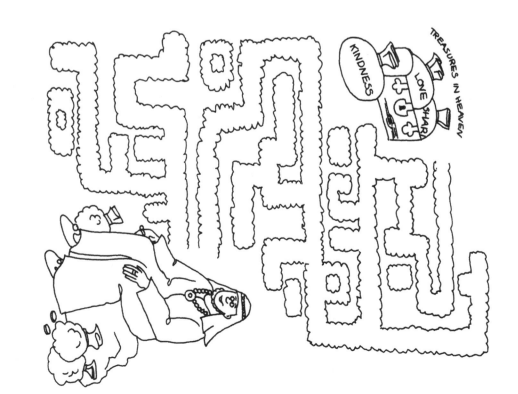

Be ready!

LUKE 12:32–48

A wise servant is always ready for his master's return!

Circle the things a servant might need to provide a meal for his master

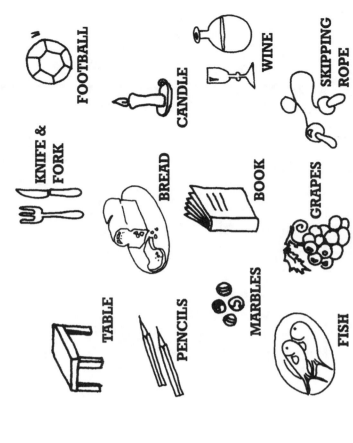

KNIFE & FORK

FOOTBALL

CANDLE

WINE

SKIPPING ROPE

BREAD

BOOK

GRAPES

TABLE

PENCILS

MARBLES

FISH

A servant who knows his master's wishes is expected to carry them out!

Use the symbols to find the words of Jesus

$\triangle$ = a

$\smile$ = be

$\Diamond$ = given

$\bigcirc$ = deal

☀ = will

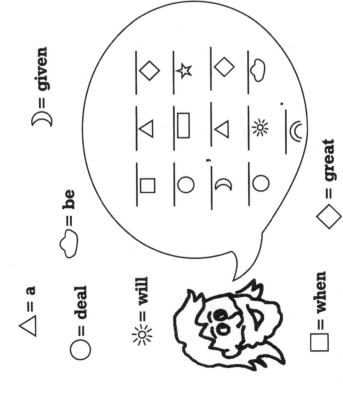

$\square$ = when

☆ = been

$\Diamond$ = great

$\complement$ = expected

$\square$ = has

LUKE 12:48

Why did Jesus tell us to ALWAYS be ready to greet him?

The servant who stayed ready was generously rewarded.

Use the code cracker to find his words in Luke 12:40

1 Z	14 M	
2 Y	15 L	
3 X	16 K	
4 W	17 J	
5 V	18 I	
6 U	19 H	
7 T	20 G	
8 S	21 F	
9 R	22 E	
10 Q	23 D	
11 P	24 C	
12 O	25 B	
13 N	26 A	

"

7 19 22   8 12 13

12 21   14 26 13   18 8

24 12 14 18 13 20   26 7

26 13   19 12 6 9   2 12 6

23 12   13 12 7

22 3 11 22 24 7 !"

These parables have the same message.
Match each picture with its story

1. The doorkeeper was told to stay awake! The master could return unexpectedly
Mark 13:34-37

[A]

2. The foolish bridesmaids took no oil with them but the wise ones were ready
Matthew 25:1-4

[B]

A.

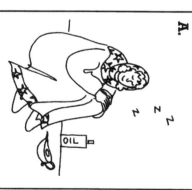

B.

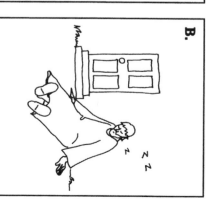

Jeremiah in the well

LUKE 12:49-53; JEREMIAH 38:3-6, 8-13

Jeremiah was one of
God's messengers sent to tell the people
about God's plans.

THINK and LOOK ahead

Next week Jesus talks
about the prophets again.

*Which other
Old Testament characters
does he also mention?*

Find out in
LUKE 13:28

Find the missing numbers to spell out the
name given to these messengers

7 = R   8 = E   11 = T   12 = H

29 = P   49 = S   72 = O

13	14	9	41	4	64	8	7
+16	÷2	x8	-12	x3	÷8	+3	x7
——	——	——	——	——	——	——	——

Add or subtract letters to check your answers

A B C D E F G H I J K L M N O P Q R S T U V W X Y Z

C-2 F-4 N+4 Z+1 C+5 I-8 J+3   E+4 O+4 W+4 D-3 B+1   Q-7 P-15 A+2 G+8 T-18

The people threw Jeremiah in a well because they did not want to listen to him!

Draw Jeremiah sitting in the well

Then solve the math problem to find out how deep this well is

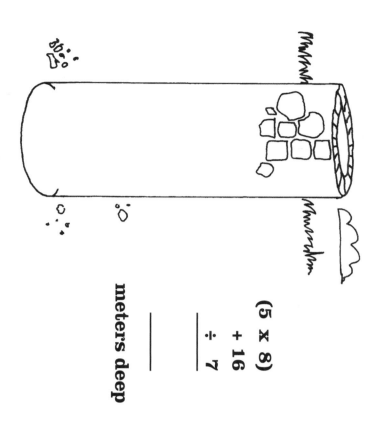

$$\begin{array}{r} (5 \times 8) \\ + 16 \\ \div 7 \\ \hline \end{array}$$

meters deep

Luckily Jeremiah was rescued and could continue God's work!

Hidden in this word search are the names of other biblical prophets.

Find and circle them

J	S	O	M	A	R
M	P	S	H	A	L
L	M	D	A	E	E
E	I	F	I	K	I
O	C	N	A	M	K
J	A	R	S	E	E
D	H	S	I	B	Z
A	E	S	O	H	E

MICAH

EZEKIEL

ISAIAH

DANIEL

HOSEA

AMOS

JOEL

Few will be chosen

LUKE 13:22–30

Jesus stopped at towns and villages on his way, to teach the people.

Use the code to find out where Jesus was going

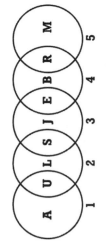

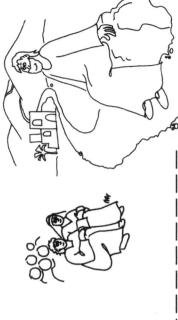

A	U	L	S	J	E	B	R	M
1	2	3	4	5

$\overline{3}$ $\overline{3,4}$ $\overline{4,5}$ $\overline{1,2}$ $\overline{2,3}$ $\overline{1}$ $\overline{2}$ $\overline{3,4}$ $\overline{5}$

THINK and LOOK ahead

Next week Jesus is invited for a meal.

FIND OUT
Who sent Jesus this invitation?
Look in Luke 14:1

Dear Jesus,
Please come
for a meal at
my home.
From
_____

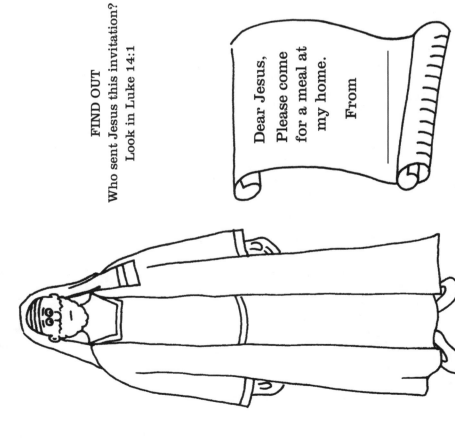

A young man stopped Jesus to ask a question

Jesus told him that many would try to enter God's kingdom, but few would succeed!

Write the remaining letters in order below to find his words

Cross out every other letter.

Start ↓								
S	A̶	I	L	R	E	W	O
I	P	L	B	L	E	O	R	N
A	L	L	Y	S	A	O	F	B
E	M	W	E	B	N	E	A	S
O	A	R	V	W	E	A	D	N

Use the code to find what else Jesus said

.	a	l	e
△	f	s	t
	1	2	3

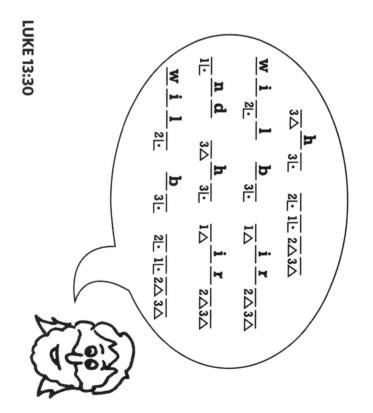

w i l l h b i r
2L· 3△ 3L· 3L· 2L· 1L· 2△3△
1△

n d h i r
1L· 3△ 3L· 1△ 2△3△

w i l l b
2L· 3△ 2L· 3L· 2L· 1L· 2△3△

"S ___ ___ ___ ___, ___ ___ ___ ___ ___ ___?"

LUKE 13:30

Put others first

LUKE 14:1, 7-14

Jesus went for a meal
with one of the leading Pharisees.

Count the place settings to find the number of guests.
Circle the answer and then color the scene

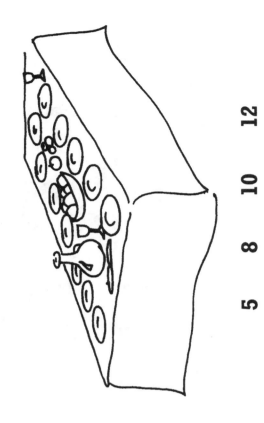

5   8   10   12

THINK and LOOK ahead

Next week Jesus tells us to
think about the cost of being his disciples.

Help this builder to work out the cost of his materials

MATERIAL LIST
2 bags of cement ____
6 tons of brick ____
4 windows ____

TOTAL
COST ____

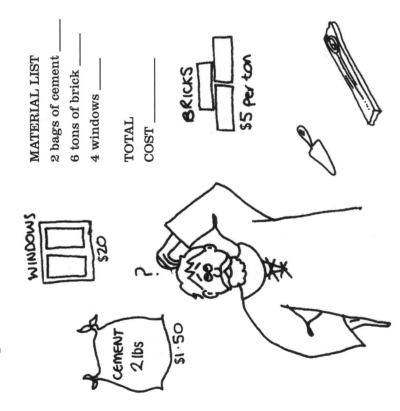

The guests rushed to take the best seats.

Which guest sat where?

Help the guests to find their places by matching the invitations and place settings

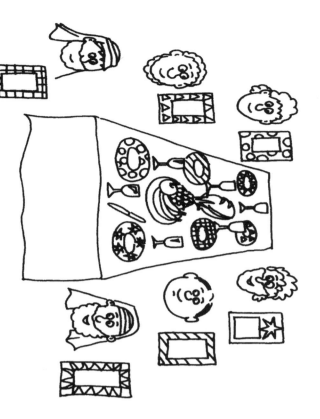

What did Jesus say to them?

Use the key to find his words

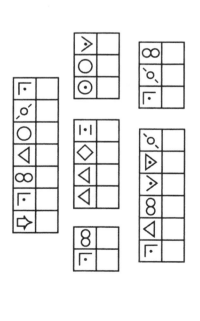

What does the last word mean?

B	U	D	E	A	T	L	M	H	N	I	W	X

Put a check mark next to the answer

A Exhausted

B Frightened

C Glorified

D Lonely

Consider the cost

LUKE 14:25-33

It is not always easy to be a follower of Jesus! He told us what he expects from anyone who follows him.

Which two people mentioned by Jesus had to consider different costs?

Use the codes to find the answers!

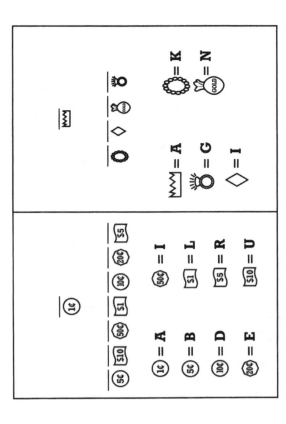

Circle the things you think are important to Jesus

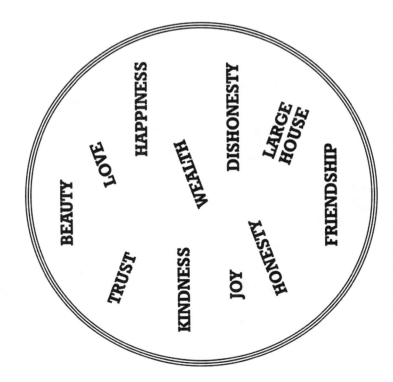

What did Jesus say a sensible builder would do?

Use the code
to find
his words

1	A	T	O	U
2	H	W	R	K
3	E	N	I	G
4	S	C	D	F
	△	□	○	◇

2□ 1○ 2○ 2◇   1○ 1◇ 1□   1□ 2△ 3△

4□ 1○ 4△ 1□   1□ 1○   4△ 3△ 3△ 2△ 3△

2△ 3△   2△ 1△ 4△   3△ 3□ 1○ 1◇ 3◇ 2△

1□ 1○   4◇ 3○ 3□ 4□ 2△   1○ 2△ 3△

2□ 1○ 2○ 2□   1□ 2△ 3△

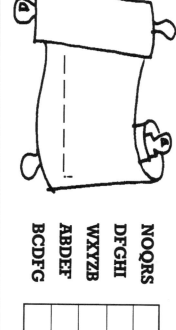

The king had a different cost to think about!

Write the missing letter in the series
to find what he decided to ask for

NOQRS
DFGHI
WXYZB
ABDEF
BCDFG

Lost and found!

LUKE 15:1-32

The Pharisees and Scribes were angry with Jesus.

Cross out the letters with odd numbers and copy the remaining letters in order on to the lines below to find what they said

Start → X T F H E I B S S M R A M N L W D E R L P C
1 4 5 8 3 2 9 6 11 4 15 22 3 14 19 16 9 12 17 12 23 6

A O C M B E M S E S O I B N C N F E L R C S
7 10 11 22 5 14 21 24 3 16 1 8 13 2 27 30 3 8 15 12 11 32

" _ _ _ _ _ _ _ _ _ _ _ _

_ _ _ _ _ _ _ _ _ _ _

_ _ _ _ _ _ _ _ _ _ _ "

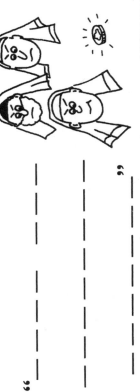

LUKE 15:2

THINK and LOOK ahead

Read Luke 16:2 to find out why this servant looks so worried!

Jesus told two parables about people who lost something but searched until they found it.

Help the shepherd to find what he has lost

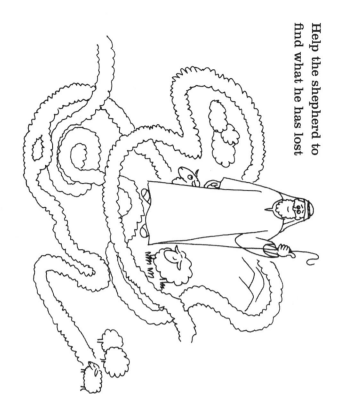

Help this woman to find her lost

It could be hidden anywhere on these pages!

How did the shepherd and the woman feel when they found what had been lost?

Give them happy faces

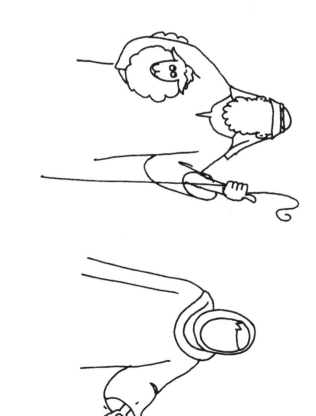

What does God do when any sinner returns to his love?

Write the first letter of each object

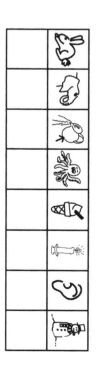

Always be honest!

LUKE 16:1-13

A rich man heard that his servant was being wasteful and decided to dismiss him.

Fit the shapes below to find out what he told the servant to do

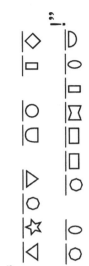

LUKE 16:2

THINK and LOOK ahead

Next week Jesus tells a parable about a rich man who dies and goes to hell.

What other name is used for hell?

You'll find the answer in **LUKE 16:23**

Unscramble the letters below

D S H A E

_ _ _ _ _

The servant cheated his master and changed the accounts so that the debtors would owe him a favor.

Jesus wants us to understand what is really important!

Add up the accounts below

A

ACCOUNTS	
Wheat	100 measures
Oil	+ 100 measures
TOTAL	_____ measures

B

ACCOUNTS	
Wheat	80 measures
Oil	+ 50 measures
TOTAL	_____ measures

✓ the correct account

A ☐
B ☐

Begin at the START arrow and write down every other word.

When you reach the RETURN arrow write down every other word, going in the opposite direction

Start   Return

IF RICHES YOU GENUINE CANNOT WITH BE YOU TRUSTED TRUST WITH MONEY WILL OHW

Luke 16:11

"____ ____ ____ ____ ____ ____ ____ ____ ____ ____ ?"

The poor man at the gate

LUKE 16:19–31

Jesus told a parable about a rich man and a poor man

Solve the clues below to find the poor man's name.
The first letter of each word will spell out the answer

CLUES

1. The opposite of hate
2. The fruit Eve shared with Adam
3. A stripy African horse
4. The opposite of never
5. A red-breasted bird
6. Something to shelter under in the rain
7. You use it to wash yourself

1.	2.	3.	4.	5.	6.	7.

— — — — — — —

— — — — — — —

— — — — — — —

— — — — — — —

THINK and LOOK ahead

What can make almost anything happen?

Cross through the word "money" and write the remaining letters
in order on the lines below to spell out the answer

For example: **MONEY**

MONEYFMONEYAMONEYIMONEYTMONEYHMONEY

— — — — —

LUKE 17:5

Find out

The rich man enjoyed a good life while poor Lazarus suffered miserably.

Use the words to fill in the blanks in this poem

**CLOTHES   HEAVEN   RICH   EAT
WEALTH   LAZARUS   SORES   HEALTH**

The _____ man lived in comfort and _____.

He always looked a picture of _____.

With elegant _____ and plenty to _____,

he did not see the man on the street.

_____ lay on the footpath outside,

hunger and sadness he could not hide.

Covered in _____, with nobody's love,

his comfort would come in _____ above.

What happened to the men when they died?

Use the code cracker to find out

```
z y x w v u t s r q p o n m l k j i h g f e d c b a
A B C D E F G H I J K L M N O P Q R S T U V W X Y Z
```

___ ___ ___ ___ ___ ___   ___ ___ ___
 o   z   a   i   f   h   d   z   h

___ ___ ___ ___ ___ ___ ___ ___ ___
 x   l   n   u   l   i   g   v   w

___ ___ ___ ___ ___   ___ ___ ___
 g   s   v   i   x   s

___ ___ ___   ___ ___ ___ ___ ___ ___ ___ ___
 n   z   m   h   f   u   u   v   i   v   w

Have faith

LUKE 17:5-19

A small amount of faith can do marvelous things!

Use the code breaker to find what Jesus said

AB	IJ	KL̇	MṄ
GḢ CD EḞ	OṖ	QṘ	SṪ
	UV̇	WẊ	YŻ

For example: L· = N

∨ = A

⊔ = W

⟩ = H

LUKE 17:6

THINK and LOOK ahead

Next week Jesus meets ten people who ask for his help.

Write the first letter of each picture to find out who they were

Check your answers in **LUKE 17:12**

Many people in the Old and New Testament had great faith in God.

Use the clues to find their names and fill in the crossword

ACROSS

3. The "rock" on which Jesus built his church
4. Isaac's father
6. He built the ark

DOWN

1. A Roman soldier commanding 100 men
2. The sister of Mary and Lazarus
5. He led the Israelites through the Red Sea

We must be ready to serve God and do whatever is expected of us.

Color the boxes to find the hidden message!

	A	B	C	D	E	F	G	H
1	L	I	A	W	I	L	L	M
2	B	E	D	O	O	R	D	F
3	K	A	E	M	W	M	Y	Y
4	P	O	B	E	S	T	M	E

COLOR: 2H, 1A, 4G, 2B, 1C, 4B, 3E, 1H, 3D, 2F, 3C, 4H, 2E, 3A, 2G, 4A, 3H, 3B, 2A

Thank you, Jesus

LUKE 17:11-19

Jesus met ten lepers who had to live apart from their families

M	O	J	E	K	S
L	N	Y	A	P	R
B	U	T	I	R	E
S	D	S	P	T	S
E	L	E	M	A	O
P	J	Q	K	M	J

Follow the arrows to spell out what they said

" J _____ ... !"

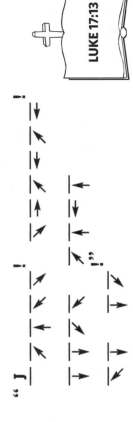

LUKE 17:13

THINK and LOOK ahead

I am someone seeking justice. *Who am I?*

Find out in **LUKE 18:3**

Arrange the letters in the correct numerical order

W₂ W₆ D₄ A₁ I₃ O₅

___ ___ ___ ___ ___ ___
1   2   3   4   5   6

Jesus told them to go to the priests and show themselves, and on the way something marvelous happened!

Copy the letters in order on to the lines above the symbols as shown

TEWRCRD / HYEEUE

Only one man remembered to thank Jesus for making him well again

Use the numbers written under the lines to find the words of Jesus.

Examples: 1 = F and 5,6 = S

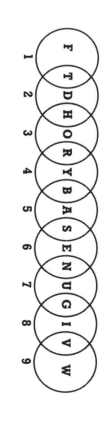

"

$\overline{7,8}$ $\overline{3}$ $\overline{3}$ $\overline{6,7}$ $\overline{4}$ $\overline{3}$ $\overline{7}$ $\overline{3,4}$ $\overline{9}$ $\overline{5}$ $\overline{4}$

$\overline{4}$ $\overline{3}$ $\overline{7}$ $\overline{3,4}$ $\overline{1}$ $\overline{5}$ $\overline{8}$ $\overline{1,2}$ $\overline{2,3}$ $\overline{2,3}$ $\overline{5}$ $\overline{5,6}$

$\overline{5,6}$ $\overline{5}$ $\overline{8,9}$ $\overline{6}$ $\overline{2}$ $\overline{4}$ $\overline{3}$ $\overline{7}$

"

Don't give up

LUKE 18:1-8

Jesus told a parable about a widow and a judge.

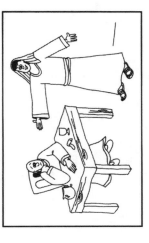

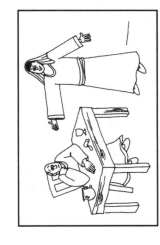

Find eight differences between these two pictures

THINK and LOOK ahead

Jesus tells a parable about these two men next week. *Who are they?*

Unjumble the letters

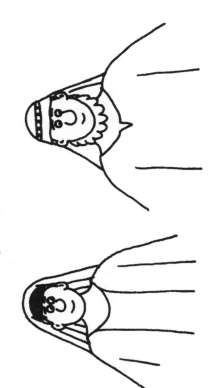

A
ESERAIHP

A
AXT LEORCCTOL

LUKE 18:10

The judge would not listen but the widow pestered him until finally he gave her what she wanted.

Use the code to find what he said

1 A	8 H	15 O
2 B	9 I	16 P
3 C	10 J	17 Q
4 D	11 K	18 R
5 E	12 L	19 S
6 F	13 M	20 T
7 G	14 N	

21 U	
22 V	
23 W	
24 X	
25 Y	
26 Z	

"

__9__

__23__ __9__ __12__ __12__ __7__ __9__ __22__ __5__   __8__ __5__ __18__

__10__ __21__ __19__ __20__ __9__ __3__ __5__   __15__ __18__   __19__ __8__ __5__

__23__ __9__ __12__ __12__   __23__ __15__ __18__ __18__ __25__   __13__ __5__

__20__ __15__   __4__ __5__ __1__ __20__ __8__ !"

LUKE 18:5

God will ALWAYS listen to our prayers!

Find the answers to the math problems and use the code to see what prayer Jesus himself taught us

1 = A   2 = D   3 = E   4 = H   5 = L   6 = O

7 = P   8 = R   9 = S   10 = T   11 = Y

```
  5      10     9
+ 5    -  6   - 6
____   _____  ____
```

```
  3      3      6    17     3
+ 2    x 2   + 2   -15    x 3
____   ____  ____  ____   ____
```

```
  5      3      9      9     15     5
+ 2    + 5   - 8    + 2   -12   + 3
____   ____  ____   ____  ____   ____
```

THIRTIETH SUNDAY OF THE YEAR, YEAR C

The Pharisee and the tax collector

LUKE 18:9-14

Where did these two men meet?

Write the letter that is missing from the second word in the box

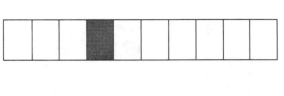

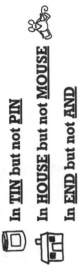 In **TIN** but not **PIN**

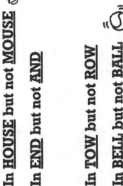 In **HOUSE** but not **MOUSE**

In **END** but not **AND**

In **TOW** but not **ROW**

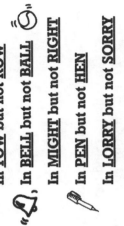 In **BELL** but not **BALL**

In **MIGHT** but not **RIGHT**

In **PEN** but not **HEN**

In **LORRY** but not **SORRY**

In **NEW** but not **NOW**

We can all be proud and boastful sometimes!

Write a prayer below.

Like the tax collector's prayer, make it pleasing to God

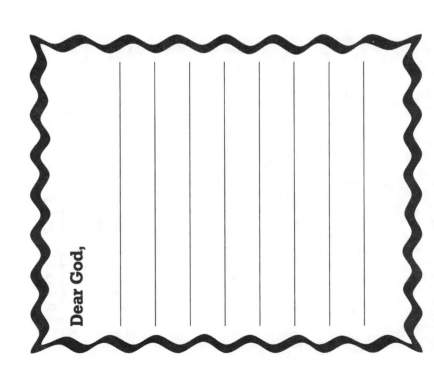

Dear God,

The two men went to the temple to pray.

Match each one with his words

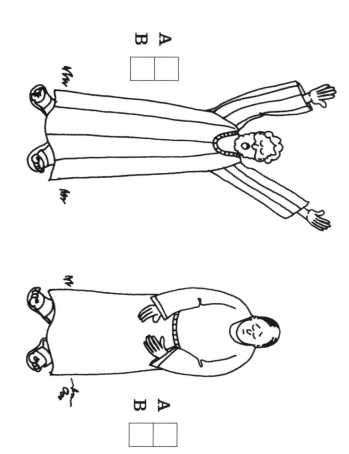

A [ ] [ ]

A [ ] [ ]
B [ ] [ ]

A

"God, have mercy on me, a sinner"

Luke 18:13

B

"Thank you for making me such a good person. I keep all your rules and am very generous!"

It was the tax collector, not the Pharisee, who pleased God with his prayer.

Use the code to find what Jesus said in Luke 18:14

CODE BREAKER

1	K	L	G	E	O
2	B	R	M	D	V
3	W	H	Y	A	U
4	F	I	S	N	T

The story of Zacchaeus

LUKE 19:1-10

Jesus went to a town where a tax collector called Zacchaeus lived.

Write the missing letter in the series to find where Zacchaeus lived

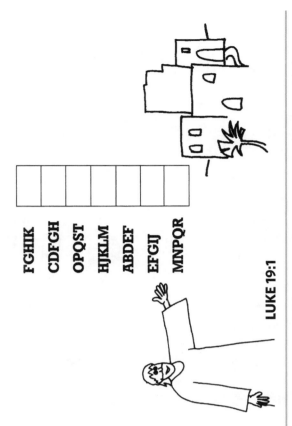

FGHIK

CDFGH

OPQST

HJKLM

ABDEF

EFGIJ

MNPQR

LUKE 19:1

Jesus called Zacchaeus to change his heart and make a fresh start.

Add or subtract letters to find what Zacchaeus decided to do!

A B C D E F G H I J K L M N O P Q R S T U V W X Y Z

G+2   Z−3   O−6   H+4   S−7   F+1   J−1   Q+5   B+3

K−3   Y+2   O−3   D+2   J+5   M−7   A+12   Z−1

F−4   F−1   K+1   T−5   K+3   R−11   E+4   X−10   F+1   R+1   Y−5   Q−2

P+4   C+5   J−5   L+4   M+2   S−4   Q+1   F−5   G+7   C+1

Q−1   X+3   Z−1   C−1   C−2   B+1   H+3   E+1   L+3   W−2   G+11

V−2   V−13   H+5   D+1   W−4   E−4   Q+2   K+2   X−3   A+2   J−2

P+4   R−3   S+1   L−4   L+3   J+9   B+3

L−3   D−1   G+1   A+4   X+3   Q+3   F−1   I−5

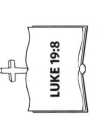

LUKE 19:8

Nobody liked Zacchaeus because he cheated people to make himself rich.

Zacchaeus climbed a sycamore tree to get a better view of Jesus.

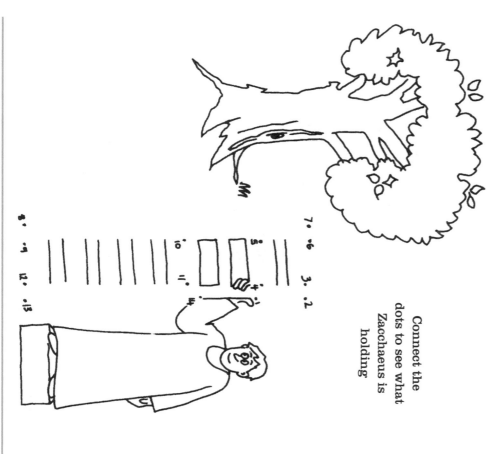

Connect the dots to see what Zacchaeus is holding

How many names of trees can you find in this word search?

A	M	L	E	O	P	Y	E	T	R
E	U	C	A	L	Y	P	T	U	S
B	N	E	C	L	O	O	P	N	Y
A	R	D	E	W	W	P	S	T	R
O	U	A	R	I	F	L	E	S	R
L	B	R	O	L	S	A	R	E	E
P	A	R	S	L	M	R	A	H	H
C	L	A	O	E	R	O	C	H	H
B	A	D	A	W	E	Y	L	M	P
K	L	K	S	W	Y	W	A	S	H

ASH
CEDAR
CHERRY
CHESTNUT

ELM
EUCALYPTUS
FIR
LABURNUM

OAK
POPLAR
WILLOW
YEW

Heaven is...

LUKE 20:27-38

These men disagreed with the teachings of Jesus.

Who are they?

Use the code cracker to find the answer!

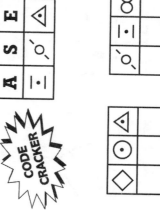

A	S	E	T	D	H	U	C

THINK and **LOOK** ahead

Jesus tells us that we will have an opportunity to do something for him.

What is it?

LUKE 21:13

Find out in

Hold this page in front of a mirror to check your answer

WITNESS!

BEAR

The Sadducees did not believe in resurrection or life after death.

Fit the pieces in the puzzle and read what Jesus said to them

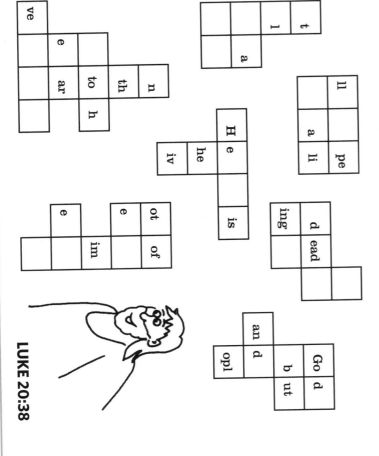

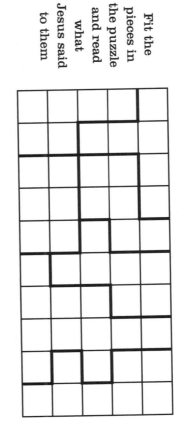

LUKE 20:38

Whose resurrection do we celebrate every Sunday?

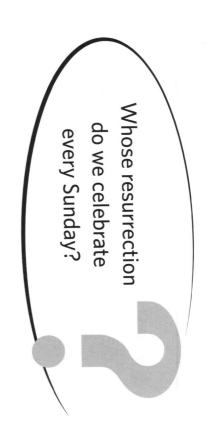

Find the answers to the clues to break the code

1. It shines in the sky and turns night to day

$\overline{1}\ \overline{2}\ \overline{3}$

2. He married Mary, the mother of God

$\overline{4}\ \overline{5}\ \overline{6}\ \overline{7}\ \overline{8}\ \overline{9}$
$\overline{15}\ \overline{16}\ \overline{17}$

3. To run after someone

$\overline{10}\ \overline{11}\ \overline{12}\ \overline{13}\ \overline{14}$
$\overline{18}\ \overline{19}\ \overline{20}$

4. They travel on tracks

4	7	13	2	20

10	9	16	18	6	15

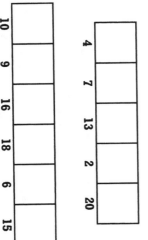

THIRTY-THIRD SUNDAY OF THE YEAR, YEAR C

Believe in me!

LUKE 21:5-19

Jesus said that it would be hard to follow his way.

Find your way through the maze to Jesus

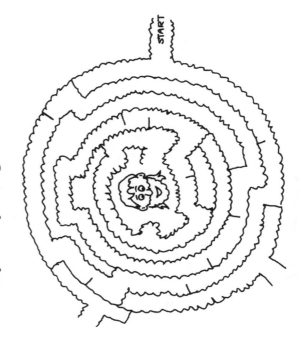

START

My name _____

THINK and LOOK ahead

In next week's gospel
what was written above Jesus?

T __ __ __ S __ __ __ N G

H __ __ __ H __ __

__ __ J __ __

LUKE 23:35-43

CLUE

There will be times when
we must stand up for what we believe!
We need not worry because Jesus
will take care of us.

Use the code to find his words below

1 A	14 N
2 B	15 O
3 C	16 P
4 D	17 Q
5 E	18 R
6 F	19 S
7 G	20 T
8 H	21 U
9 I	22 V
10 J	23 W
11 K	24 X
12 L	25 Y
13 M	26 Z

$\overline{9}$ $\overline{19}\ \overline{8}\ \overline{1}\ \overline{12}\ \overline{12}$

$\overline{7}\ \overline{9}\ \overline{22}\ \overline{5}$ $\overline{25}\ \overline{15}\ \overline{21}$

$\overline{1}\ \overline{12}\ \overline{12}$ $\overline{20}\ \overline{8}\ \overline{5}$

$\overline{23}\ \overline{15}\ \overline{18}\ \overline{4}\ \overline{19}$ $\overline{1}\ \overline{14}\ \overline{4}$

$\overline{23}\ \overline{9}\ \overline{19}\ \overline{4}\ \overline{15}\ \overline{13}$ $\overline{25}\ \overline{15}\ \overline{21}$

$\overline{23}\ \overline{9}\ \overline{12}\ \overline{12}$ $\overline{14}\ \overline{5}\ \overline{5}\ \overline{4}$

LUKE 21:15

Add the missing words from the list below

We will be
rewarded for our courage
and faith.

Not a _____ on your _____

Your _____ will be _____ .

_____ will win you _____ life.

LUKE 21:19

HEAD

FAITH

HAIR

EVERLASTING

HARMED

King of the Jews

LUKE 23:35-43

The soldiers and the crowd made fun of Jesus as he hung on the cross.

Arrange their words in the right order below

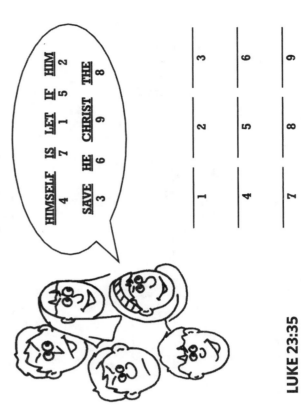

HIMSELF IS LET IF HIM
   4   7   1   5   2

SAVE HE CHRIST THE
  3   6   9   8

— — —
1 2 3

— — —
4 5 6

— — —
7 8 9

LUKE 23:35

THINK and LOOK ahead

Next Sunday we begin our preparations for celebrating Christmas. *To which church season do the next four Sundays belong?*

Solve the clues below.

The first letter of each word will spell out the answer

CLUES

1. The opposite of before
2. A bird that quacks
3. Grapes grow on these
4. We use these for hearing
5. The opposite of old
6. Someone in charge at school

[1.] [2.] [3.] [4.] [5.] [6.]

— — — — — —

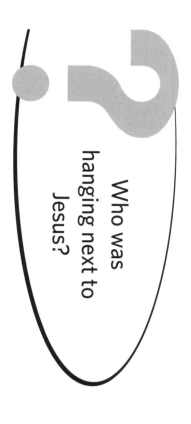

Who was hanging next to Jesus?

One of the criminals asked Jesus to remember him in his kingdom.

The letters in some of these words have been written back to front. Write them in the correct order on the lines below to find Jesus' reply

"I esimorp you, taht

_____

yadot you lliw be with

_____

em ni esidarap"

_____

Write the first letter of each object in the box

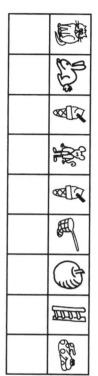

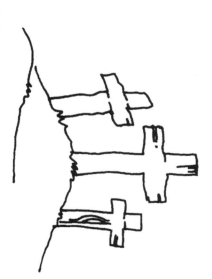

LUKE 23:43

Special Feasts for Years A, B, and C

Mary, Mother of God

LUKE 2:16-21

God chose Mary to be the mother of Jesus his Son.

List below some of the things mothers do to care for their babies

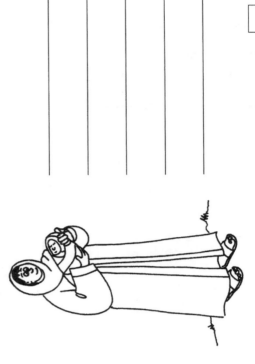

_____

_____

_____

_____

Do you think Mary did these things?

YES ☐

NO ☐

Color the picture using the number key given below

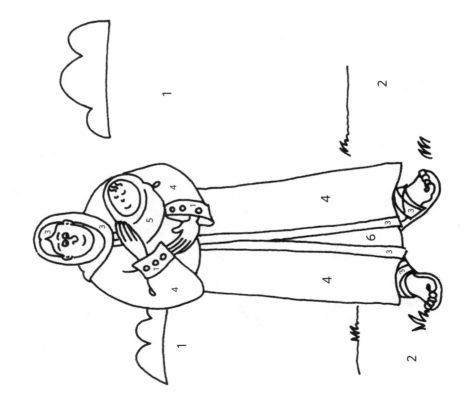

1	2	3	4	5	6
Blue	Green	Brown	Yellow	Orange	Red

YEARS A, B, C • MARY, MOTHER OF GOD (JANUARY 1)

How much do you know about Mary?

Use the clues to fill the crossword

ACROSS
1. The town in Galilee where Mary grew up
4. The town where Mary gave birth to Jesus (Clue – Luke 2:4-7)
5. The prayer said to Mary using a set of beads

DOWN
2. The angel who brought Mary some good news
3. Mary's husband
6. Mary's cousin

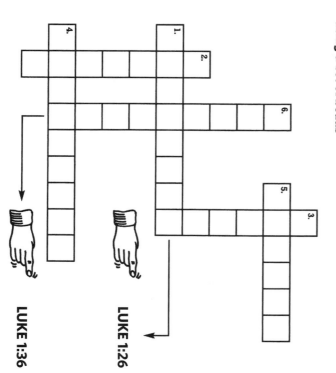

LUKE 1:26

LUKE 1:36

Here are some pictures of events in Mary's life, but they have been jumbled into the wrong order!

Put the number of each picture in the correct order on the lines below

1. Birth of Jesus

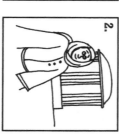
2. Mary in the Temple

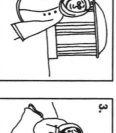
3. Mary at the foot of cross

4. Angel Gabriel appears to Mary

5. Journey to Bethlehem

6. Mary visits Elizabeth

_____ _____ _____ _____

God sends his Son Jesus

JOHN 1:1-18

In today's gospel Jesus is called by many different names.

Find the different titles used for Jesus

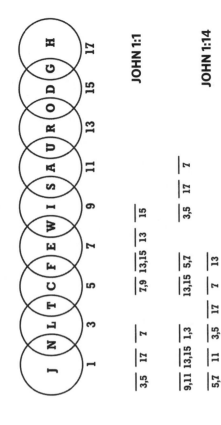

J	N	L	T	C	F	E	W	I	S	A	U	R	O	D	G	H
1	3	5	7	9	11	13	15	17

$\overline{3,5}$ $\overline{17}$ $\overline{7}$ $\overline{7,9}$ $\overline{13,15}$ $\overline{13}$ $\overline{15}$ — **JOHN 1:1**

$\overline{9,11}$ $\overline{13,15}$ $\overline{1,3}$ $\overline{13,15}$ $\overline{5,7}$ $\overline{3,5}$ $\overline{17}$ $\overline{7}$ — **JOHN 1:14**

$\overline{5,7}$ $\overline{11}$ $\overline{3,5}$ $\overline{17}$ $\overline{7}$ $\overline{13}$ $\overline{3}$ $\overline{9}$ $\overline{15,17}$ $\overline{17}$ $\overline{3,5}$ — **JOHN 1:9**

$\overline{3,5}$ $\overline{17}$ $\overline{7}$ $\overline{5}$ $\overline{17}$ $\overline{13}$ $\overline{9}$ $\overline{9,11}$ $\overline{3,5}$ — **JOHN 1:17**

$\overline{1}$ $\overline{7}$ $\overline{9,11}$ $\overline{11,13}$ $\overline{9,11}$

God made our world and sent Jesus to show us how to take care of it and each other.

Find eight differences between the two pictures

God sent Jesus to rescue us from our wrongdoings and to be our Savior.

Use the clues to find the missing letters and decode another word which means Savior

Something you wear on your head in cold weather

You use your eyes to . . .

Opposite of woman

They swim around in ponds

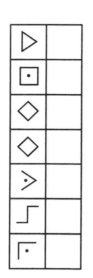

The Jews were waiting for the

—— —— —— —— to come!

Who shows us what God wants us to do?

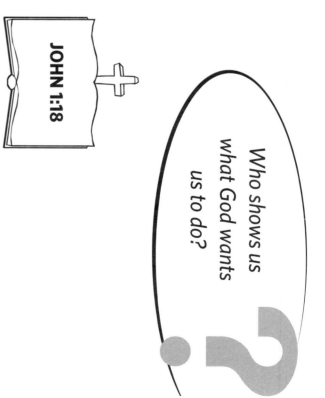

JOHN 1:18

Use the code to spell out the answer

z y x w v u t s r q p o n m l k j i h g f e d c b a
A B C D E F G H I J K L M N O P Q R S T U V W X Y Z

" —— —— —— —— —— —— —— —— —— —— ——
   r g   r h   g s v   l m o b

—— —— —— —— —— —— ——
 h l m   q v h f h

—— —— —— —— —— —— —— ——
 d s l   n z p v h

—— —— —— —— —— —— —— —— —— —— ——
 u z g s v i   p m l d m "

Visitors for Jesus

MATTHEW 2:1-12

Three wise men came from the East to find a newborn King.

Use the numbers written under the lines to find the missing letters and spell out their names

For example, 1=M and 3,4=P

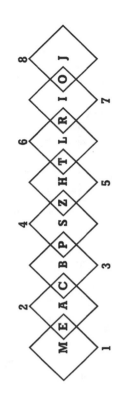

1	2	3	4	5	6	7	8
M E	A C	B P	S Z	H T	L R	I O	J

___ ___ ___ ___ ___ ___ ___
1   1,2 6   2,3 5   7   7,8 6,7

___ ___ ___ ___ ___
2,3 2   4   3,4 2   6,7

___ ___ ___ ___ ___ ___ ___ ___
3   2   6   5,6 5   2   4,5 2   6,7

They each brought a gift fit for a king!

Find out which wise man brought which gift and fill in the blanks

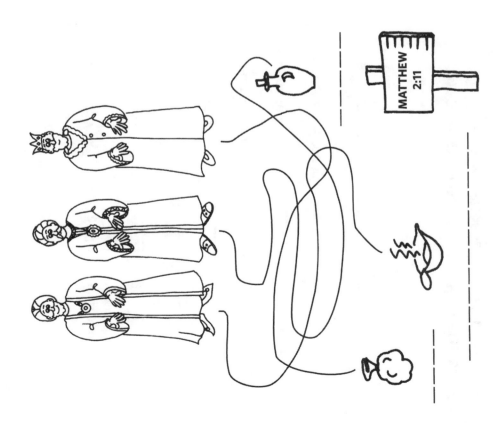

MATTHEW 2:11

Someone was not pleased to see them!

Use the clues to complete the crossword and find out his name

The wise men had followed a star to Bethlehem.

Read
MATTHEW 2:6

Use the words to fill in the blanks and find out what the prophet Micah had foretold

And you, ___ ___ ___ ___ ,

in the land of ___ ___ ___ ___ ,

you are not least ___ ___ ___ ___ ___ ___

among the ___ ___ ___ ___ of Judah.

Because from you will come a ___ ___ ___ ___ ___

who will ___ ___ ___ ___

my people ___ ___ ___ ___ ___ ___ .

IMPORTANT   ISRAEL   JUDAH   BETHLEHEM
LEADER   PEOPLES   SHEPHERD

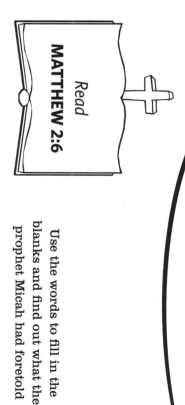
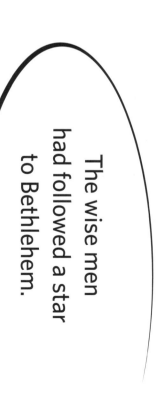

Jesus is presented to the Lord

LUKE 2:22-40

Why did Mary and Joseph take baby Jesus to the Temple in Jerusalem?

Fit the shapes into the puzzle below to find out!

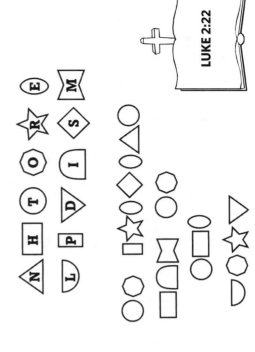

LUKE 2:22

Mary and Joseph took Jesus home to Nazareth.

Complete their directions for the journey

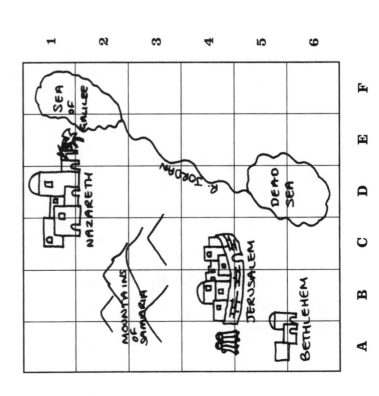

A   B   C   D   E   F

Directions: B5, B4, C4, _____

Who did they meet at the Temple?

Write the first letter of each picture in the box

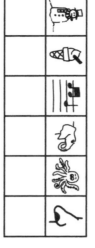

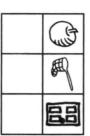

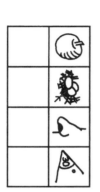

They were filled with the Holy Spirit and praised God when they saw Jesus!

Use the code cracker to find Simeon's words to Mary and Joseph

CODE CRACKER

A B C D E F G H I J K L M N O P Q R S T U V W X Y Z
1 2 3 4 5 6 7 8 9 10 11 12 13 14 15 16 17 18 19 20 21 22 23 24 25 26

"
13 25   5   25 5 19   8 1 22 5

19 5 14   20 8 5

19 1 12 22 1 20 9 15 14   23 8 9 3 8

25 15 21   8 1 22 5   19 5 14 20

6 15 18   1 12 12

20 15   19 5 5
"

LUKE 2:30

Peter and Paul

MATTHEW 16:13-19

Jesus asked his disciples to tell him what the people were saying about him.

Who did they think Jesus might be?

The answers below have been written back to front. Copy the letters in the correct order to read the names

NHOJ EHT TSITPAB

_____

EHT TEHPORP HAJILE

_____

RO HAIMEREJ

_____

MATTHEW 16:13

Peter and Paul traveled far and wide preaching the good news!

Help them to find their way to Jerusalem. Complete the directions they have been given

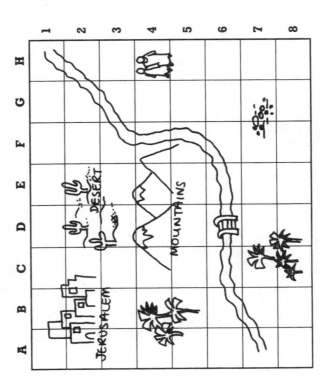

Directions to Jerusalem: 5H, 6G, 7F

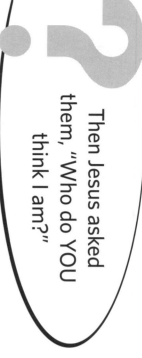

Then Jesus asked them, "Who do YOU think I am?"

Use the code to find out which disciple knew the right nswer

z y x w v u t s r q p o n m l k j i h g f e d c b a
A B C D E F G H I J K L M N O P Q R S T U V W X Y Z

" h r n l m   k v g v i   h z r w
  __ __ __ __ __   __ __ __ __ __   __ __ __ __

  b l f   z i v   g s v
  __ __ __   __ __ __   __ __ __

  h l m   l u   t l w "
  __ __ __   __ __   __ __ __

Jesus chose Simon Peter to lead his church.

Find the words of Jesus using the key below

L	M	C	E	O	U	W	T	H	R	Y	N	B	I	P	D	K	A

God's glory on the mountain

MATTHEW 17:1-10

Jesus took three of his disciples to the top of a mountain to see something amazing!

Follow the arrows to spell out their names

B	P	A	J	E	S	J →
A	M	E	S	R	T	E	S
P	T	E	A	R	E	P	A
M	E	N	O	S	N	M	E
S	D	J	J	H	O	E	R

P ___ ___ ___ ___ ___ ,
___ ___ ___ ___ ___
___ ___ ___ ___ ___ ___

MATTHEW 17:1

A cloud covered them with a shadow and God spoke!

Write the words in order on the lines to see what God said

1 ___ 2 ___ 3 ___
4 ___ 5 ___
6 ___ 7 ___
8 ___

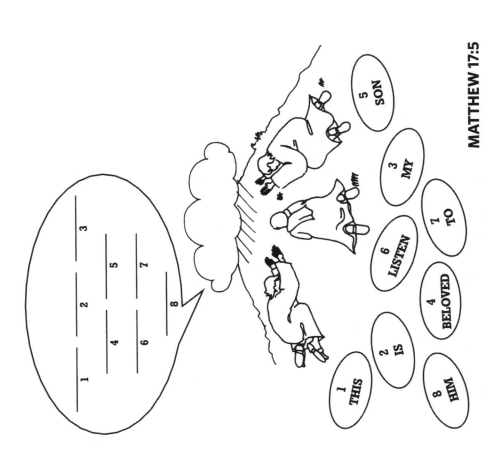

1 THIS
2 IS
3 MY
4 BELOVED
5 SON
6 LISTEN
7 TO
8 HIM

MATTHEW 17:5

How did Jesus appear to change?

Use the code cracker to find the answer

19 22 — 8 19 12 13 22

15 18 16 22 — 7 19 22

8 6 13 — 19 18 8

24 15 12 7 19 22 8

25 22 24 26 14 22 — 26 8

4 19 18 7 22 — 26 8

15 18 20 19 7

CODE CRACKER

1 Z   14 M
2 Y   15 L
3 X   16 K
4 W   17 J
5 V   18 I
6 U   19 H
7 T   20 G
8 S   21 F
9 R   22 E
10 Q   23 D
11 P   24 C
12 O   25 B
13 N   26 A

Two men appeared and talked to Jesus. Who were they?

Solve the math problems and find their names using the key

KEY

3 = J   4 = I   5 = S   8 = H   9 = L

10 = E   12 = A   16 = M   24 = O

$$
\begin{array}{cccccc}
5 & 12 & 10 & 3 & 4 & 16 \\
\times 2 & -3 & -6 & +0 & \times 3 & -8 \\
\hline
\end{array}
$$

$$
\begin{array}{ccccc}
4 & 12 & 15 & 2 & 3 \\
\times 4 & +12 & -10 & \times 5 & +2 \\
\hline
\end{array}
$$

Mary is taken into heaven

LUKE 1:39-56

After the angel left her, Mary set off to visit her cousin.

Write the first letter of each picture in the box

What was her cousin's name?

Who was her cousin married to?

LUKE 1:40

What do we believe happened when the time came for Mary to join Jesus in heaven?

Unscramble the answer by writing down every second word on the lines below

Start

IF	SHE	HE	WAS	COULD	TAKEN	BE	UP
SAW	TO	AS	HEAVEN	BY	BODY	EARTH	
AND	MARY	SOUL					

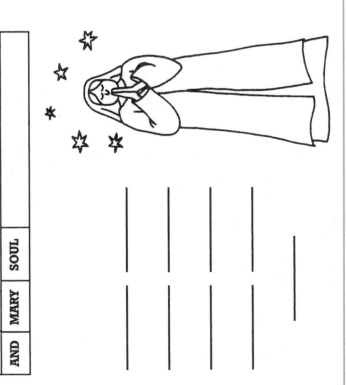

What did Elizabeth say when she heard Mary's greeting?

Use the code to find her words

△	T	O	Y	U	B	M
○	R	W	S	F	A	E
□	N	I	D	H	L	K

| ↓ | ← | ↑ | → | ↗ | ↘ |

"

"

Elizabeth's words are repeated in a well-known prayer

Add or subtract letters to spell out its name

A B C D E F G H I J K L M N O P Q R S T U V W X Y Z

O + 5	M – 5	L – 7	

A + 7	I – 8	Z – 17	K + 1

Q – 4	C – 2	F + 12	Z – 1